Television
mockumentary

Manchester University Press

Television mockumentary

Reflexivity, satire and a call to play

Craig Hight

Manchester University Press
Manchester and New York
distributed in the United States exclusively by Palgrave Macmillan

The right of Craig Hight to be identified as the author of this work has been asserted by him in accordance with the Copyright, Designs and Patents Act 1988.

Published by Manchester University Press
Oxford Road, Manchester M13 9NR, UK
and Room 400, 175 Fifth Avenue, New York, NY 10010, USA
www.manchesteruniversitypress.co.uk

Distributed in the United States exclusively by
Palgrave Macmillan, 175 Fifth Avenue, New York,
NY 10010, USA

Distributed in Canada exclusively by
UBC Press, University of British Columbia, 2029 West Mall,
Vancouver, BC, Canada V6T 1Z2

British Library Cataloguing-in-Publication Data
A catalogue record for this book is available from the British Library

Library of Congress Cataloging-in-Publication Data applied for

ISBN   978 0 7190 7316 8   hardback

ISBN   978 0 7190 7317 5   paperback

First published 2010

The publisher has no responsibility for the persistence or accuracy of URLs for any external or third-party internet websites referred to in this book, and does not guarantee that any content on such websites is, or will remain, accurate or appropriate.

Typeset
by Toppan Best-set Premedia Limited
Printed in Great Britain
by CPI Antony Rowe, Chippenham, Wiltshire

Dedicated to David Brent

Contents

Figures

All illustrations are screen grabs from DVDs

Preface

This book builds from arguments outlined in detail in *Faking It: Mock-documentary and the Subversion of Factuality*, a book I co-authored with Jane Roscoe, the first sustained exercise in exploring the nature of mockumentary texts. *Faking It* offered an initial foray into defining the mockumentary form and examined a number of key film and television texts and the nuances of their relationship with documentary culture. The book was written to fill a gap in the field of documentary theory, and to inspire media studies students to approach the mockumentary form with an appreciation of its complexity and significance.

Like *Faking It*, this volume is the product of many hours of watching mockumentary texts, some produced since the publication of that book, supervising students in making their own mockumentaries and engaging in a dialogue with colleagues over recent developments in wider documentary culture. This volume is intended to continue debates over the nature of mockumentary, and discussions in the chapters which follow have in part been inspired by the proliferation of literature focused on fact-fiction forms and their significance as evidence of a broadening (or weakening) of documentary culture. This volume is also intended to serve as a resource for producers of mockumentary, amateur filmmakers, those within the film and television industries who are engaged in designing mockumentary texts and the emerging group of digital producers who draw upon televisual fact-fiction forms as templates for online programming and content.

And finally, this book is intended to serve as a resource for media studies students, particularly those engaging with the intersection of television and documentary theory. Documentary culture has exploded since the early 1990s, increasing the profile of the documentary genre as an art form, at the same time as its most treasured aesthetics are being appropriated toward very different agendas. The emergence of compromised factual forms in television and online digital forms suggests an expanded field for documentary theory itself and the need to develop innovative critical frameworks in response. The chapters which follow do not attempt to provide a comprehensive overview of recent developments in the critical exploration of mediations of the real. Readers unfamiliar with the broader complexity of documentary and its many associated forms are encouraged to seek out the many excellent publications in this area (and to consult the bibliography for suggested further reading).

Acknowledgements

The key acknowledgement for the work that follows is Dr Jane Roscoe, my co-author for the first book on mockumentary: *Faking It: Mock-documentary and Subversion of Factuality*. Since the publication of that book in 2001, Jane and I have continued to develop arguments and conduct research into the form. Jane has since left academic life to pursue opportunities in the Australian television industry. We had always intended to co-author this book, and many of the discussions contained here are the product of a number of intensive brainstorming sessions, workshops and conversations over three years. Juggling a project such as this with a new career proved untenable but I have drawn on her energy and continued support throughout the drafting of the manuscript, and her presence remains in the discussions contained in this volume.

This book has also benefited hugely from the work of colleagues at Visible Evidence conference over a number of years, especially those who have been working in the area of documentary hybrids. This includes John Corner's now extensive and authoritative work on the relatively neglected area of television studies, including a number of highly perceptive pieces on the expansion of the real into hybrid genres; the valuable work of Derek Paget and Steve Lipkin on docudrama; Jon Dovey's distinctive analysis of popular factual television; Annette Hill's research into audience readings of non-fiction television; Richard Kilborn's extensive research into television reality forms, especially his perceptive work on docu-soaps; Gareth Palmer's writings on reality television and governmentality; and Brett Mills' work on television comedy vérité, which served as a key reference point for discussions in this volume. These works are discussed in various parts of the chapters below and my hope is that this volume continues their rich debates over hybrid forms. Some of the revisions in theoretical work in the chapters below were aided by Michael Zyrd's detailed questioning of the central arguments of *Faking It* in a panel at Visible Evidence, December 2002.

I would also like to give my thanks for the continued support of colleagues in the Screen and Media Studies Department at the University of Waikato. And to the staff at Manchester University Press – not least for their patience in waiting for me to complete this manuscript.

And most of all I would like to thank my partner, Cathy Coleborne, for keeping me on track during the long months of drafting this manuscript, providing inspiration when needed, and giving me the gift of our daughter Cassidy.

Introduction

Mockumentary has emerged as a common and distinctive part of the contemporary mediascape. Comprised of a corpus of texts across a variety of media that do not quite make a genre it has reached a point where it is an accepted part of the mainstream, particularly for cinema and television. The proliferation of mockumentary texts range from the banal and quickly forgotten to those which generate critical interest for their apparent insight into the contemporary *zeitgeist*. Where once *This is Spinal Tap* (1984) was invariably listed as a key influence by mockumentary filmmakers, now film and television producers have a broader and richer vein of innovative texts from which to draw inspiration. From popular cinematic exemplars such as horror film *The Blair Witch Project* (1999) and the satiric comedy *Borat: Cultural Learnings of America for Make Benefit Glorious Nation of Kazakhstan* (2006) to critically acclaimed television series such as the British and American versions of *The Office*, the mockumentary has arguably come of age, achieving a degree of prominence and often sophistication that deserves greater critical appraisal.

Mockumentary appropriation of documentary aesthetics has a long history. Depending on how one defines mockumentary, the form could be seen to date from the beginnings of the documentary genre itself. As Lebow notes, in reference to the easy integration of reconstructed and dramatised scenes by early practitioners,

> If the histories of the nonfiction film are to be believed then *all* of the most exemplary early documentary films, whether those of Flaherty, Grierson, Vertov, or even Edison's and Lumières' actualities, are also exemplary mockumentaries. (Lebow, 2006: 232)

Winston notes an apparent early use of the label 'mockumentary' in reference to Robert Flaherty's *Man of Aran* (1934) by at least some members of Flaherty's own crew (Winston, 1999: 73). More definitively, however, mockumentary is a term that identifies a deliberate blurring of an assumed fact-fiction dichotomy, and cannot be usefully applied to a context and time before there were discourses and conventions that rigorously demarcated the modes of fact and fiction. Sobchack has argued that 'documentary is primarily indexical, fiction primarily iconic and symbolic' (Sobchack, 2004: 245), a distinction that implicates mockumentary as playing somewhere in the spaces in between. Such a dichotomy suggests how mockumentary challenges theorists with issues of how to identify, define and position such texts, given the impulse to develop categories that provide a safe haven for documentary itself from the encroaches of fictional manipulation and artifice.

It is more fruitful to instead consider fact and fiction as poles on a continuum, to recognise that there are a variety of 'in-between' forms distinguished by an often complex divergence of agenda, collectively exhibiting the full range of techniques of audio-visual construction, and often asking audiences to engage in layered modes of reading. Mockumentary can be seen as a key example of 'documentary hybrid', a term which encompasses a variety of fact-fiction texts which are closely or loosely associated with the broader concerns and aesthetics of documentary culture. The label 'documentary hybrids' could include early forms such as nature documentary (Bousé, 2000) and drama-documentary (Paget, 1998; Lipkin, 2002) which tend to either draw explicitly from documentary aesthetics and associated discourses or identify with key parts of the documentary agenda. These hybrids have always been central to the development of documentary as a genre, despite the efforts of some theorists to position them outside documentary proper (as does Bousé in discussing the factual claims of what he terms 'wildlife films').

More recent documentary hybrids include the explosion of globalised television formats which integrate documentary aesthetics with more established entertainment formats, and occasionally pay lip service to a documentary agenda. Reality gameshows (or 'gamedocs'), docusoaps, video diaries, reality sitcoms, situation documentaries, documentary musicals and the plethora of lifestyle programming which incorporates some aspect of documentary aesthetics could all come under this broader label. Corner has usefully grouped these more recent television hybrids according to their primary function of 'documentary as diversion', to denote their departures from the more conventional politics and aesthetics of documentary practice (Corner, 2002a). Mockumentary's relationship to all of these developments is often dismissed as a parasitic one, although it does not simply draw from but comments upon and contributes to changes within this broader documentary culture. As documentary aesthetics, discourses and practices have continued to broaden, so too have mockumentary forms.

Mockumentary has also easily adapted to more fundamental changes within the contemporary mediascape, particularly the increasing dominance of digital platforms. These include digital video disc (or digital versatile disc or DVD), the World Wide Web, and a variety of mobile platforms. The convergence between these digital platforms and the more established mass media of film and television has initiated an apparently inevitable transformation of documentary culture as whole. Both the expansion of mediations of the real which is associated with digitality, as new media forms appropriate the culture and forms of documentary, and their convergence (and divergence) across digital platforms effectively provide new space for mockumentary to freely roam. Conversely, the task of defining mockumentary becomes much harder within digital media that offer more contingent and fleeting support for the assumed dichotomy between fact and fiction that still drives documentary culture.

This volume is partly a necessary updating and extension of the theoretical work first developed in *Faking It: Mock-documentary and the Subversion of Factuality* (Roscoe and Hight, 2001), a book co-authored by Jane Roscoe and this writer. The current volume addresses the problem of identifying and positioning mockumentary within a greatly expanded and more dynamic realm of the mediation of the real across analogue and digital media. The chapters below extend our original arguments on the nature and significance of the mockumentary form.

Faking It outlined a definition of mockumentary as those fictional texts 'which make a partial or concerted effort to appropriate documentary codes and conventions in order to represent a fictional subject'. We discussed patterns within mockumentary as broadly falling into three overlapping tendencies, defined in terms

of the degree of reflexivity which their appropriation of documentary aesthetics constructed toward factual discourses. These three
'degrees' of mockumentary were illustrated through discussion of
key mockumentary texts, particularly classic mockumentaries such
as *David Holzman's Diary* (1967), *The Falls* (1980), *Zelig* (1983),
This is Spinal Tap, *C'est arrivé près de chez vous* (*Man Bites Dog*)
(1992), *Bob Roberts* (1992) and *Forgotten Silver* (1995). There was
some discussion of the difficulties of identifying mockumentary as
a genre in its own right, and we concluded instead that

> it is more productive to think of mock-documentary as a *discourse*:
> informed and shaped through the particular relationships it con-
> structs with documentary proper, with the discourses of factuality,
> and especially through the complexity of its engagement with viewers.
> (Roscoe and Hight, 2001: 183, original emphasis)

Our grading of patterns within this discourse serves adequately as
an initial framework, but confused some readers who assumed that
it offered a taxonomy of texts, rather than foregrounding the
dynamic interplay between different senses of intertextuality within
specific texts, and especially the variety of positions afforded to
viewers of mockumentary.

In our concluding remarks, we made much of the apparent subversive potential of the mockumentary form toward documentary,
as it appeared then;

> We argue that all mock-documentary texts contain the potential for
> critical reflexivity, as an inherent part of their appropriation of docu-
> mentary aesthetics, and that it is this role constructed for the viewer
> that consistently marks the mock-documentary out from other fact-
> fiction forms. (Roscoe and Hight, 2001: 184)

As noted above, mockumentary has broadened to include references to the full range of factually based texts, mutating into a
myriad number of forms across different genres and media. It is no
longer sufficient to define mockumentary largely through its reflexive potential toward documentary as a (cinematic and televisual)
genre.

As discussed in the following chapter, the complexity of the audience's engagement with mockumentary is still crucial, and the
discourse still 'offers the audience an opportunity to reflect on
the wider cultural acceptance of factual and sober discourses and
potentially to move towards a position of critical awareness, distrust

or even incredulity of such discourses' (Roscoe and Hight, 2001: 185). Instead of mockumentary retaining a distinctive subversive edge, however, it has become just one part of a broader reflexivity toward factual forms within visual culture as a whole. Arguably the most common and naturalised forms of reflexivity have been in the incestuous and highly competitive realm of television documentary hybrids, themselves a key spark for the emerging variety and sophistication of the examples of television mockumentary which are the primary focus of this volume.

Such changes mean that some of the more sweeping predictions from *Faking It* have not come to pass:

> In the next few years, we suggest that there is likely to be continued exploration of mock-documentary. One possibility is that this form will eventually become exhausted, with audiences tiring of its irreverent stance towards factual aesthetics, and filmmakers moving to explore other modes of expression. Mock-documentary might be considered as a transitional discourse, a form that takes full advantage of technological developments and our insecurities concerning factual discourse. Having pushed those issues to their logical endpoint, the form itself could easily give way to new configurations within the fact-fiction continuum, alternatively, the continued emergence of mock-documentary could lead to a more fundamental reappraisal of the essentials of documentary proper. In the near future, might we conceivably think of mock-documentary as the offspring of documentary, a member of the 'next generation' that emerges and is inspired by the exhaustion of the documentary genre itself? (Roscoe and Hight, 2001: 189)

Lebow makes a similar argument, suggesting that this is a relationship in which mockumentary is not necessarily merely an irritant and inferior form:

> I find problematic the assumpion that underpins mockumentary: namely, that it depends on and responds to the 'real' or 'true' original, documentary. The idea that the category of documentary supports and sustains mockumentary as its 'straight' or 'upright' other – that documentary in effect props mockumentary up – is troubling to me [...] Could it be *mockumentary* that is doing the propping, setting a stage by which documentary may finally appear as a stable and coherent category? (Lebow, 2006: 224, original emphasis)

Unfortunately for such arguments, there has been a distinct failure of mockumentary to date to centre on truly transgressive examples of popular deconstructive form which operate as a direct critique of documentary either by design (*Man Bites Dog, The Falls, David Holzman's Diary*) or through context (*Forgotten Silver*). The failure of mockumentary to fulfil its full subversive potential suggests not only the limited ways in which such forms have tended to be explored by filmmakers and television producers, but also a rapidly changing context for documentary and audio-visual non-fiction. It is a measure of the complexity and paradoxical nature of wider documentary culture that examples of mockumentary discourse have proliferated, together with other hybrid forms, at the same time as there has been a rise in the popularity and appreciation of feature film documentary itself.

This book, then, addresses a variety of developments which prompt the need for a revision of our initial framework. In the chapters that follow the definition of mockumentary as a discourse is expanded upon. A key focus here is the variety of ways in which mockumentaries generate, both in isolation and collectively, a commentary on the nature of the transformation of documentary genre by the plethora of television documentary hybrids. Mockumentaries are exploring the new terrain of hybrid agendas, distinctive aesthetics, forms of participation and interaction by participants and audiences, together with the variety of representational and ethical issues associated with these developments. Crucially, however, such hybrids typically incorporate a high degree of self-reflexivity themselves, and this begs the question of whether television mockumentary offers any kind of challenge to such texts that they do not already make themselves. Does mockumentary have any special status as a 'subversive' discourse within television, or has it evolved into another naturalised style within the broader hegemony of television aesthetics?

What has become obvious is that there is an increasingly incestuous playing field of hybrid forms, to the extent that the matter of identifying and assessing mockumentary discourse is no longer a trivial or straightforward task. Such a task has now become one of identifying how various hybrid traditions are utilised in a given text, rather than of attempting to rigidly apply a taxonomy, an exercise that always risks missing the more innovative and problematic texts in favour of praising the formulaic as exemplars of an assumed canon of texts. The need for a revised and updated treatise on mockumentary is partly in response to the emergence of film and especially television examples which suggest less of a rigid division between mockumentary and other hybrids, and even between mockumentary and documentary proper (in the case of reflexive documentary and documentary comedy). Such new texts challenge the certainty of existing simplistic definitions of mockumentary and require greater subtlety in our theoretical approach.

This book contributes to a small but vital literature on mockumentary. Apart from the occasional critique of specific texts, early theoretical exploration of mockumentary includes Nichols' collapsing of mockumentary patterns into his discussion of the reflexive mode of documentary representation (Nichols, 1991) and Jacobs' analysis of an odd combination of the 'pseudo-documentary' and the neo-western in the same volume of Studies in History and Criticism of Film (Jacobs, 2000). After *Faking It*, the major volumes on mockumentary have been the edited collections *Docufictions: Essays On the Intersection of Documentary and Fictional Filmmaking* (Rhodes and Springer, 2005) and *F is for Phony: Fake Documentary and Truth's Undoing* (Juhasz and Lerner, 2006). The *Docufictions* collection looks primarily at examples of mockumentary and docudrama (Lipkin, Paget and Roscoe, 2005), and attempts to use such fact-fiction categories to re-examine the complexity of patterns within documentary itself. The book brings together a variety of perspectives, but perhaps most chiefly demonstrates the confusion and lack of consensus on how to define and apply notions of mockumentary. The Juhasz and Lerner collection in comparison is very much focused on avant-garde and independent examples of 'fake documentary' and it consequently deals almost exclusively with feature and short film, largely ignoring television. The editors seek to escape any trivial or popular associations of the label 'mock-documentary', insisting that such texts play a distinctive and subversive role within documentary culture.

Paul Ward's brief but useful overview of contemporary documentary production, *Documentary: The Margins of Reality*, includes an interesting take on documentary and comedy, referring to these as distinct but intersecting modes, and consequently positioning mockumentary as 'one of the more prevalent forms of comedy documentary' (Ward, 2005a: 72). And there are a number of useful volumes focused on individual mockumentaries, the most substantial of which are the edited collection *Nothing That Is: Millennial Cinema and the* Blair Witch *Controversies* (Higley and Weinstock,

2004), focusing on a variety of perspectives on *The Blair Witch Project*, and Ben Walters' excellent discussion of the UK series of *The Office* (Walters, 2005). Other shorter, but still worthy, pieces include Thomas Doherty's brief overview on the history of the mockumentary (Doherty, 2003), Ethan de Seife's online history of mockumentary, Carl Plantinga's excellent piece on the archetypal mockumentary *This is Spinal Tap*, detailing how it operates as both a parody of rockumentary and a satire of heavy metal masculinity (Plantinga, 1998), John Caldwell's efforts to delineate various kinds of 'docu-real' television programming (including texts which can also be categorised as mockumentary), and Brett Mills' discussion on *The Office* (UK) as an exemplar of sitcom innovation he terms 'comedy vérité' (Mills, 2004).

Despite, or because of, this increased interest in the form, however, a clear critical consensus on mockumentary or its significance has yet to emerge. There is no singular sense of where to position mockumentary: either inside of documentary itself and grouped with reflexive documentary and documentary comedy or a distinctive subgenre (Bayer, 2005: 169); as purely fictional texts; or operating in a blurred boundary between fact and fiction. The popularising of the term 'mockumentary' seems to date from critical responses to *This is Spinal Tap* (Doherty, 2003: 23), although this term is often rejected by theorists in favour of labels such as 'pseudo-documentary' (Jacobs, 2000), or 'fake documentary' (Juhasz and Lerner, 2006) as a means of more clearly distinguishing a particular corpus of texts, or avoiding the implication that such texts' primary agenda is simply to 'mock' existing cultural forms.

In *Faking It: Mock-documentary and the Subversion of Factuality* (Roscoe and Hight, 2001), we favoured the term 'mock-documentary' largely for theoretical reasons, to emphasise the discourse's relationship to the documentary genre and its implicitly reflexive agenda toward factual culture as a whole. 'Mockumentary', however, has become the more definitive and favoured term among both practitioners and audiences. It is also a label which usefully moves us away from a simplistic relationship with documentary itself. Mockumentary does not exist simply to 'mock', in either of its senses, documentary. It has evolved into a more subtle and more complex discourse, in part because of the now much broader series of intertextual references which mockumentary forms make, outside of simply replicating familiar documentary representational styles.

Within popular commentary the term 'mockumentary', however, is often misused. The label is frequently thrown at a documentary by critics because of their frustration with its arguments, as a means to dismiss a text as a polemic which has moved outside of a fidelity to the truth in order to score political points. Michael Moore's popular political documentaries such as *Bowling for Columbine* (2002) and *Fahrenheit 9/11* (2004) seem to attract the most opprobrium on these terms, not least because they appear capable of reaching and persuading a wide audience. In a more general sense, however, this kind of casual use of the label derives not only from an inadequate understanding of the potential subtlety and complexity of the best examples of mockumentary, but from an undervaluing of satire and other forms of comedy. As noted above, there is the common assumption that mockumentary is merely a parasitic form (Jacobs, 2000: 2), both feeding off the much more valuable and worthy genre of documentary (which partly also explains its relative neglect within documentary theory) and propagating a suspect postmodern sensibility (McClure and McClure, 2001).

There are three parts to this book, and these also form a useful summary of its objectives: Part I defines mockumentary discourse and outlines some of its key patterns across different media; Part II positions mockumentary within the wider spectrum of televisual space, in particular in relation to traditions of documentary, dramatic and comedic forms; and Part III assesses the aesthetics and agenda of specific television mockumentary programmes, with a particular focus on television mockumentary series.

In a broad sense, mockumentary always involves a 'call to play', but this has been manifested in a number of often contrasting ways, reflecting the complexity of audience readings which they prompt. As outlined in chapter 1, mockumentary practitioners have employed the discourse for a variety of reasons, at some times for novelty or promotional purposes, at other times for dramatic ends or incorporating the complexity of parodic and satiric agendas. The discourse has been used within diverse genres, serving as an experimental and innovative form within long-established generic traditions across a variety of different media.

The difficulties of defining mockumentary partly stem from the fact that, as the discourse has become more established, it has widened to incorporate and reflect changes in the nature of the mediation of reality itself. The discourse has focused on the full set of codes and conventions associated with non-fiction-related media; it has grown to reflect the full continuum of fact-fiction forms. There is a consequent difficulty in identifying the 'boundaries' of mockumentary, or trying to state what is and is not a mockumentary text. Chapters 1 and 2 introduce these arguments and they are returned to throughout the following chapters. From one perspective the 'core' examples of mockumentary are those which reference documentaries, while the more problematic in terms of a coherent definition of the discourse are those that reference documentary hybrids such as docusoaps and reality gameshows. Each of these reality-based forms involves an often quite distinctive intersection of production practices, aesthetics and forms of audience engagement, interaction and participation. As the nature of the genre has broadened and been remediated, particularly across digital-based media, so mockumentary has broadened its set of textual strategies in response.

The key focus of this book is on a mapping of the range of applications of mockumentary within a specific medium; the explorations of mockumentary form by often innovative television producers and programme makers. Television is relatively neglected in critical traditions, often dismissed as a medium increasingly governed by a commercial agenda favouring a spectrum of disposable spectacle, exploitation and trivial entertainment over the possibilities of quality informative and educational programming. Such attitudes have certainly informed the approaches of most documentary theorists toward the medium until relatively recently.[1] While the more established traditions of cinematic studies are able to draw upon both a wider critical appreciation of the medium and a more sustained set of discourses supporting the academic study of cinematic texts, there is a lack of 'a strong, sustained tradition of critical appraisal' of television programming (Geraghty, 2003: 30–1). As Jacobs argues, however,

> The continued sense that the television text is mostly inferior to the film text and cannot withstand concentrated critical pressure because it lacks 'symbolic density', rich *mise-en-scene*, and the promotion of identification as a means of securing audience proximity, has to be revised in the light of contemporary television. (Jacobs, 2001: 433)

There is a need to reiterate that television is capable of being viewed as a site for artistic expression as well as communication

(Jacobs, 2001: 429). Such a claim is best demonstrated through the discussion of the aesthetics of particular texts, rather than relying on the broader narratives of television (Geraghty, 2003: 29), which is as ridden with contradictions and banalities as any aspect of popular culture. As outlined in chapter 3, television provides an environment uniquely designed to foster mockumentary. Televisual space is partly defined through a high degree of intertextuality, with television forms constantly commenting upon themselves and other cultural forms, in the process repeatedly foregrounding themselves as acts of mediation. Television mockumentary provides distinctive forms of play within this frame in relation to television representations of the real (see chapter 2). Despite the higher profile accorded cinematic mockumentary, the televisual medium has served as a key site in the genealogy of the discourse. Mockumentary has some of its origins in the constant experimentation within particularly comedic television forms, although typically initiated for commercial reasons rather than a commitment to experimentation for its own sake.

The discourse has intersected with a number of key televisual generic traditions, including recent transformations of television documentary prompted by the proliferation of hybrid formats, and their influence in reshaping the expectations surrounding television documentary itself (see chapter 4). The challenges of addressing television documentary hybrids have preoccupied documentary theory since the mid 1990s, and there is no doubt that mockumentary discourse as a whole has responded to and added to the aesthetics, practices and commentary over this part of the fact-fiction continuum. Mockumentary also intersects with specific aesthetic traditions within the broad spectrum of television drama (chapter 5), including drama-documentary, and the rich variety of comedic forms based on parody and satire (chapter 6).

The remaining chapters address detailed analyses of television mockumentaries, focusing especially on the more extended forms of mockumentary available in television series within different national contexts. The emergence of these series, where a mockumentary premise is central to the aesthetics and agenda of a sequential and layered narrative, suggests that the discourse has become naturalised within the mainstream of television narrative styles, rather than lapsing as an occasional gimmick or stunt style. Some of the richer examples of mockumentary discourse as a whole are in fact to be found in television serial form, generating a number of layers of meaning at a textual level, and prompting overlapping modes of reading and appreciation by audiences. A discussion of any television mockumentary series consequently offers insight into distinctive aspects of the medium, revealing the centrality and complexity of hybridity as an everyday programming and production strategy and suggesting one way of discussing the transformations of the relationships between mediations of the real and other forms within television programming.

Note

1 My thanks to Derek Paget for suggesting this discussion.

Part I
Defining mockumentary

I

Mockumentary discourse:
a call to play

Mockumentary is as difficult to define as any rich symbolic form, and is becoming even more so as it broadens to intersect with a greater number of genres and emerges in digital media forms. In simple terms, it could be defined as the corpus of fictional texts which engage in a sustained appropriation of documentary aesthetics, but more texts than mockumentary can fall into such a definition. Referenced to the continuing expansion of the documentary culture, mockumentary poses the same difficulty of identifying a shifting set of codes and conventions. Central to any mockumentary text is the relationship which is established with the specific form or forms which it appropriates, and while in a broader sense we could say that mockumentary is thus 'parasitic' it is also inherently reflexive, offering a potential subversion of the very forms it references. In most cases, however, audiences tend to label the discourse as merely playful.

A more useful and suitably nuanced definition follows from labelling mockumentary a discourse, and considering not only the broad patterns to its agenda and aesthetics but also how mockumentary has been continually reshaped within specific texts, genres and media. The definition of mockumentary discussed here is informed by Nichols' still useful three-part definition of the documentary genre (Nichols, 1991: 12–31). Nichols offered a coherent definition encompassing an institutional practice developed by a 'community of practitioners', a specific 'corpus of texts' which demonstrate a set of codes and conventions typically identifiable through modes of representation (the core being expository, observational and interactive or participatory modes) and a 'constituency of viewers' who bring specific expectations and assumptions to their reading of these texts.

Because of the natural slippage that occurs between these three aspects of media practice, documentary is consistently identified through not just one of these aspects but the intersection of all three, even though they are not necessarily all required for a specific text to be assumed to be a documentary. For example a text can be accepted as 'real' even if no documentary modes are used; it could be acknowledged by audiences as such for its agenda, or through its insights or collective sense of the socio-historical world. By the same token a documentary can be dismissed as fiction by an audience that is suspicious of its content.

This definition also implies broader support for the genre from 'discourses of sobriety' (Nichols, 1991: 5) or ways of conveying knowledge about the world which are so naturalised as to disguise their grounding in positivist discourses. The potency of such discourses derives from their ability to structure the world they appear to merely reflect. Integral to the genre is an assumed indexical bond to the socio-historical world, based on a deeper cultural belief in the validity and integrity of photographic forms of evidence. Documentary draws from such wider discursive support for the notion of a mechanically centred notion of objectivity, a sense that the moving image camera can function as an impartial observer of reality. The genre maintains the rhetorical stance that it can serve as a 'window on reality', a claim to audiences that 'this is how things are' and that to watch documentary is to encounter direct representations of the world. The genre seeks a special status for its representations, based on both a set of assumed ethical practices central to its production practice and the nature of its codes and conventions.

This rhetorical stance remains, despite widespread awareness of the issues inherent in any act of mediation involving the real. The roles of the filmmaker in selecting pieces of evidence, positioning the documentary frame and composing sequences of audio-visual evidence in the service of a persuasive argument are all understood by audiences – but these tend to sit in a natural tension with an apparently common-sense belief in photographic indexicality. The paradox at the centre of documentary is that it offers acts of mediation that aspire to appear unmediated, a paradox that allows for both its continued salience with contemporary audiences and the potential for forms such as mockumentary to play with its less-than-innocent relationship with socio-political knowledge.

Mockumentary plays a complex role in relation to the broader dynamics of documentary culture. It sets out to take the three parts of Nichols' definition as a given, but then turn them back on each other. To separate the codes and conventions from a community of practitioners and their efforts to engage with and communicate perspectives on reality. To open the space between practitioners and their audience, for purposes particularly of entertainment (as do other fact-fiction hybrids). To add to debates over the mediation of reality – which paradoxically can also strengthen documentary against hybrid forms. To make plain what documentary as a genre tends to deny: the fluidity between fiction and non-fiction, between the indexical relationship with reality promised by documentary, and the iconic and symbolic forms generated in fiction.

If we reconceptualise Nichols' definition of documentary as a frame for approaching the broader field of documentary culture, mockumentary in turn can be defined not as a genre or subgenre, but as a complex discourse similarly identified through reference to three levels of media practice:

1. Mockumentary arises from a variety of agendas on the part of fictional media producers. While it draws in particular from parodic and satiric traditions, it is not reducible to these.
2. At the textual level, mockumentary appropriates representational styles not only from the codes and conventions of documentary proper but from the full spectrum of non-fiction, including hybrid forms across different media.
3. And mockumentary is capable of providing for a complexity of modes of reading, inherently (but not always explicitly) involving different senses of reflexivity toward the non-fiction and hybrid forms which it appropriates.

The core agendas of mockumentary producers

The wider agendas of mockumentary need to be delineated not only from the everyday manipulations inherent in documentary filmmaking, but also from those examples that are ultimately revealed to be a deliberate lapse in standards for documentary proper. The term 'fake documentary' tends to be applied to those texts which are intended to be read and accepted as a part of the documentary genre, to be accepted as adhering to its political and ethical standards, but which involve deliberate efforts to fake specific pieces of evidence (Mapplebeck, 1997; Kilborn, 1998b). Winston has discussed the many examples of documentary which are labelled as 'fake', including those that are labelled as such by commentators ignorant of the ways in which documentary filmmakers obtain footage and construct sequences in the service of an argument (Winston, 2000: 9–39). Media coverage of this latter category of apparent 'fakes' has been a frequent feature of documentary but, as Winston notes, this arises from an ignorance of the ways in which conventional documentary practice naturally involves creative endeavour. He expresses frustration over a collapsing of distinctions between 'downright fabrications through less heinous misrepresentations to reconstructions to previously witnessed events and the everyday interventions of filmmaking'. The debate over these has lacked understanding that 'moral difference could be drawn between total fictionalising on the one hand and reconstructing actual events on the other', or that 'everyday filming required repeated actions, requested if necessary, so that moving-image editing norms could be obeyed' (Winston, 2000: 9).

With mockumentary, in contrast, there is always a point where audiences are intended to recognise and appreciate the fiction. Juhasz and Lerner argue that mockumentaries (confusingly, they prefer the term 'fake documentaries') are distinguished by this very moment of revelation.

> Although a significant subset of 'real' documentaries certainly can and do self-reference their artifice, as well as the deceptions that can and do organize the moral and social, this revelatory action is the *definitive* project of the fake documentary. (Juhasz and Lerner, 2006: 2, original emphasis)

Often the point, in fact, is to delay this flagging of fictionality, or to put the viewer in a position where their initial reading of a text requires them to make continual assessments over what is real and what is not. Instead of documentary's call to action based on the presentation of socio-political issues, the ultimate agenda of mockumentary is typically a call to play.

While all mockumentary forms share this wider playfulness, there are also more specific agendas followed by filmmakers and other media producers. Mockumentary cannot be reduced to a simple exercise in 'mocking' whatever it references. Media producers may be aiming for some form of metanarrative critique (Bayer, 2005: 164), an exploration of the contradictions of non-fiction mediation, or simply looking for a particular production style for more banal reasons. The clearest patterns in mockumentary to date are discussed below, but it is important to note both that within any given text these may overlap, and that each of these could also be further delineated into more subtle tendencies marked by production techniques, the nature of appropriation and the specific forms of engagement which are established for audiences.

Stunt or novelty mockumentary

This agenda tends to be associated with the more trivial or banal examples of mockumentary, in the sense that filmmakers and producers are here not looking to engage in complex, subtle and sustained efforts at reflexivity toward the forms which are appropriated but are employing representational styles that are immediately familiar to audiences. Such texts aim to create a media event, inevitably using mockumentary as little more than a gimmick, or a one-joke premise rather than an integral part of narrative structure and character development in the conventional sense. An early example is the infamous 1938 radio broadcast of *War of the Worlds* (discussed further in chapter 2), in which a regular drama slot featured an aural mockumentary approach as a novel way of presenting a well-known story. More recent examples of the stunt agenda range from employing a mockumentary form for a skit within a television comedy programme, to the number of examples of one-off episodes of an established dramatic television series, such as the live premiere of the 1997 series of *ER* (1994–). As discussed in chapters 5 and 6, there are similar episodes from series as varied as *M.A.S.H.* (1972–83), *The X-Files* (1993–2002), *The West Wing* (1999–2004) and at least two episodes of *The Simpsons* (1989–).

Other texts that have used mockumentary as the basis of a media stunt include the television programmes *Alternative 3* (1977), *Ghostwatch* (1992), *Alien Abduction: Incident at Lake County* (1998),[1] and *Opération Lune* (*Dark Side of the Moon*) (2002) (discussed further in chapter 3). They attempt to generate audience interest by delaying as long as possible the revelation that they are not based on fact. These programmes all derived their effectiveness from the context for their initial broadcast – they are inevitably less interesting when viewed again or by audiences that are already aware of their status as fiction. (A similar agenda clearly informs the small number of so-called 'snuff films' which briefly captured public attention in the early 1970s.)

In a more satiric vein the stunt agenda is at the centre of *Borat: Cultural Learnings of America for Make Benefit Glorious Nation of Kazakhstan*, itself a close relation to innumerable hidden-camera stunt-based television programmes (Torchin, 2008). More trivial, everyday and immediately disposable examples of the comedic stunt agenda include the myriad of April Fool's Day news stories that appear each year in news bulletins across a variety of media. As Humphrys suggests, 'the classic form of April fool hoax is to present some improbable situation in such a convincing manner that people fall for it on the spur of the moment, then later cannot understand why they did so' (Humphrys, 1999). The April-fool news story relies upon a non-fiction mode of presentation, typically using a known newsperson to present the story with a straight face, and some of the best stunts have involved television. Within news broadcasts these are invariably flagged by the programme, by presenters pointedly reminding viewers of the date or through their placement at the end of a bulletin (with human-interest and other light-hearted items). Such items are notable for the latitude given to media professionals to play outside their own strict guidelines and expectations and involve various levels of complicity on the part of producers, publishers and broadcasters.

Such examples have become something of a tradition in contemporary news production, continuing a long history of similar stunts (hundreds of years old, according to online sources such as The Museum of Hoaxes[2]). They demonstrate the malleability of mockumentary discourse, where precisely the same agenda can be repeated across different media, employing distinct but overlapping representational forms that are nonetheless intended to be received in the same way by differently situated audiences. Exactly the same news item can be repeated across different media, using different forms of 'evidence' to justify their claims to authenticity.

The Museum of Hoaxes website lists the greatest April-fool hoax as a television one: the 1957 BBC news programme *Panorama*'s report on a 'spaghetti harvest' in southern Switzerland, which featured footage of spaghetti apparently growing on trees. This is still remembered fondly and celebrated because of its effectiveness,

apparently a reflection of the BBC audience's comparative ignorance at the time of how spaghetti was actually produced.
Interestingly, there tends to be greater involvement on the part of
television, newspaper and radio news professionals in Britain than
in the United States (partly a legacy of the negative publicity
surrounding the *War of the Worlds* radio broadcast, with both
voluntary controls and eventual US Federal Communications
Commission policy insisting on clearly demarcating fake news from
the real). Such stunts are even the basis of informal competition
between media professionals, with appreciation centring on those
that are best able to exploit topical news stories to enhance their
effectiveness. Their high profile – with new bulletins reporting on
such seasonal stunts in other media – mean that audiences have
become accustomed to expecting such diversions.

Using mockumentary for promotion

This agenda overlaps with the stunt agenda, but is more clearly
focused on using mockumentary discourse for more specific marketing purposes (although there are occasional examples in political campaigns where the intended effect is somewhat similar: buy
our product). This agenda encompasses well-established traditions
of appropriating immediately recognisable forms of non-fiction
presentation for advertising purposes – a staple technique involving
cultural references and various degrees of seriousness or intended
commentary. Examples on radio and television can vary quite
widely, from using mock-interviews as testimony for a product, or
a serious address to highlight more clearly absurd content, to mild
efforts at parodying contemporary fact-fiction forms. As discussed
in later chapters, these traditions perhaps operate more effectively
within television, where intertextual references are characteristic of
the visual discourses, generic modes and forms of address which
help to define the televisual space.

Advertising campaigns which have employed mockumentary
discourse typically play to a knowing, sophisticated audience. For
example, airline carrier JetBlue's 2003 campaign sought to distinguish it in a highly competitive market by demonstrating both its
sophistication and also its apparent lack of image construction
by mocking its competitors' use of employee testimonials and suggesting low consumer expectations of all commercial airlines
(Reed, 2004). Car maker Volvo's 2003 'mystery of Dalaro' campaign

included an 8-minute online documentary claiming to be an investigation into the 'collective unconsciousness' that explains how 32 families from the same eastern Sweden village could supposedly buy the same model of car from the same dealership on the same day in October 2003. And there is an emerging tradition of using mockumentaries to promote other fictional media using short (typically trailer-length) film segments. X-Box used a 7-minute film about a 'motion capture artist' as a 2003 promotion for a video game called *Midtown Madness 3*. ESPN's flagship sports news programme, *Sportscenter* (1979–), has employed a consistent mockumentary style in its promotions, recruiting high-profile North American athletes for self-mocking pieces riffing on behind-the-scenes skits on the programme's production (Farrell, 1999). These are all part of a continued effort by advertisers to employ something which is edgy and distinctive, while still referencing familiar stylistic templates.

Although generally trivial examples of mockumentary discourse, the more interesting examples derive from concerted attempts to generate an aura of innovation around another media text. The advertising campaign for Stephen King's television series *Kingdom Hospital* (2004) included a mockumentary entitled 'Investigating Kingdom Hospital: The Journals of Eleanor Druse', which operated parallel to the series itself, featuring an interview with a fictional character whose journals purported to serve as the basis for the film's supernatural theme. In a more satiric frame the director of the investigative documentary *Wal-Mart: The High Cost of Low Price* (2005), Robert Greenwald, used mock testimonials from fake employees and neighbours to feature the film's irreverent take on Wal-Mart, using actual Wal-Mart locations and mimicking the soft-focus Americana style of the corporation's commercials (Edwards, 2005).[3]

A variation on these promotional pieces is the number of mock 'making of' documentaries typically made available online and packaged onto DVD releases of film and television texts. The intention here is partly to engage in a commentary upon wider filmmaking practices, or at least to play to audiences aware of the less-than-honest testimonies of participants in film marketing campaigns. Often these are little more than an in-joke, with knowing performances by celebrities and complicit figures. The more sustained and sophisticated examples use mockumentary as the basis for the broader premise of a campaign, such as the marketing for *The Blair Witch Project*, which operated at a number of levels and included mockumentary texts such as the television programme *Curse of the Blair Witch* (1999) (as discussed in detail in the following chapter).

Mockumentary as an innovative dramatic style

This agenda encompasses the variety of non-comedic uses of the discourse, examples where media producers have employed a number of representational strategies centred on a convincing simulation of documentary aesthetics. As with other agendas, this also incorporates a variety of more specific production practices, partly determined by the modes of representation which are referenced, partly by more conventional issues of narrative and character construction and overall thematics.

There are a variety of advantages to the use of specific 'documentary' effects within fictional texts. Mimicking the observational mode of documentary draws upon a sense of 'liveness' or spontaneity that occurs in direct cinema and cinéma vérité (such as with Woody Allen's *Husbands and Wives* (1992), which intercuts apparent vérité sequences with interviews with characters explaining their motivations and responses to the action). The result can be a dramatic fiction which appears to be unfolding in real time on the screen. Varying drama through an apparent documentary lens can serve useful narrative ends; constraining the perspective of audiences and providing them with limited amounts of information about characters and events. Such a device allows a director to build dramatic tension through omission and encourage the viewer to imagine what is outside of the frame. A roving, point-of-view camera is a formulaic trope of the horror genre, of course, which is why *The Blair Witch Project* is partly an innovation within existing horror conventions (as discussed in the following chapter).

Using a wider array of documentary devices, particularly fake archival footage or interviews, often also allows for an economical narrative style. Using a 'voice of god' narrator typical of an expositional mode of documentary can provide a shorthand introduction to characters and situations, similar in effect to a direct address to the audience. An on-screen or voice-over narrator becomes a storyteller who is free to address the audience directly but may still have an ambiguous relationship with the on-screen fictional world.

A film such as *Bob Roberts* is an exemplar of this technique, allowing for a complex set of perspectives on a central character, where secondary characters can immediately convey their perspectives to a central reporter, and hence to the audience (in this sense *Bob Roberts* updates the reporter-as-narrator premise of *Citizen Kane* (1941)).

In other cases, appropriating a documentary mode of presentation is used to increase a sense of verisimilitude and hence plausibility for an improbable story. In many instances this involves a film also attempting to tap into wider subcultures of superstition and folklore, particularly in the genres of horror and science fiction. An apparent documentary on an event or entity which is outside of human knowledge has much to exploit here in opening confusion over its ontological status. Key examples here include the vérité horrors of *Blair Witch*, and its apparent predecessor *The Last Broadcast* (1998), and the alien visitation premise in mockumentary texts such as *Alien Abduction, The Wicksboro Incident* (2003) and *Cloverfield* (2008). Here the collision between the rational and the irrational is used to create not comedy but suspense, to give credence to the threat posed by the supernatural and extraterrestrial.

This agenda also incorporates those efforts to use mockumentary form not for innovations in storytelling technique but to develop some form of socio-political critique. Documentary serves here typically as an assumed rational form that allows for an 'investigative' feel to a text, or a focus on socio-political aspects of communication (including commentary on documentary). There is an overlap here with satire (see below), but there are notable cases of mockumentaries which use the documentary form for serious political intent, including the mock-autobiography *David Holzman's Diary*, or the Dogme 95 film *Fuckland*, constructed as a video diary of an Argentinean in the Falkland Islands.[4] One of the more thought-provoking mockumentaries in this vein is *Zero Day* (2003), which uses the video diary form to explore the deliberations and motivations of two American teenagers planning a Columbine-style massacre at their high school. Other examples include the assassination conspiracy films *Nothing So Strange* (2002), *Interview with the Assassin* (2002), and the briefly controversial *Death of a President* (2006), which speculated on the assassination of George W. Bush.

As discussed in chapter 5, there is an obvious overlap here with drama-documentary, not just in their broader project to engage with aspects of historical narrative through fictional means, but the occasional sharing of textual strategies.

The dominance of parody and satire

Most mockumentaries, and certainly the most popular examples, derive from the intention to use documentary and reality-based forms to generate parody and satire. There are useful distinctions to be made here between these two terms, despite the lack of a clear consensus among theorists on their respective definitions. Both parody and satire sample something of their textual targets in order to offer forms of commentary, but they can be distinguished by their agendas, the nature of their appropriations and ultimately the readings they encourage of audiences.

For Hutcheon, 'parodic art both deviates from an aesthetic norm and includes that norm within itself as backgrounded material' (Hutcheon, 2000: 44). She suggests that parody is 'related to burlesque, travesty, pastiche, plagiarism, quotation, and allusion, but remains distinct from them' (ibid.: 43). At the heart of her definition is a sense of the conservatism of parody, the awareness of the ambivalence which parodic texts often have towards their target(s), within an overall nostalgic appreciation at the heart of their mimicry. There are plenty of mockumentary texts which exhibit these tendencies, including those that include cameos from celebrity and other public figures, such as *The Rutles – All You Need is Cash* (1978), an affectionate parody of the Beatles mythology; the variety of films of Christopher Guest both as actor (*This is Spinal Tap*) and director (*Waiting for Guffman* (1996), *Best in Show* (2000) or the subtle humour of *A Mighty Wind* (2003)); and the Woody Allen mockumentaries *Take the Money and Run* (1969) and *Zelig*.

Hutcheon refers to this as the paradox of parody, in that such texts contain both authority and transgression, both similarity and difference, in relation to their subjects: 'Even in mocking, parody reinforces; in formal terms, it inscribes the mocked conventions onto itself, thereby guaranteeing their continued existence' (Hutcheon, 2000: 75). Accordingly, Hutcheon defines parody as essentially parasitic, even if parodic texts are capable of transcending their origins, of moving beyond mere mimicry. Harries sees wider possibilities for parody, which he defines as 'the process of recontextualizing a target or source text through the transformation of its textual (and contextual) elements, thus creating a *new* text' (Harries, 2000: 6, original emphasis). The distinctions between Harries and Hutcheon over parody are not major, and crucially both acknowledge the primary role played by the audience in determining the effect of any transgressions. For both writers, part of the task of evaluating a parodic mockumentary text involves identifying the extent to which it achieves a clear distinction from its target.

Both Harries and Hutcheon argue that parodic discourse has become quite formulaic, that such texts form a canon focused on familiar methods of 'reiteration, inversion, misdirection, literalization, extraneous inclusion and exaggeration' (Harries, 2000: 37). Hutcheon insists that parody is central to an era of postmodernism, arguing that the prominence of parodic texts suggests a wider sense of ideological instability (Hutcheon, 2000: 82). Both parody and satire imply some ironic, critical distancing from the object that is their focus, and therefore both imply value judgements, but 'satire generally uses that distance to make a negative statement about that which is satirized' (Hutcheon, 2000: 44), containing an expectation of the power of the satire to influence change in its target. Such distinctions are not always obvious, not least because specific texts may contain both tendencies. Plantinga's excellent analysis of *This is Spinal Tap* is a good illustration here, as he details how the film engages in a satire of heavy metal discourse on masculinity and a parody of a particular documentary format (in this case 'rockumentary') (Plantinga, 1998: 321).[5]

All of these agendas share appropriation as a strategy to put into play the representational styles from a variety of non-fiction and related forms. Despite the frequency of promotional and stunt mockumentary, and the many examples of dramatic mockumentary, there is no question that mockumentary is popularly identified as couched within parodic and satiric traditions. The corpus of mockumentary texts is generally at odds with the sober agendas of documentary and other non-fiction; it serves as the playfully irrational counter to the rationality of factual discourse. Part of what makes the discourse so dynamic and complex, however, is that all of the agendas outlined above can be contained to varying degrees within a single mockumentary text. The key point to reiterate here is that we can see from just this initial listing that mockumentary discourse has evolved into a variety of often conflicting strategies and agendas,

encompassing texts ranging from the trivial application of mockumentary form to densely layered and innovative constructions
which look to engage audiences in a multitude of ways.

The corpus of texts which we might label 'mockumentary' has
also proliferated. What constitute what we might call mockumentary proper are those texts which consistently apply mockumentary
discourse, which offer a sustained appropriation of reality-based
forms for their entire length. There is also a whole range of texts
which only partially use the discourse, which arguably operate at
the margins of mockumentary despite often sharing similar agendas.
These take elements of factual forms and incorporate them spas-
modically into fictional texts for a variety of effects (see especially
chapter 7). Such examples challenge any formation of a comprehensive canon of mockumentary. Where, for example, does the
March of Time sequence from *Citizen Kane* fit, or similar isolated
sequences of mockumentary within fictional (or non-fictional)
texts? Such texts do not involve a sustained, seamless appropriation, they are not intended to be read as if they were documentary
or related forms, even if the intentions underlying such a limited or
partial appropriation share some of the agendas of mockumentary
proper.

Mockumentary discourse, then, has been integrated into a
number of generic codes and conventions and used in often quite
contrasting ways, in both sporadic and sustained forms of appropriation and simulation. Often the discourse has been integral to
reinvigorating a genre if only in a stylistic sense, taking a distinct
textual strategy which ultimately transcends aesthetics to provide
a fresh perspective on a conventional topic (*Blair Witch* for horror,
The Office for sitcom). More recently, television series using the
form suggest that mockumentary can serve primarily as a narrative
form within dramatic and comedic texts, useful for exploring thematic issues other than a reflexivity toward documentary.

Mockumentary: referenced to an expanding fact-fiction continuum

Mockumentary in general entails a call to play. It reflects an impulse
to engage with elements of the fact-fiction continuum, to manipu-
late and perform these for a contrasting series of agendas. And the
discourse offers at least the potential to disrupt the expectations

that are associated with this broader continuum. Although the core of mockumentary has consistently centred on the satiric and parodic treatment of non-fiction forms, it is important to recognise that the discourse is not necessarily exclusively parasitic. There are many examples derived from a more experimental agenda, particularly from filmmakers looking to explore wider issues of representation using mockumentary forms.

Jim Lane's useful discussion of autobiographical documentary, for example, argues that *David Holzman's Diary* 'is a fictional film which paradoxically anticipates an entire group of autobiographical films and videos' that he terms 'the journal entry documentary film' (Lane, 2002: 33). The film reflects upon 'direct cinema's claim to truth', a quote deliberately initiating a reflexive discussion about the nature of these films as it playfully explores the nature of people's relationships with new forms of (documentary-making) technology (Roscoe and Hight, 2001: 161–6). This is not to suggest that director Jim McBride was prescient, more that he was responding to currents within documentary culture that were already becoming evident, recognising also that the audience was more open to toying with the notion that autobiographical films offered a greater sense of authenticity (Figure 1). This is one case where a mockumentary filmmaker added to the lexicon of factual forms. Lane argues that '[d]espite its fictional status, *David Holzman's Diary* created a simulated, intimate mode of narration that proved viable for actual autobiographical documentarists' (Lane, 2002: 45). Similarly, it has been argued that Luis Buñuel's 1933 film *Las Hurdes (Land Without Bread)* to some extent anticipated the emergence of the voice-over documentary that it parodies (Russell, 2006: 102). Here Buñuel looked to play with a form that was not yet firmly established as a generic convention.

Mockumentary is now part of the lexicon available to both fictional and non-fictional filmmakers and producers. The discourse now freely references from throughout the fact-fiction continuum, shaped by the variety of agendas outlined above, drawing from and reflecting the increasing instability and fluidity of the contract between documentary makers and audiences which is central to wider documentary culture. While most definitions of mockumentary focus only on those texts that reference and potentially develop a reflexive commentary toward the documentary genre itself, mockumentary discourse can now be seen to draw upon a greatly expanded

1. L. M. Kit Carson introduces his experiment to discover the 'truth' of his life through film, from *David Holzman's Diary* (1967), a mockumentary film that anticipated the emergence of autobiographical documentary.

range of representations of the real, involving contrasting styles, agendas, forms of rhetorical address codes and conventions. These include not only documentary modes of representation but closely related modes of presentation from news and current affairs (including older forms such as newsreels), amateur videography and home videos, the range of video and camcorder forms and surveillance footage that form the basis of the 'reality' claims of television documentary hybrids, and a variety of reality-based forms proliferating on digital platforms.

In this sense, mockumentary has been part of, and is responding to, a broadening of documentary-related media. These are typically marked by both a continuation of an assumed centrality of the indexical image as a signifier of reality and a fracturing of the aesthetic and agenda of documentary proper. The intention here is not to survey all of these trends, but to note the increasing fluidity of boundaries between genres and between media in a variety of contradictory and mutually reinforcing trends. This is part of what Corner has termed 'post-documentary' culture.

This is a culture in which the modernist project of documentary, a project which is anyway crucially split across its defining cinematic and televisual moments, is relocated and reworked with a whole new diversity of other popular uses of recorded reality. Its aesthetics, its institutional supports and its public goals are all subject to a more profound instability than its most unstable of genres has previously faced. (Corner, 2001b: 358)

It is still debatable whether this constitutes a transformation of the documentary genre itself, as there are paradoxical trends here. Such trends within documentary culture also need to be couched within an acknowledgement of wider social and cultural patterns of engagement with mediations of the 'real'. There are too many factors to properly survey here, but they include a quite dynamic interaction between the wider cultural practices of surveillance, autobiography and creative expression.

At one level, there has been an expansion of intimate and auto-biographical forms of documentary filmmaking, derived from both amateur and professional explorations of first video and then digital camcorders.[6] Jonathan Caouette's *Tarnation* (2003) is an oft-cited example of an 'amateur' filmmaker able to participate in a broadening documentary mainstream through using the iMovie non-linear editing software bundled with the Apple computer operating system. The result is something like Dziga Vertov playfully exploring a video diary format.

Documentary culture is also increasingly integrated with a wider and disquieting naturalisation of surveillance practices within modern societies, most clearly demonstrated by the increased acceptance of surveillance footage within television programming (Palmer, 2003). Together with the emergence of an amateur surveillance culture centred on camcorders, webcams, videologs and phonecams, such trends suggest (among other things) a collapse of distinctions between public and private space and an increased realm for personalised forms of confession and expression. Although clearly intersecting with more established traditions of personal media production such as amateur photography (Hight, 2001), it is the aesthetic of amateur video – grainy, hand-held, accidental and partial perspectives on typically trivial events – which is increasingly reinforced as the key marker of authenticity. The broader surveillance culture sharing this aesthetic encompasses everything from amateur surveillance with webcams and phonecams to journalistic exposés using 'caught on tape' forms of sensationalist appeal, terrorist camcorder propaganda posted on websites (such as in the brutal aftermath of the 2003 American invasion and occupation of Iraq) and the faking of apparently accidental capturing of footage by fans of *America's Funniest Home Videos* (1990–).

Such examples partly suggest an extension of amateur film practices (Zimmermann, 1995), involving a global audience that are engaged not simply through the commercial dictates of television. This naturalisation of nonprofessional footage is itself a natural consequence of increased access by audiences to technologies which effectively allow them to play the role of producers, publishing content directly online, and outside of the practices which define professional journalism. Documentary aesthetics, then, are increasingly appropriated and transformed as modes of practice within online, emergent models of broadcasting.

It is a paradox of this new documentary culture that there has also been a rise in the popularity and profile of feature film documentary. Films such as *Le Peuple migrateur* (*Winged Migration*) (2001), *Touching the Void* (2003), *Spellbound* (2002), *Capturing the Friedmans* (2003), *Super Size Me* (2004), *An Inconvenient Truth* (2006) and especially the work of Michael Moore (*Bowling for Columbine, Fahrenheit 9/11*) have found easy distribution in film multiplexes and later home rental and retail markets. Moore's work has to some extent helped to establish popular expectations of feature documentary for American audiences (high production values and pointed political commentary, but in an entertaining vein) and offered a template for political documentary which sparked a variety of other independent, partisan political documentaries. Such features often follow a familiar trajectory, beginning with initial limited release to the film festival circuit, then wider release to commercial theatre distribution, then possible screening on television. Distributors and funders have belatedly recognised that documentary could constitute a profitable market, leading also to a proliferation of DVD sales, while new digital distribution platforms (DVD and World Wide Web) have made self-distribution also more viable.[7]

All of these trends are overlapping in complex and not always easily predicted ways. In general terms we can say that there are continuities with more conventional documentary forms, even where the nature of production practice, the platform for dissemination and distribution and the materiality of texts themselves (into digital code) have been transformed. The implications of such an expanded and transformed documentary culture are potentially extremely significant, in that they reflect increasingly fluid discourses of public and private forms of socio-political knowledge and the means for articulating these.

A key issue within this expanded realm of the real, one that is directly relevant to mockumentary, is the manner in which a new, broader, more fractured documentary culture foregrounds and often prioritises forms of reflexivity toward any mediation of reality. Mockumentary's appropriation of documentary codes and conventions contains an inherently reflexive potential toward the broader field of documentary, offering the potential for audiences to engage in a commentary on core aspects of the genre itself. Everything from the ethics of documentary filmmakers and their agendas, to the validity of core aspects of documentary modes of representation, to the assumptions and expectations that we have as audiences, becomes subject to mockumentary's call to play.

Forms of reflexivity have become especially prominent in television documentary hybrids, but instances of reflexivity have a long tradition within documentary filmmaking. Nichols has outlined the reflexive mode of the genre, which he defines as inflections of expository, interactive, observational modes of documentary representation which entail a metacommentary about the process of representation itself. Reflexive moments in documentary can be 'self-conscious not only about form and style, as poetic ones are, but also about strategy, structure, conventions, expectations, and effects' (Nichols, 1991: 56–7). These are the moments where documentary reveals itself as a construction. This obviously involves a direct challenge to documentary viewers' expectations of nonfiction forms:

> The reflexive mode of representation gives emphasis to the encounter between filmmaker and viewer rather than filmmaker and subject. This mode arrives last on the scene since it is itself the least naïve and the most doubtful about the possibilities of communication and expression that the other modes take for granted. Realist access to the world, and the ability to provide persuasive evidence, the possibility of indisputable argument, the unbreakable bond between an indexical image and that which it represents – all these notions prove suspect. (Nichols, 1991: 60)

Nichols speculates that the arrival of the reflexive mode in documentary entails a 'maturation of the genre', with the incorporation of traditions of satire, parody and irony. (The overlap with mockumentary here is obvious, although Nichols himself conflates fictional and non-fictional reflexive texts. Both he and Ruby, writing much earlier (Ruby, 1977), tend to discuss mockumentaries *David Holzman's Diary* and *No Lies* (1974) purely as forms of reflexive documentary.)

Nichols' discussion of a reflexive mode of documentary involves a useful outline of different senses of reflexivity, involving overlapping but distinct techniques designed towards different effects. We can think of a useful continuum between milder forms of 'formal' or stylistic reflexivity and 'political' reflexivity. For Nichols, 'formal reflexivity' involves employing documentary aesthetics for an affectionate parody of the documentary form, creating an awareness and appreciation of the nature of documentary filmmaking (in accord with Hutcheon's insistence on the conservatism inherent in parody as a discourse).[8] This doesn't necessarily directly challenge a faith in the documentary form, but involves 'those strategies that break received conventions', introducing 'gaps, reversals, and unexpected turns that draw attention to the work of style as such and place the obsessions of illusionism within brackets' (Nichols, 1991: 70). Such strategies are not new to the genre, with early works in actuality forms, such as Vertov's *Chelovek s kinoapparatom (The Man with a Movie Camera)* (1929), offering a template for revealing and commenting upon the act of mediation itself.

'Political reflexivity', in contrast, ranges from an expression of unease with documentary pretensions, through to an open attack on the central premises of the genre and its associated sober discourses. The agenda here is to engage with documentary as an institutional form, to highlight that it should be distrusted for that very reason. More fundamental aspects of factual discourse are often also the targets here, including a calling into question of the integrity of the photographic image itself, or at least our often naïve, immediate and common-sensical belief in the ability of the camera to accurately and objectively document the socio-historical world. In more detailed and sustained attacks, this can involve the 'revealing' of documentary as simply another form of fiction.

Nichols retains a subtlety to this discussion. The forms of reflexivity he discusses, only briefly outlined here, serve as ways of inflecting documentary modes for multiple purposes. An instance of formal reflexivity may in certain circumstances also be politically reflexive; as he notes, the effects of reflexivity ultimately depend on audiences themselves. In fact, it is possible for there to be unintentional reflexivity, or for a reflexive moment to be associated with a text whether or not that has been the intention of the filmmakers themselves. This may occur where an event is staged and not acknowledged (but subsequently revealed), or simply where audiences become confused about where the boundary lies between fiction and documentary in a particular film.

Mockumentary and layered readings for audiences

Complicating the identification of mockumentary practice is the fact that a specific mockumentary text can operate at a variety of levels simultaneously and be open to interpretations from differently situated audiences. A single text can cue different layers of interpretation and pleasure for audiences: in fact the more popular forms of mockumentary often have this as a central aspect of their appeal. One difficulty in building a complex model of the interplay between documentary and mockumentary is the relative paucity of empirical research into forms of spectatorship associated with the broader continuum of documentary forms. This discussion assumes that mockumentary operates to play with, and put into play, assumptions and expectations associated with a 'documentary mode of reading' (of the sort outlined by Nichols in his three-part definition of documentary). Unfortunately, most of the work offered by Nichols and later writers is drawn largely from textual analysis, based on speculation derived from anecdotal evidence or derived from critics' own perspectives. There are few examples of empirical audience research in this area.[9]

Much of documentary theory draws from a collective sense that there are fundamentally different modes of reading associated with fact and fiction. Sobchack argues that viewers engage with a '"documentary consciousness": a particular mode of embodied and ethical spectatorship that informs and transforms the space of the irreal into the space of the real' (Sobchack, 2004: 261). She insists that

> In sum, what the generic terms *fiction* and *documentary* designate are
> an experienced difference in our mode of consciousness, our atten-

tion toward and our valuation of the cinematic objects we engage. (Sobchack, 2004: 261, original emphasis)

At base, her argument rests on an assumption that our engagement with documentary is about recognition of our own socio-political experience. In a wider discussion of texts which combine fictional and non-fictional elements, Sobchack argued that the nature of viewers' engagement

> with and determination of film images as fictional or real may be experienced either preconsciously or consciously, idiosyncratically or conventionally, momentarily or for relatively sustained periods of time – and, furthermore, it suggests that whatever the textual incentives offered by the film, this engagement and determination depends always on the viewer's existential knowledge of and social investments in the context of a lifeworld that exceeds and frames the text. (Sobchack, 2004: 268)

She argues that each viewer brings to such texts her own experiences with all media images, not just those of documentary. The key is to acknowledge the contextualised nature of the viewing experience, in relation to traditions of codes and conventions that are accepted as conveying a recording of reality.

> The charge of the real is always an *ethical charge*: one that calls forth not only response but responsibility – not only aesthetic valuation but also ethical judgement. It engages our awareness not only of the existential consequences *of* representation but also of our own ethical implication *in* representation. It remands us reflexively to ourselves as embodied, culturally knowledgeable, and social invested viewers. (Sobchack, 2004: 284, original emphasis)

Central to documentary is consequently a call to action, based on this recognition of our ethical responsibilities within the address of documentary, both implicit and explicit in modes of representation. What needs to be emphasised, however, is that this is not just a rational or cognitive process of interpretation. Documentary entails an emotional charge as well. Here she recognises the complexity of our engagement with documentary as a genre, and the levels of cognitive and emotional investment that it entails.

Complicating these assumptions about a documentary mode of reading are the possibilities for viewers to acquire degrees of critical awareness toward documentary practice. Consequently, it is possible to consider a number of interpretive responses toward documentary texts, accessible to all documentary audiences given the right circumstances and textual or extra-textual prompts. Viewers may challenge the nature of evidence that a filmmaker collates and presents, particularly if the audience has existing knowledge, experience or belief about the subject. We could view this as an experience-based, contextualised form of reflexivity that might not extend to a critique of documentary form itself. Viewers could also draw upon an awareness of the constructed nature of documentary, such as an understanding of the ways in which it is contextualised within wider value systems and institutional constraints, and aimed at specific audiences.

Potentially, audiences may have a deeper sense of doubt about the integrity of the photographic image itself, most typically through an awareness of either the capabilities of digital technologies to fake images, or simply through a wider sense of distrust of journalism (in other words, this highly reflexive stance toward documentary could come from quite narrow, highly politicised readings, not just because these viewers may be more 'sophisticated' in their understanding of media practices). The point is that the range of potential modes of readings by viewers is complicated not just by intellectual or cognitive responses and interpretations of form and content, but also, crucially, by emotional responses tied to common-sense understandings of the mediation of reality. And this complexity of audience responses is only becoming more complicated in a digital era. A common paradox within documentary culture as a whole is the coexistence between a naturalised belief in the indexical nature of images and a widespread awareness of how easily images can be digitally manipulated (Fetveit, 1999).

There are other aspects to documentary construction which could complicate audience responses. For example, there is a host of issues inherent to notions of 'performance' in documentary. We could delineate distinct forms of performance within documentary proper, such as those inherent in some everyday sense of role playing (we all perform different roles in our everyday lives, as fathers, daughters, employers, consumers and so on). Consider the distinctions between conscious and unconscious forms of self-representation in the presence of a camera crew, the performance aspects involved in dramatic reconstructions, and forms of professional performance (say by musicians or politicians) that are being documented.

Intersecting with these are subtle notions of authenticity. How do we respond if what has been filmed is a staged performance, but we are encouraged to believe that it gives insight into a performer? What if the performance has the emotional resonance of truth, or there appears to be slippage in the façade? When aging former socialite Edie performs a cheer, or sings a song from her past for the Maysles brothers in *Grey Gardens* (1975), these are performances that are perhaps more revealing than an interview. They are suggestive of a relationship with these filmmakers that shows a high degree of trust and intimacy (particularly as they are interspersed with scenes of her whispering to the Maysles). But these are performances that are also remnants from her past that she is wanting to present to them. They are an opportunity to demonstrate the vibrancy of her memories, and in a sense to relive part of the experience itself. As viewers, we feel that we understand her motivations, her nostalgia and the sense of enjoyment she gains from performing before not just the camera but the wider film audience. Similar assessments of the nature of what is being presented on screen are inherent in our interpretation of autobiographical films (Lane, 2002) and other forms of documentary where a participant's subjectivity is foregrounded (Renov, 2004).

Such concerns of performance, personalised narrative, other forms of subjectivity and their intersections with assumptions about authenticity in the words and actions of social actors are even more central to the modes of reading associated with television documentary hybrids. Here viewers are more deliberately positioned to make complicated assessments of performance, often because of the staged and constructed elements of the environment and activities that are being filmed (these issues are discussed in more detail in chapter 4).

There are other aspects to audience readings of documentary proper, often neglected within documentary literature, particularly a host of issues surrounding notions of viewer pleasure. These could involve narrative pleasures, in the sense of the satisfaction of a solution to a puzzle (often central to expositional mode), perhaps involving the 'capture' (even if only on camera) of an aberrant socio-political figure, or the host of natural dramatic qualities associated with social actors. There are often elements of voyeurism inherent in the documentary gaze itself, if not in its sexual connotations, then in terms of a curiosity with the exotic, with social and cultural spectacle outside of the cultural norms of assumed audiences (documentary as tourism of the Other). Documentary also offers clear ideological pleasures, as in the comfort of seeing one's value systems being validated (is Michael Moore influencing audiences to change their political beliefs, or providing a confirmation of what they already believe?). Finally, the notion of 'play' within documentary proper is inadequately acknowledged, and typically only in reference to distinct representational styles such as performative and reflexive modes. If we associate mockumentary with a call to play rather than the call to action inherent in the documentary project, is this a distinction that is central to audiences' engagement (and which audiences in particular)?

Mockumentary discourse engages with this complexity of modes of reading, offering a space for audiences to play with their own assumptions and expectations generated around documentary and reality-based texts. These possibilities are shaped by the specific agenda(s) pursued by the makers of mockumentary texts. Hutcheon and Harries, each writing in relation to parodic discourse, argue for the need to consider the complexity of reading practices associated with parodic texts. Hutcheon notes that 'readers are active cocreators of the parodic text in a more explicit and perhaps more complex way than reader-response critics argue that they are in the reading of all texts' (Hutcheon, 2000: 93). She argues that the producers of parody must assume a degree of familiarity with cultural norms in order for them to be recognised, and that there is inevitably a degree of sophistication demanded of readers. (Unfortunately, Hutcheon seems to conclude that only an elite audience can therefore fully appreciate parody.)

Harries similarly argues for a particular mode of spectatorship associated with parody

> Not only do parodies create 'something' (new textual configurations as well as modifications to pre-existing canons), they also foster 'ways' to view texts, developing and nurturing *critical* spectatorial strategies. While parody does indeed rely on and cannibalize other texts, its reworkings affect not only the viewing of previous textual systems but also the construction and viewing of future related canonical texts. (Harries, 2000: 7, original emphasis)

For Harries, the range of reading responses to a parodic text can include those readers who do not recognise the target and therefore do not realise the film is a parody, a reader who realises a text is parody but does not get the exact reference, one who recognises the intent and the target but does not appreciate the irony and, finally, the reader who is able to actually enjoy the ironic position in relation to the targeted text (Harries, 2000: 108, citing Rose). He insists that a certain amount of linguistic competency is required of the viewer to 'recognise the doubly-coded signifiers and understand their juxtaposition', a 'generic competence in order to understand what logonomic system is being parodied or ironically played with', and an ideological competence in comprehending the nature and implications of a norm violation (Harries, 2000: 109).

The difficulty with both of these writers' positions is that they tend to equate complexity at a textual level with sophistication at the level of audience interaction. They neglect to marry these assumptions with a model of audience interaction that incorporates an awareness of the complexities of possible *in situ* readings. It is not necessarily the case that a sophisticated audience will be making a variety of simultaneous readings at different levels. It is more useful to suggest that such texts remain open to repeated viewings and layered forms of appreciation, open to the possibilities of engaging with the variety of contextual knowledges and extra-textual cues which audiences may bring to specific viewing encounters. It is also useful to acknowledge the 'interpretative repertoires' that viewers utilise, based particularly on their familiarity with different visual traditions.

In terms of mockumentary, viewers may obviously bring to a text a familiarity with documentary codes and conventions, but also various degrees of awareness of mockumentary discourse itself. Viewers who have encountered texts which undertake exercises in deconstructing documentary and reality-based forms of construction can be assumed to be more readily familiar with and able to recognise such tendencies in other texts. More than this, any audience that is familiar with documentary as a genre will have varying degrees of understanding of the conditional and contingent issues of authenticity, indexicality and ethical practice. Where a viewer sits in relation to the core tensions and paradoxes of documentary culture can be assumed to shape their response to the various intentions of documentary appropriation performed by mockumentaries.

Experiences which viewers may have of mockumentary, and the host of complications to textual readings which these bring, may simply teach viewers to be more suspicious of particular kinds of documentary apparatus. Students often ask whether a documentary such as *American Movie: The Making of Northwestern* (1999) is in fact a mockumentary, precisely because it takes a satiric perspective on its key subject and seems to move beyond the rational, empathetic perspective typically adopted toward the documentary's participants.[10] Other examples where satiric discourse is employed in documentary, such as Mark Lewis' work (for example *Cane Toads: An Unnatural History* (1998) and *The Natural History of the Chicken* (2000)), suggest an overlap between reflexive documentary and mockumentary. It may be that audiences simply accept each of these as part of a broader set of strategies employed by filmmakers and programmer makers, or they may seek more definitive categories of texts with clearly defined modes of reading.

Obviously this discussion raises more questions than it answers and is by no means exhaustive, but there are some key points here. Firstly, that there is a need for a richly textured model of spectatorship for documentary itself, one which acknowledges modes of readings associated with the more hybrid forms within the broader fact-fiction continuum. Secondly, it is obvious that mockumentary puts these modes of reading potentially into play with each other, suggesting that audiences are increasingly being asked to engage in greater cognitive activity in determining the ontological status of both mockumentary and the full continuum of fact-fiction texts.

The complexity of mockumentary discourse lies not just in its play with documentary and reality-based modes of reading but with the ability of the more richly textured mockumentaries to offer layered forms of engagement, to provide a variety of pleasures for viewers which can bear repeated viewing. For example, audiences can enjoy a mockumentary's intertextual references to documentary culture or to wider socio-political discourses associated with the thematics of the text. Many mockumentaries also work purely in conventional narrative terms, engaging audiences through identifiable characters and compelling stories. Viewers, then, may appreciate the craft involved in replicating documentary form, the collision of documentary form with incongruous content, the accuracy, insight and effectiveness of the parodic treatment of its targets, and the sheer playfulness of the exercise in representation. For example, the classic mockumentary *This is Spinal Tap* can be enjoyed for its parodic references to the classic rockumentaries D. A. Pennebaker's *Don't Look Back* (1967) and Martin Scorsese's *The Last Waltz* (1978), for its satire of 1980s heavy metal bands or for its effectiveness in getting us to identify with the quasi-familial community of Spinal Tap itself (see Plantinga's excellent discussion of this film, Plantinga (1998)). The extent to which any such text is formally or politically reflexive (in Nichols' terms) is partly determined by the audience, and by the context in which the text is viewed.

A wider question here is whether contemporary culture is increasingly suited to such layered texts. Johnson argues that popular culture as a whole has become a realm requiring greater cognitive endeavour than in the past in 'the kind of thinking you have to do to make sense of a cultural experience' (S. Johnson, 2005: 14). He insists, for example, that television is growing increasingly rigorous in its construction of meaning, a result of wider changes in the nature of the industry itself, its economics and a direct response to devices such as DVDs and TiVo which allow repeated, time-shifted viewings of television programming. Johnson cites the emergence of multithreaded narratives in prime time, following from the template established by series such as *Hill Street Blues* (1981–87) (S. Johnson, 2005: 68). These featured a greater degree of subtlety in conveying information crucial to understanding narrative, an emphasis on creating texture within narratives, and especially an acknowledgement of the pleasures of viewers 'filling in' narrative gaps left for them. Johnson suggests that key to this complexity is the need for viewers to be able to track multiple relationships between characters: 'many popular television dramas today feature dense webs of relationships that require focus and scrutiny on the part of the viewer just to figure out what's happening on the screen' (S. Johnson, 2005: 109). More generally, he sees a drift toward increased complexity in what is made available to the viewer, as individual episodes incorporate references such as to previous incidents in the series' fictional world (S. Johnson, 2005: 84–7). The result is a serial text which is capable of enduring, even requiring, repeated viewings in order to appreciate its layers of meaning.

These are teasing speculations, but again, they are largely derived from selective textual analysis. Whatever the universal applicability of Johnson's conclusions, certainly audiences appear to have become more adept at dealing with intertextual references and capable of drawing upon a variety of modes of reading when engaging with contemporary popular culture, including mockumentary. A key issue here is whether mockumentary in these terms suggests greater audience 'sophistication' or 'savvy'; whether mockumentary is addressing a visually and politically sophisticated audience or simply one that is accustomed to stylistic play within media forms. While the potential exists to engage in a complex and layered engagement with a text, it is not necessarily the case that such texts are evidence of a wider increase in critical literacy in relation to popular culture. If mockumentary entails a call to play, what are the socio-political implications, if any, of this play? Does it simply encourage more participatory forms of media involvement, or are there political implications as well? Certainly the proliferation of mockumentary across a variety of media suggests that the discourse, which has become naturalised within avant-garde and mainstream filmmaking and within primetime television programming, is capable of evolving into more emergent and interactive forms of narrative.

Notes

1 *Alien Abduction* is discussed in Roscoe and Hight, 2001: 151–2.
2 See http://museumofhoaxes.com/.
3 See www.walmartmovie.com/wmtv, with the advertisements also available through YouTube.
4 This is a rare Dogme film that is actually a mockumentary. See chapter 5.
5 In *Faking It* (Roscoe and Hight, 2001), these kinds of distinctions informed the effort to identify the specific tendencies of reflexivity toward documentary expressed as degrees of mockumentary.
6 Michael Renov's work is particularly useful in conceptualising developments along this trajectory (Renov, 2004).
7 These new digital platforms directly facilitate layered forms of audience engagement, most explicitly in DVDs. The release of documentary on DVD often allows for a potential reframing of a documentary's core arguments by pairing a feature with 'extra' materials offering insights into the complexities of documentary practice itself (Hight, 2005).

8 Nichols further distinguishes formal reflexivity into stylistic reflexivity, deconstructive reflexivity, interactivity, irony, parody and satire.

9 As is discussed in chapter 4, Annette Hill's work in relation to television reality programming remains significant (Hill, 2005; Hill, 2007; Hill, 2008).

10 See also Middleton, who discusses *American Movie* in relation to *This is Spinal Tap* and *Roger & Me* (1989) in a discussion on documentary comedy (Middleton, 2002).

2

The mockumentary across media

The previous chapter provided broad outlines for a definition of mockumentary discourse, covering the variety of agendas behind media producers' use of the discourse, the range of forms that are referenced within the broader fact-fiction continuum and the complexities of audience readings of mockumentary texts. This chapter looks at the ways in which the discourse has emerged across different media, necessarily employing different textual strategies and often exhibiting distinct patterns in thematics within key fictional genres. Mockumentary discourse has proven itself malleable enough to be applied over a broad range of media forms, involving mimicking production practices associated with reality-based media or simply simulating their aesthetics with varying degrees of skills and subtlety. There are distinct trajectories in the development of mockumentary within each medium, as briefly discussed below. There are overlapping and mutually reinforcing trends here, all of which are converging and diverging across digital platforms in new configurations such as the possibilities of cross-platform or 'transmedia' storytelling.

This chapter is not attempting a comprehensive genealogy of mockumentary across all media. Such a task is beyond this volume and in fact self-defeating, as it is difficult to speak of a definitive corpus of texts within such a rapidly expanding and dynamic set of textual strategies. Instead the aim here is to suggest some of the broader patterns in mockumentary practice, to note key reference points in each medium and especially to begin to situate television mockumentary within this wider context. The more specific history of television mockumentary is the task of later chapters.

Mockumentary draws upon audiences' familiarity with codes and conventions associated with the fact-fiction continuum appropriate to each medium. In general terms, it is possible to identify an overall trajectory in the development of the discourse, marked by an increasing density of the field of symbolic forms referenced from these continua, and consequently some distinct changes in the relationships of mockumentary texts with audiences. Viewers appear to have become more accustomed to engaging with the sense of play generated by mockumentary, more adept at identifying cues to fact and fiction and anticipating intertextual references. Since the 1990s viewers have become users and navigators (rather than simply viewers) within entertainment environments across digital platforms that allow more flexible and customised forms of interaction and participation in mockumentary texts. Increasingly, users have become producers, capable of more direct and creative forms of participation in engaging with mockumentary's call to play. The later part of this chapter discusses such examples of mockumentary's development within the wider set of participatory possibilities inherent in emergent online media, which Henry Jenkins has termed 'convergent culture' (Jenkins, 2006).

Radio

Any history of mockumentary would need to acknowledge one of the more celebrated cases of appropriating non-fiction codes and conventions for dramatic purposes: the 1938 radio broadcast of *War of the Worlds* typically associated with Orson Welles. The broadcast is an example of aural mockumentary, drawing on what Renov has termed 'acoustic indexicality',[1] and has been extensively discussed elsewhere (Cantril, 1940; Roscoe and Hight, 2001: 78–9). Welles helped to write and perform this radio version of H. G. Wells's famous novel on Halloween Eve in 1938. Despite disclaimers that the play was another dramatic fiction, and performed in a regular timeslot for Welles's dramatic troupe, its simulation of a news broadcast of an apparent Martian invasion caused panic among listeners, and later, political controversy. The broadcast was constructed as a series of 'live' links to reporters, including interviews with panicked eyewitnesses on location in towns along the Eastern coast of the United States. Its effectiveness derived from listeners' familiarity with the aural codes and conventions associated with news reporting, within a cultural context that reinforced most listeners' complete faith in the integrity of radio as a default voice of authority. These factors apparently precluded any real critical modes of reading toward the institutional voice apparent in the authoritative tones of the radio announcer on the part of a sizeable portion of the broadcast's audience. The key advantage of radio mockumentary over audio-visual media is that it allows listeners greater freedom to employ their imagination – in the case of *War of the Worlds* this was prompted by the excited tones of the studio announcers, the panic in the voices of 'eyewitnesses' and, perhaps most effective of all, the use of static and silence to suggest a link that has been cut by violent, extraterrestrial means.

The 1938 broadcast is still an apparently rare example of a dramatic radio mockumentary. The medium has retained a key role in the history of mockumentary as a discourse, but more as a site for comedic experimentation. Many of the examples of British mockumentary (or part mockumentary) series were trialled first as radio series, with performers honing their skills in mimicking voices, developing characters and narratives based around the appropriation of such non-fiction tropes as 'voice of god' narration and on-location interviews. There is also a long history of the use of mock announcements within radio comedy programmes, a feature used, together with more surreal sound effects, in the popular BBC radio comedy series *The Goons*. Created and co-written by Spike Milligan, the hugely inventive series ran from 1951 to 1960, featuring especially the vocal talents of Milligan, Harry Secombe, Peter Sellers and Michael Bentine. It was enormously influential in the development of British comedy, inspiring not only other radio comedy series but also a variety of television descendants. The series served as a key inspiration and precursor to a similar use of non-fiction conventions in the *Monty Python's Flying Circus* (1969–74) television series, itself a key reference point within television comedic mockumentary (see chapter 6).

On a more banal and pervasive level, radio has incorporated something of the promotional agenda for mockumentary, with announcements, vox-pop and 'expert' testimony used as staple elements within the variety of styles employed in radio advertising.

Feature film

The most well-known and popular examples of mockumentary are comedic feature films (Doherty, 2003). While these largely shape popular understandings of the mockumentary form, there is a long and rich history of the discourse that also includes more dramatic and serious fictions, and avant-garde and experimental work that often comprises the more reflexive or satirical examples of all mockumentary. Cinema also has a long history of the sporadic use of the discourse within more conventional narratives, with fake news broadcasts and interviews featuring in a number of mainstream films (Roscoe and Hight, 2001: 93–7).

The archetypal cinematic mockumentary is *This is Spinal Tap*, a richly layered film referenced to the often formulaic documentary subgenre of rockumentary. There have been many other examples similarly inspired by non-fiction media. Albert Brook's *Real Life* (1979), subtitled 'An American Comedy', parodied *An American Family* (1973), a classic observational television series that itself anticipated the docusoap format (Ruoff, 2002). Brook's film foregrounds the same concerns about ethics and voyeurism which dominate debates over the emergence of television documentary hybrids (see chapter 4). The production of the feature film *Series 7: The Contenders* (2001) predated the emergence of *Survivor*, but developed a satire of the tendencies of television hybridity through extrapolating that hybrid's premise to one 'logical' conclusion: 'contestants' fight for their lives after being selected and armed by a fictional television series titled *Series 7* (Hight, 2003).

More complex examples of mockumentary have come from auteur filmmakers who are generally not looking to attract a mainstream audience, but are preoccupied with aesthetic and cultural concerns. They tend to use mockumentary discourse for commentaries not only on specific tendencies within documentary culture, but also on broader issues related to visual culture. These range from the early mockumentary *David Holzman's Diary*, which anticipated developments in cinéma vérité,[2] and Peter Greenaway's exhaustive deconstruction of the expositional mode of documentary representation in *The Falls*. Greenaway's work on *The Falls* and other mockumentary-inflected texts such as *Vertical Features Remake* (1978) were informed by his own frustrations with documentary production while working on British public service and information films. Other key texts here include the nostalgic recreation of 1930s America in Woody Allen's *Zelig*, the political satire of *Bob Roberts* and the black comedy of the Belgian student production *C'est arrivé près de chez vous*

(*Man Bites Dog*), in which a film crew profile a serial killer (Roscoe, 1997).

Within cinematic mockumentary there is a corpus of films pre-occupied with the nature of feature film production itself. These include *The Making of... And God Spoke* (1993), *Welcome to Hollywood* (1998), *Slaves of Hollywood* (1999), *They Shoot Movies, Don't They?: The Making of Mirage* (2000), *R2PC: Road to Park City* (2000), *The Independent* (2000) and *Lisa Picard is Famous* (2000). Clearly inspired by the emergence of 'making of' documentaries (Arthur, 2004) that have proliferated as DVD extras (Hight, 2005), they tend to function as 'in-jokes', feature cameos by Hollywood figures and suggest that it is the film industry itself which constitutes their main audience. Many of these are amateur productions and they tend to tell similar stories of frustrated ambition, in part demonstrating how familiar the mockumentary style is to budding filmmakers. In this they can be seen as longer-form (and bigger budget) cousins of similar examples of early career efforts in short film.

Short film

This is a medium where mockumentary also has a particularly rich and long history, demonstrating all of the agendas and textual strategies associated with mockumentary discourse, ranging from experimental approaches involving mockumentary to the (unfortunately more numerous) trivial, banal and novelty-based examples of the form. The more celebrated examples include the black comedy of *A Sense of History* (1992), with Jim Broadbent in confessional mode as the epitome of upper-class amorality, and the fake interview with a rape victim at the centre of Mitchell Block's challenging *No Lies*. Short films are the site for the greatest explosion of mockumentaries in terms of participation by more amateur, low-budget productions. There are far too numerous examples here to mention in any detail, not least because the vast number of amateur productions have typically had very limited local release. Often these underestimate the satiric potential of mockumentary and rely on such modest budgets that they invariably involve the filmmaker's friends and family members as cast members and funders. There are now mockumentary film festivals dedicated to the form,[3] but the real growth in this medium has been prompted by the emergence of online sites which allow for the easy upload of user-generated content, such as YouTube (see below).

DVD and the World Wide Web

The digital platforms of DVD, and the World Wide Web offer a further array of possibilities for the expansion of mockumentary discourse. These need to be seen within the wider complexities of the relationship between digital and earlier media, which can be usefully approached with Bolter and Grusin's notion of 'remediation' (Bolter and Grusin, 2000). Their perspective on the nature of digital media, and particularly the complex relationships it establishes toward audio-visual media such as film and television, is rich and provocative. It includes the argument that any new medium tends to appropriate existing cultural forms, taking familiar modes of media construction and ways of creating meaning in order to refashion these into new forms that exploit the capabilities afforded by the new medium. Certainly this broad pattern appears to be at work with digital examples of mockumentary. While in many cases mockumentary on these platforms involves referencing completely new fact-fiction (digital) forms, there are familiar patterns of mockumentary agenda and practices here.

As within cinematic mockumentary, *This is Spinal Tap* anticipated the potential of mockumentary discourse on DVD and online. The special edition DVD release for the film includes a number of extras that maintain the fictional premise of the film, including audio commentaries from the lead actors in character, offering comments on the making of the 'documentary'.[4] This matched the film's promotional material, which generally sought to maintain a documentary frame, making no explicit reference to its status as a parody. Harries, for example, notes that the film's distribution company even released a fictional discography of the band Spinal Tap (Harries, 2000: 118). An official *Spinal Tap* website was less seamless in maintaining the fiction. Established not just to promote the film, but to allow for the distribution of actual CDs of the fictional band's music, it eventually also included a touring schedule (the success of the film having prompted a real tour by the fake band). Although not initially intended, the cumulative effect of such additions to the cinematic release was to encourage further layers of direct participation by its growing base of fans. They could continue to play along with the parody, playing the band's music when they liked, buying other merchandise and even taking the opportunity to see Spinal Tap live on tour. The 1993 sequel to the film, *The Return of Spinal Tap* (1993), in fact is largely a recorded performance from one of the band's actual concerts, held to promote the release of one of the band's real albums (Roscoe and Hight, 2001: 120–4). Some fans continued their appreciation online, through discussion groups, building tribute websites and uploading their short film parodies and homages of the film.[5]

In terms of this discussion, *Spinal Tap* is of interest as an example of a cinematic mockumentary which successfully expanded its presence into other media, building upon and contributing to its status as a cult film. The DVD release allowed fans to explore the wealth of materials developed through the film's improvisational practice, edited down to form the narrative of the film itself. The film's deleted scenes, many of which are of a similar standard to those included in the film itself, serve almost as an extended narrative, as we see more of the lead characters within different situations (such as at the monkey enclosure at a zoo, or Elvis Presley's grave in Graceland). These scenes not only draw attention to the craft of the film's director (Rob Reiner) in creating a narrative from such disparate materials, but support the sense that these are characters who plausibly exist outside of the specific frame of the film.

In this sense, *Spinal Tap* demonstrates how mockumentary can potentially play with the possibilities which DVD provides to re-present, and hence reframe, cinematic texts. Brookey and Westerfelhaus (2002) contend that the most significant aspect of DVDs is the manner in which they deliberately blur the lines between what constitutes the primary text of the film and these secondary texts of 'extra' or 'supplementary' materials. The inclusion of a variety of extras on DVD releases allows for the reframing of a cinematic or televisual text by providing additional layers of information and the means to easily access these layers even during the playing of the 'primary' text itself. In the case of *Spinal Tap*, this layering is designed to 'flesh out' the original fictional premise, to expand the plausibility of this milieu by providing access to the original 'evidence' of their position in the socio-historical world.

The more typical use of mockumentary on DVD, however, has been to use the form to simply package as extras those promotional materials associated with a cinematic release (mockumentary extras either for a 'straight' film or for mockumentary texts themselves). In many cases this means the inclusion of a parody of documentary biographic and autobiographic chronicles of film industry figures, or short film in-jokes that were composed by a film's cast and crew while on location. One example well known to *Star Wars* fans is *R2 D2–Beneath the Dome* (2001), a one-off that was included on the DVD release for *Star Wars II: Attack of the Clones* (2002) and subsequently released as a stand-alone text.

A different practice was followed by the producers of the science-fiction film *Donnie Darko: the Director's Cut* (2001), who sought to draw upon the cult following of the feature film by holding a competition in 2004 for viewers to submit short films explaining why he/she was the number one fan of the film. The winning short would be included on the 2004 Director's Cut DVD release. The film ultimately selected and included on the two-disc DVD is titled *#1 Fan Darkomentary* (2005) and is a superb example of short-form mockumentary, with director Daryl Donaldson playing an obsessed fan documenting his stalking of cast and crew of the film. The pen-ultimate scene, where he meets and clearly disturbs *Donnie Darko* director Richard Kelly, is a perfect encapsulation of Hollywood production meeting playful amateur production, where it is only the amateur who knows what is going on.

A distinctive feature of mockumentary on digital platforms is the potential to explore different dimensions of the discourse's 'call to play'. Short film enables direct forms of participation from ama-teurs, while mockumentary feature films often include short cameos from public figures (such as George Harrison's gleeful role as an interviewer in the Beatles parody *The Rutles – All You Need is Cash*). The example of the *Spinal Tap* fan culture suggests that the possibilities for more direct forms of audience engagement with such media also partly depend on extra-textual events (the CDs and tours). The DVD medium does allow for more interactive engagement with all of these materials at once (we can watch the film, listen to the music and access promotional materials, all from the same DVD text), but only in the limited sense of choosing the order in which we can view them. The senses of play that are avail-able to each of these media, in other words, tend to be limited to exploring the layers of a particular mockumentary fiction, to exploiting the discourse's potential for different modes of reading. In the case of *Spinal Tap* some fans have gone further to immerse

themselves into the fiction, largely through more creative initiatives, including detailed website tributes,[6] online discussion threads
or material inspired by the original film (as noted above).

Such examples begin to touch on the range of participatory roles
that are inherent in what Jenkins terms 'convergence culture':

> Convergence does not depend on any specific delivery mechanism.
> Rather, convergence represents a paradigm shift – a move from
> medium-specific content toward content that flows across multiple
> media channels, toward the increased interdependence of communi-
> cations systems, toward multiple ways of accessing media content,
> and toward ever more complex relations between top-down corpo-
> rate media and bottom-up participatory culture. (Jenkins, 2006: 243)

Jenkins views the more radical potential of digital media as lying
in the tension between the production cultures dominated by con-
centrations of large media corporations, typically creating media
content reliant on large budgets and retaining tight control over
copyright, and the emerging participatory cultures that are being
fostered by the many online sites that tend to be grouped under
the loosely defined label 'Web 2.0'. For Jenkins, convergence
culture entails new productive linkages between these different
trajectories of creative activity, 'enabling new forms of participation and collaboration' (Jenkins, 2006: 245) centred on the encour-
agement of participation from communities of viewers and users
outside of institutional control. He draws heavily on Pierre Levy's
notion of 'collective intelligence' in describing the potential for
these new 'bottom-up' cultures.

The potential for mockumentary discourse to operate within
such a climate is enormous. But there is a central paradox here. The
emergence of media that are more directly playful, more participatory is also marked by an absence of the conditions which helped
to create this discourse. In particular, mockumentary has difficulty
remaining distinctive in an environment where there are few stable
and familiar modes of representation, where the convergence
between non-fiction and fictional content is such an integral feature
of this new mediascape. Mockumentary inevitably cannot have the
same 'kick' and tends to exist simply as surface play, rather than
having the potential to tap into the 'charge of the real' identified
by Sobchack (see chapter 1). Within online media there is often a
confusion between forms that in previous media could be assumed

to be more clearly delineated between common-sense dichotomies of fact and fiction, objective and subjective or authoritative and amateur.

Such dichotomies are more difficult to maintain on the World Wide Web, and hence mockumentary is inevitably on more slippery representational ground. Where do we position a site such as the online version of *The Onion* satirical newspaper, or the plethora of parody newspaper, television or other fake media institutional websites that employ the full range of audio-visual techniques (especially animation)? Labels such as 'documentary' tend to serve only as reference points for the origins and discourse of online forms (Hight, 2001), rather than to suggest a clearly identifiable genre of online sites that can be appropriated by mockumentary producers.

Users engaging with a variety of sites are not utilising a documentary mode of reading in the same way as they might do for film and television, although this always remains one of the possibilities for interpretation. Audiences engage within online forms with degrees of play and reflexivity as a matter of course, as the foregrounding of mediation is inherent in the ability to directly interact with such texts. The World Wide Web allows for a wider continuum of interactive participation than do media such as film and television. Interaction here can range from simply clicking on a hypertext link and exploring pre-designed pathways through online content, to contributing feedback to site designers, through to more open forms of participation such as the uploading of user-created content. The referentiality of online texts is also of a different order, with references to the actual socio-historical not always able to convey the same sense of indexicality. Forms such as webcam, blogs and vlogs rely on a sense of authenticity, but these are more tenuous than audio-visual media positioned as fragments within interfaces designed from graphic design principles rather than documentary practice. This kind of culture, then, necessarily entails a collapse of distinctions between codes and conventions, just as it does between producers and users. The playful mashup of different traditions is almost the *raison d'être* of contemporary online culture. The mockumentary possibilities here are suggested by the YouTube series uploaded by the user known as 'lonelygirl15', which attracted an appreciative fan base before its belated revelation that it was not a video diary but in fact a scripted drama (Newman, 2006).

Mockumentary has always been at the centre of amateur forms of audio-visual and online production – from student productions looking to experiment with a form that appears quite transparent and straightforward, to efforts to engage in playful mashups of fact and fiction. The future of mockumentary is perfectly attuned to online participatory culture. User-created mockumentaries build upon and seem a natural part of the emergence of wider cultures of surveillance (including forms of self-surveillance with digital devices such as phonecams, webcams and camcorders) that are such a strong feature of sites that operate within the broad dynamics of Jenkins' convergence culture. The teasing of fact and fiction and play between notions of performance and authenticity all become natural extensions of the constant recording of everyday life and the monitoring of a socio-political sphere which has long since discarded any meaningful distinctions between public and private space.

Mockumentary producers have also recognised the rich possibilities that such an environment offers for using the discourse in online promotion campaigns (in Jenkins' terms, 'top-down' online mockumentary production). These range from the relatively trivial, such as the producers of *Borat: Cultural Learnings of America for Make Benefit Glorious Nation of Kazakhstan* exploiting the natural marketing potential of MySpace by providing Sacha Baron Cohen's lead character with an apparent 'home page' (www.myspace.com/borat). Other online materials associated with feature film mockumentaries look to generate a similar effect to viral marketing through teasing user expectations (see the discussion on *The Blair Witch Project* below), but most promotional websites tend to 'flag' their status as fiction, often by including sections of a website that provide information on cast biographies, while other pages offer straight-faced messages from the characters they play. The more detailed examples look to develop and maintain a post-viewing relationship with the viewers of the mockumentary text that they promote. There is the accompanying website to the Australian television parody series *CNNNN: Chaser Non-Stop News Network* (2002–3) (see chapter 8), which continues the series' targeting of the global news network CNN by replicating the CNN website. Another example is the set of webisodes produced for nbc.com as online fragments of the fictional world of the US version of *The Office* (see chapter 9).

Some of the more interesting examples of mockumentary promotion have emerged where producers look to exploit the possibilities for extending a mockumentary premise onto digital platforms.
The mockumentary feature film *Nothing So Strange* centred on the
fictional assassination of then Microsoft CEO Bill Gates and the
investigation of the conspiracies surrounding the cover-up of this
event. Included on the DVD release are extended forms of apparent evidence such as photographs and video from the assassination,
audio files from police interviews with a key witness and clips from
apparent news discussion programmes featuring conspiracy theorists. The DVD includes links to what it terms a 'virtual 2nd DVD'
of materials on the pseudo-event, consisting of a number of inter-
connecting promotional websites. The official website is www.noth-
ingsostrange.com, which allows for a download of the entire film
itself and contains more conventional promotional material such as
a plot synopsis, filmmaker's biography and press releases, but all
scripted as if the film where an actual documentary covering real
events. There are links to other websites from the film's central
protagonists (the fictional Citizen's for Truth organisation), partial
archiving of a document from a Los Angeles District Attorney's
investigation into the assassination and frequent references to
other apparent literature covering similar positions. Collectively
these sites are intended to echo the proliferation of conspiracy
theories generated by the November 1963 assassination of US
President John F. Kennedy. The sites are all cross-referenced, using
each other as reinforcement and support, and are designed to
appear as if they have been spontaneously produced by disparate
groups that share common interests in the Gates assassination.

Cross-platform mockumentary

A more extensive and higher-profile example of a sustained mockumentary discourse across media platforms is *The Blair Witch
Project*.[7] Directed by Daniel Myrick and Eduardo Sanchez, the film
itself is an innovative horror narrative,[8] which famously begins with
a full-screen caption stating:

> In October of 1994, three student filmmakers disappeared in the
> woods near Burkittsville, Maryland, while shooting a documentary
> called '*The Blair Witch Project*'. A year later their footage was found.

The remainder of the film consists of what appears to be a carefully edited narrative oscillating between 16mm film footage from the unfinished documentary by the three filmmakers and video footage for an intended 'making of' documentary on the process of their filmmaking. The ending of the film appears to suggest (without actually showing) the murder of the three by supernatural forces.

An example of dramatic mockumentary, *Blair Witch* was produced through an improvisational production technique where the actors were taken out into the woods and left deliberately ignorant of what the producers were going to subject them to next (McDowell, 2001). The directors, in interviews about the film, have themselves blurred the lines between what they were doing and documentary filmmaking. Myrick comments: 'Most of the film was serendipity. However, the process we created allowed these moments to be captured. Much like a real documentary' (Rickard, 1999: 39). This form of preparation, combined with the simple use of a vérité aesthetic controlled by the actors themselves to capture the action, makes for an extremely effective horror film.

The film's narrative conforms to familiar conventions of the horror genre in having a group of unwitting innocents put themselves in danger and then struggle to survive. However, the sense of immediacy provided by an apparently condensed version of real-time recording plays with this sense of expectation. Adhering strictly to the limited frame of a documentary camera builds tension through omission, through the withholding of knowledge about the specific nature of the threat the three 'filmmakers' encounter and attempt to document.

The mockumentary approach thus allows an innovative take on the conventional clash between the rational/scientific and irrational/supernatural at the core of classic horror narrative. At one level, it is the rational objectivity associated with photographic evidence which contrasts with the film's portrayal of the irrational (Roscoe, 2000: 6). However, the aesthetic of the film also reflects a tension between different types of knowledge. The two kinds of cameras operated by the filmmakers – black and white 16mm film for the 'real' documentary footage and a digital camcorder for the behind-the-scenes footage – immediately set up familiar dichotomies between analogue film and digital video and their associations with public and private knowledge. The digital camcorder records moments of intimate confessions, particularly the points of emotional tension and confrontation that are so closely associated with a grainy, hand-held aesthetic in documentary hybrids. Heather's widely parodied, tearful, desperate confessional address to her camcorder late in the film, for example, falls within the visual template for video diaries. The gaze of the documentary film camera, in contrast, represents the authoritative perspective which these film students are attempting to achieve. It is the documentary camera that they use to record the 'evidence' of the apparent presence of a supernatural entity, evidence that they desperately attempt to interpret and put into a rational, meaningful frame (and in turn, the audience attempt to interpret both the evidence the camera records and the reactions of the filmmakers to their plight).

The students are novices, and the film as a whole is like a training film on how to make a documentary, from their initial discussions of their strategy toward the Blair Witch legend, to tensions over how to film things and how useful their interview materials are. It is a documentary combined with a making of documentary (in a further layering, with the film's DVD audio commentaries the film in fact becomes its own making of documentary, with the cast describing the process of documenting their fright in the woods). In fact, the film, if it *were* a documentary, would be classified as a classic example of Nichols' reflexive mode of representation. It highlights the means of production and the gaps in the representation that it offers. As a 'documentary' formed from a documentary that is never completed, we are given the sense that we are seeing the 'raw', unmediated footage that might have been polished into the more distanced perspective of authoritative documentary that the filmmakers aspire to. The film camera is revealed as a tool whose power is beyond them, a tool that is only meaningful within a prescribed positivist practice, while the video camcorder offers an easy way to capture emotional experience, but without the sense of being positioned within a comforting metanarrative (Banash, 2004: 113–14).

The film, in other words, serves as a site for a variety of competing discourses on the nature and significance of documentary footage. Their cameras are central to all the interaction between the students whom we see on screen. The tension within the film draws partly from the absence of a clear perspective on the entity which appears to be stalking them and from the desperate and ultimately futile attempts by Heather, the director, to maintain a sense of control over their fears through the act of filming itself. At key points in the film Heather, for example, insists on recording, as if this in itself might provide some security, or a stability of perspective that the camera is meant to convey. This is in contrast to Mike, who begins to view the camera as a means to avoid the reality in front of the lens or even as an instrument of voyeurism.

While the rest of the crew abandon the documentary camera, Heather insists on continuing the pretence of an investigative documentary expedition, despite the failure of such a practice to provide a comforting pathway to the truth, to any useful knowledge about the Blair Witch (at least any knowledge that will allow them to escape). Similarly, the audience are denied any comforting sense of distance and objective perspective on what is actually happening. Ultimately neither camera provides a sense of closure, in the form of definitive evidence and an ultimate revelation of the Blair Witch, that is expected from generic conventions of both horror and documentary.

The layers to the film (a commentary on contemporary documentary culture, the documenting of an encounter with a horrific supernatural entity, the narrative of three terrified students lost in the woods) suggest the varieties of forms of engagement available to its audience, which are perhaps central to the film's popular success. Schreier's research suggests that audiences, despite knowing that the film is fiction, are still able to engage with its horrific premise and enjoy the quality of its faked representations. She identifies three groups of viewers within a study of online newsgroups:

> First of all, there are those who know perfectly well that the film is fiction; they watch it as a horror film and evaluate it according to the standards of the genre. A second group of viewers also realizes that the film is a fiction; yet they appreciate the film's special status as a hybrid and enjoy the oscillation between fact and fiction that it provides. And a third group of viewers, while eventually coming to realize the film's fictionality, are nevertheless temporarily confused as to its ontology. (Schreier, 2004: 331)

As Higley and Weinstock note (Higley and Weinstock, 2004: 16), the type of engagement which viewers had with the film itself depended very much upon any intertextual knowledge that they brought to their viewing. In particular, the initial engagement of audiences, at least in the United States, appeared to be shaped by one of the more successful publicity campaigns ever conducted by an American studio.

> Months before the official release of the film, there were a number of dedicated websites filtering various pieces of information to an internet audience intrigued by the rumours about the film, the witch and the students. Many of these sites had been set up by people who had not seen the film but believed it to be a true story. These websites effectively participated in the creation of a hoax, either unwittingly because they believed the film to be a real documentary about a real disappearance, or through colluding with the filmmakers to manufacture and maintain the hoaxes' hype. (Roscoe, 2000: 4)

There is some uncertainty over whether Haxan studio initiated the hoax, or the filmmakers simply recognised early on the promotional possibilities that these online equivalents of 'word of mouth' testimonies offered. In any case, the success of the *Blair Witch* film was obviously part of a carefully orchestrated publicity campaign that replicated an online fan base. An initial website set up in June 1998 included sections on a timeline of historical events in the Blair Witch mythology, and biographical details on 'the filmmakers' (in this case pretending to be the three missing students Heather Donahue, Joshua Leonard and Michael Williams) (Roscoe, 2000: 4). The film also benefited from the appearance of online details which may or may not have been accidental, such as the original Internet Movie Database listing which suggested that the actors/characters were actually dead (Rickard, 1999: 37). On April Fools Day 1999 the original website was relaunched to include additional documents of their disappearance, including photos, audio from the DAT tapes used by the students, images and quotes from Heather's journal and segments of the film supposedly shot by them (Castonguay, 2004: 74).

Other key aspects of the promotion for the film and its sequel included a widely seen television mockumentary, *Curse of the Blair Witch*, which aired on the Sci Fi Channel two days before the film opened (12 July 1999) (Figure 2). Intended as an extended trailer or teaser for the film's release, it provided a detailed 'history' of the Blair Witch, included clips from the film and was constructed in a more conventional expositional format with structured interviews intercut with a variety of forms of evidence (in fact, this was the

2. A photograph of a hunting party in the Black Hills of Burkittsville, Maryland, one of the many 'documents' which *Curse of the Blair Witch* (1999) used to present the historical mythology of the Blair Witch.

original model for the feature film itself, before the directors realised that the observational approach worked perfectly for their purposes).[9] The television programme included excerpts from the 'lost reels' of the students' film, interviews with members of their family and friends and testimony from folklore experts, in a format that Hopgood suggests was obviously modelled on the style of the 1970s Leonard Nimoy-presented programme *In Search Of...* (1976–82) (Hopgood, 2005: 241–2).

The full array of promotional texts associated with the film includes a 'missing' poster for the three leads (for many audiences, one of the first signs of the marketing campaign) and, later, a comic book presented as the account of a lunatic attacked by the Blair Witch, a CD 'soundtrack' of the songs supposedly found on tapes in the students' car and books by D. A. Stern, *The Blair Witch Project: A Dossier* (Stern, 1999) and *The Secret Confession of Rustin Parr* (Stern, 2000). The *Dossier* volume, supposedly compiled by investigators, replicates both the website and the film in offering fragments which the reader must collate to build a picture of the disappearance and wider history of the Blair Witch. Subsequent mockumentaries, *The Burkittsville 7* (2000) and *Shadow of the Blair Witch* (2000), were intended to promote the release of the (non-mockumentary) sequel to the film.

Director Daniel Myrick later claimed that the branding of *Blair Witch* formed part of a carefully crafted campaign, part of what he termed the directors' and Haxan studio's 'prime directive':

> We tried to create a fake legend, complete with multiple points of view, sceptics, and unexplained mysteries. Nothing about the legend could be provable, and everything had to seem like it could have a logical explanation (which the reader would be led away from as quickly as possible). (Cited in Jenkins, 2006: 102)

Each of the various texts surrounding the 'primary text' of the feature film itself[10] works to support the supernatural premise of its narrative. Each of the television, print and online texts references appropriate non-fiction conventions to present particular, overlapping aspects of a coherent, if incomplete story. Crucially, a core aspect of all of these texts is their withholding of a definitive conclusion about the disappearance of the three students, a denial of closure to their collective narrative. The film itself partly offers the pleasures of a detective story, but one in which a final revelation is deferred, while the other texts provide a wealth of further evidence to explore. This collective of *Blair Witch* texts encourages audiences to explore this evidence (a more dispersed 'call to play') through the various pathways provided by the website and the narratives of the film and television texts. Morgan in fact refers to the film, website, book and DVD recording as four 'phases' in the same text, each adding to the wider body of evidence concerning the disappearance of the three filmmakers. The DVD provides for more direct pathways through this material by both grouping these texts together (including providing links to online material) and allowing easy access to the chapters of the two key audio-visual texts (the film and television mockumentaries).

Unlike the possibilities afforded by Jenkins' model of cultural convergence, however, the types of interactivity possible within this group of texts are comparatively limited. The key objective of this collective of texts is the building of a 'closed, inclusive world' (Brooker and Jermyn, 2003: 326) that positions the audience as readers, if not quite passive viewers. Telotte critiques the role played by the film's website along similar lines (Telotte, 2004). He suggests that the site works to 'frame the film narrative within a context designed to condition our viewing or "reading" of it, even to determine the sort of pleasures we might derive from it' (Telotte, 2004: 38). The website and other secondary texts not only generated interest before the film was released into theatres, but provided the opportunity for an ongoing relationship after an initial viewing, providing more detail of the film's purported event and a means to promote and distribute additional merchandise for film and for eventual DVD distribution.

Telotte argues that ultimately the website in fact did little more than construct an ongoing, typically consumerist relationship for audiences within the marketing agenda of Haxan studio. The pathways through this system are tightly prescribed, and in fact, in order to participate actively (through discussion and creative practice), audiences need to go outside the closed world which is provided. There were no links, for example, from the official website to the variety of fan sites, discussion groups which offered detailed assessment of the *Blair Witch* evidence and the wealth of short film parodies inspired by the film (Castonguay, 2004: 69).

Most other critics have effectively agreed with such an assessment. Schreier refers to the non-film materials as part of the *Blair Witch* 'paratext' (Schreier, 2004: 319), texts which form part of the wider fiction, with the film at its centre. S. Johnson more generally refers to the websites associated with traditional media as 'parasites' to denote their secondary status, and also their dependent relationships to film and television media (S. Johnson, 2005: 169). Booker talks of the idea of 'overflow', to describe the pattern of 'media producers to construct a lifestyle experience around a core text, using the Internet to extend audience engagement and encourage a two-way interaction' (Brooker and Jermyn, 2003: 323). Different experiences are offered by DVD and internet, with the internet encouraging 'more exploration, ongoing involvement, interaction, and community involvement than does a DVD, however many featurettes that DVD has' (D. Johnson, 2005: 39).

Walker takes a much broader perspective of the forms of engagement provided by this series of wider-associated *Blair Witch* texts. He refers to this collective as a 'metatext', which should be viewed as offering:

a complex interweaving of at least three levels of narrative 'reality' (the film itself, the auxiliary fictional texts, the production and reception history of the film), each further fragmented by multiple perspectives, none of which can claim authority or primacy. There is no centre and no predetermined point of entry. It is a heteroglossic space, a multimedia version of collaborative hypertext. (Walker, 2004: 166)

Despite the limited parameters for participation, we can look back now on *The Blair Witch Project* as a limited prototype for cross-platform forms of mockumentary. Jenkins has introduced the notion of 'transmedia storytelling' (Jenkins, 2006: 93–130) to describe the deliberate crafting of a narrative across different forms of media, not just encouraging but requiring audiences to engage with all texts in a wider fiction in order to make sense of its overarching narrative. *The Blair Witch Project*, in these terms, is an incomplete transmedia mockumentary allowing for limited senses of the word 'play'.

Mockumentary, documentary games and ARGs

In fact, there is an interesting comparison to be made between this mockumentary and some forms of narrative emerging within gaming cultures. Poole's discussion of the difference between diachronic (or 'back story') and synchronic stories in some game genres is a useful starting point (Poole, 2000). The back story of a game is the algorithm of play that includes limitations on actions of characters, the different levels that must be traversed in a particular sequence and so on.

For the purposes of talking about videogames, the 'back-story' is the diachronic story, and the story that happens in the fictional present is the synchronic story – an ongoing narrative constituted by the player's actions and decisions in real-time. (Poole, 2000: 106)

The closeness of this description to the 'metatext' of *Blair Witch* suggest how it could be reconfigured as a game. The website, television mockumentary and print materials can be seen to offer the 'back-story' of the *Blair Witch* narrative, while the film itself offers the immediacy of a vérité journey through one part of this wider narrative. As noted above, each of the texts within the *Blair Witch* fiction entails engaging with the pleasures of different constructions of evidence. While the film provides an intimate experience as the eyes of the various characters, as cinéma vérité is intended to do, the television mockumentary and website place the viewer more in the position of distanced observer that is the conventional place for documentary viewers. For Murray, 'a game is a kind of abstract storytelling that resembles the world of common experience but compresses it in order to heighten interest' (Murray, 2000: 142). This is particularly apt to describe *The Blair Witch Project*, where our fears of the unknown and the supernatural are offered in ways which replicate their representation through non-fiction forms.

On the other hand, this cross-platform mockumentary does not offer the same control in terms of authorship that is a feature of more collaborative game narratives. The film, in the sense of Poole's quote above, would serve as one pathway through a *Blair Witch* game, a kind of First Person Shooter synchronic narrative (with the shooter as a camera person and the frame a documentary lens). Such a comparison reveals the limited nature of interaction available to audiences of this text. A more games-oriented version of *Blair Witch*, for example, might have featured direct participation by allowing users to role-play an investigative team looking to solve the mystery of the students' disappearance by sifting through a field of possible evidence to decide on a plausible explanation for the filmmakers' disappearance.

Galloway (2004) argues that '[g]ames signal a third phase for realism. The first two phases were realism in narrative (literature) and realism in images (painting, photography, film). Now there is also realism in action. Whereas the visual arts compel viewers to engage in the act of looking, games compel players to perform acts.' Although Galloway's argument offers a broader perspective for game narratives, there are obvious implications here for factual discourse within game environments. To begin to consider the implications of mockumentary discourse within digital media environments, we need to think of the construction of narrative in terms of space. For Jenkins, game designers 'don't simply tell stories; they design worlds and sculpt spaces' (Jenkins, 2007: 56); they should be viewed as 'narrative architects' (ibid.: 60). Game architecture involves particularly the creation of opportunities for more direct interaction on the part of users in this space, as a means to help engagement with a narrative. There is a key issue here of whether the ability to play with a narrative, in whatever sense, encourages a sense of belief or a greater willingness to suspend disbelief in the world of the narrative.

In discussing the forms of engagement provided by digital narratives Janet Murray offers the terms 'immersion', 'agency' and 'transformation'. Immersion involves the 'experience of being transported to an elaborately simulated place' (Murray, 2000: 98). She notes the pleasures that come from testing the boundaries between fact and fiction, provided by texts which tease the reader or viewer into a confusion over its ontological status (Murray, 2000: 105). Agency is 'the satisfying power to take meaningful action and to see the results of our decisions and choices' (Murray, 2000: 126). The key here is the degree to which a fiction provides a space for players to perform their agency. This goes beyond simple participation and 'the pleasures of navigation', involving the ability to follow pathways through aspects of a wider narrative text. Finally, transformation involves providing opportunities for role-playing different characters or positions within a wider text, so that, for example, the same action or event is available in a number of different ways. The greater the sense of spatial depth and temporality the more immersive is the experience (Murray, 2000: 159).

The possibilities for constructing mockumentary narratives within the broader field of game spaces partly derive from the emergence of documentary-inflected game narratives. Some writers argue that there is a developing corpus of texts which could be termed 'documentary games' or 'docu-games' – those based especially around reconstructing historical events. Here players are provided with layered forms of engagement with realistic behavioural and visual simulations (Raessens, 2006; Fullerton, 2008). In providing the means for players to reconstruct history, in a variety of ways, docu-games naturally create opportunities for reflexive perspectives on the notion of historical narrative itself, something which Bogost and Poremba (2008) suggest have at least the potential for enhancing players' skills in media literacy and cultural critique (familiar arguments for mockumentary audiences – see chapter 1).

The deliberate confusion between real and fictional spaces is already a central objective and criterion of one type of game narrative, still emerging as a coherent form, generally known as 'pervasive', 'immersive' or 'ubiquitous' games. McGonigal's suggested taxonomy of definitions is useful here. For her, pervasive games are those based on a blurring of game and real environments, using mobile, ubiquitous and embedded media technologies to reframe everyday spaces as virtual playing fields. Within this broad category there is the more specific form of immersive games, or alternate reality games (ARGs), which operate under the rhetorical stance of 'this is not a game' (McGonigal, 2003) and deliberately challenge players to engage with specific modes of action within a distinctive gamespace.

One of the first ARGs was associated with the release of Steven Spielberg's feature film *Artificial Intelligence A.I.* (2001), a game design nicknamed The Beast by its designers. As Szulborski notes, the distinctive nature of this gaming experience was that '[i]nstead of creating either a representational or abstract gamespace for the players, the designers overlaid their narrative and gameplay atop the real world, effectively making reality the gamespace for the experience' (Szulborski, 2007: 228). Sparked by teasing messages in the trailer for the film and a message in the film's credits (referring to a 'Sentient Machine Therapist' named Jeanine Salla), players were required to sift through clues sent through e-mail, phone calls and text message prompts, which led them through thirty fictional websites. The ultimate objective was to gather together and give coherence to the various narrative fragments they encountered.

The more complex ARGs are designed around the interplay between an array of analogue and digital media technologies:

> displays that can make digital content available to players as they move through the physical world, including mobile phones, handheld computers, earphones, wearable computers and interactive projections and tangible interfaces that are embedded into the surrounding environment; wireless communications that enable players to communicate with remote servers and other players; and sensing technologies that capture players' contexts, including positioning technologies such as GPS, cameras, microphones and potentially even physiological sensors. (Benford et al, 2007: 248)

Crucially, while other game genres address players as citizens in a fictional world, ARGs deliberately look to address players as themselves, as individuals uniquely positioned within the socio-historical world. Players do not need to adopt a particular character, one with superpowers or abilities that only make sense within the game's synthetic world. Instead they are typically addressed as social actors, with the gamespace targeting them with personalised information as game prompts.

The myriad of possibilities within this kind of game paradigm are only just beginning to be explored, but there are a variety of possible trajectories for game designers to take. Referring to games media as a whole, Jenkins notes that 'the gamespace becomes a memory palace whose contents must be deciphered as the player tries to reconstruct the plot' (Jenkins, 2007: 60). The complexity of the wider fields of evidence that are provided by ARGs means that more 'emergent' examples of this game form require extensive collaboration between players across different regions and countries (a prime example of Pierre Levy's 'collective intelligence'). The Beast, in fact, unexpectedly generated an online community of players calling themselves The Cloudmakers, a community that survived and prospered despite the end of the game itself.[11]

The challenges inherent in an overlap between virtual and physical space also lie not just in being sent messages through everyday media such as mobile phones, but in being required to engage in social interactions with people who may or may not be part of the game. Dena outlines what she terms the 'alternative reality design aesthetic', suggesting that, with these interactive spatial narratives, 'the design goal is to reduce signs of the game's fictional status while enhancing elements that trigger gamers to treat it as they would real life' (Dena, 2007: 238). Björk's definition for a pervasive game in fact is one 'whose spatial, temporal, social or interface-related characteristics are ambiguous' (Björk, 2007: 277), where the deliberate intention of the designer is to make it difficult for players to determine what kinds of social or media interactions are or are not part of the game.[12]

McGonigal notes that players are not 'seduced' by a narrative, becoming hopelessly confused by what is real and what is not, but are instead knowing and active participants in the creation of the fiction, in effect performing their belief in a plausible narrative (McGonigal, 2003; 2007). There is obvious and significant overlap here with elements of the agenda and complexity of forms of engagement generated by mockumentary discourse. Both look to encourage layered forms of engagement, the taking of players (viewers) through a matrix of fact and fiction, forcing them to make constant assessments of what is real and not, and in the case of

ARGs involving a more embodied 'call to play', with players required to make choices in their physical environment.

On one hand, then, there are obvious possibilities within gaming culture for drawing upon the complexity of mockumentary narratives. The promotional possibilities here are already being explored by film producers – the mockumentary *Cloverfield* used an ARG as the basis of its promotional campaign (Walters, 2007) – but it is interesting to speculate on the forms of mockumentaries which could emerge further along such trajectories. Instead of mockumentary filmmakers using and reframing fragments from visual culture and bringing them into a two-dimensional, linear narrative text, what happens if fictional fragments are instead attached to real-world locations and users are asked to directly engage with the fiction through engagement with physical space? What are the possibilities for gamespaces where players are required to piece together an alternative historical narrative for real locations, to treat everyday artefacts as evidence for social and historical realities that are created by a game design team? What if there are efforts to construct fictional digital archives of the sort suggested by Murray's definition of hyperserial (Murray, 2000: 253–8), prompting the emergence of new breeds of cyber play? We could term these 'ludic mockumentaries', constructed by designers creating the parameters to a fiction and the rules of play, which govern interactions between players and other media, amongst collaborative communities of players and between the game and non-players within specific spaces.

We can imagine, for example, an ARG approach to *The Blair Witch Project* using hand-held devices that require players to travel to Burkittsville and directly engage with apparent locations from the film, while interacting with pieces of evidence made available through everyday media technologies (some viewers of the film did make this journey, but were dismissed as unknowing dupes of the film's narrative and promotional campaign, rather than accepted as possible players in an unintended gamespace). What other mockumentaries can be re-imagined as games which blur the line between the fiction and the real? What would it be like to play a real-world version of *Borat: Cultural Learnings of America for Make Benefit Glorious Nation of Kazakhstan* in which players replicated Sacha Baron Cohen's performance as an inept Kazakhi filmmaker, documenting their creative encounters with non-players? These would be familiar narratives for games players schooled in existing forms of film and television mockumentaries.

On the other hand, such speculations reveal, again, the central paradox of mockumentary discourse when faced with digital media. Such mockumentary gaming narratives would be indistinguishable from ARGs and similar gaming experiences that already exist. The various notions of play, interaction, collaboration and performance that are so central to mockumentary are already key characteristics of these new digital realms. Mockumentary discourse is both a useful reference point for categorisation and analysis of these digital forms of play and such a naturalised aspect of online and gaming media that its identification is somewhat redundant. The collective effect of ARG cultures is to transform the real, sober, rational public sphere into a space for play, in the process effectively colonising a digital medium before it can be dominated by non-fiction gamespaces that attempt to use digital technologies toward more sober, informative and educational agendas. In contrast to film and television media, then, in games media it is the documentary genre which must address suspicions of being parasitic of more dominant forms.

Notes

1 Writing on the significance of sound as the basis of indexicality within the wider field of animated documentary, Ward quotes Renov's use of the term 'acoustic indexicality' (Ward, 2005a: 98).
2 'Cinéma vérité' is translated literally as 'cinema truth', derived from Dziga Vertov's term KinoPravda.
3 Such as the Faux Film Festival in Portland, Oregon (www.fauxfestival. com), or MocDocs festival in Toronto (www.mocdocs.com) and the many short film festivals which provide recognition for mockumentaries as a form.
4 The full list of DVD extras includes theatrical trailers, audio commentary (with Derek Smalls aka Harry Shearer, David St Hubbins aka Michael McKean and Nigel Tufnel aka Christopher Guest), Catching Up with Marty Di Bergi featurette, deleted scenes (14 chapters' worth in all), a 1960s 'Flower People' press conference, Spinal Tap on The Joe Franklin Show, music videos for 'Gimme Some Money', '(Listen to the) Flower People', 'Hell Hole' and 'Big Bottom', fake commercials for their album 'Heavy Metal Memories', 'cheese rolling' trailer, three TV spots and three commercials for Rock 'n' Rolls brand food pockets,

all packaged with animated film-themed menus with sound effects and music.

5 See de Siefe for details of other fan activities inspired by the film in print, music and online, such as the longevity of the Usenet discussion group alt.fan.spinal-tap (de Siefe, 2007: 36–8).

6 The official site for the film, www.spinaltap.com/, is now defunct, with all traffic now directed to one of the main fan sites, www.spinaltapfan.com/.

7 For a detailed history of the film and its reception, see the introduction to Higley and Weinstock (2004), and Roscoe (2000). Higley and Weinstock question whether the film is a mockumentary – they note the lack of a satiric agenda and conclude that the label of 'mock direct cinema' is more appropriate.

8 There is some controversy over the originality of the film. Both the film and its promotional website bear a close resemblance to that of the earlier mockumentary *The Last Broadcast* (1998), and both films and their websites in turn resemble the documentary on witch hysteria *Paradise Lost: The Child Murder of Robin Hood Hills* (see Kendzior, 1999, and Higley, 2004). Certainly the 'found footage' premise has been used in earlier horror predecessors such as *Cannibal Holocaust* (1980), and has been central in later alien conspiracy mockumentaries such as *Alien Abduction: Incident at Lake County* (1998), *The Wicksboro Incident* (2003) and *Cloverfield* (2008).

9 This programme follows a similar format to the television mockumentary *Alien Abduction: Incident in Lake County*, where video footage of the apparent alien abduction of a family itself is spliced into the text and becomes the focal point of discussion between various experts over its legitimacy. *Alien Abduction* is notable partly for its inclusion of expert testimony from ufology figures who did not realise they were taking part in a mockumentary (Roscoe and Hight, 2001: 151–5).

10 Keller argues instead that the television text is the primary text (Keller, 2004), based on the director's admission that it reflects the original plan for the film's structure (McDowell, 2001: 144).

11 See www.cloudmakers.org/, and the ARG site www.unfiction.com/.

12 The possibilities for confused and unexpected encounters formed the basis of the narrative of the David Fincher-directed thriller *The Game* (1997), starring Michael Douglas, Sean Penn and Deborah Kara Unger.

Part II

Mockumentary in televisual space

3

The televisual space

This part of the book introduces and frames its particular focus: an introduction to the complexities of mockumentary discourse operating within the medium of television, with a particular emphasis on television series. The wider frame for this discussion is the exploration of contemporary television, which shapes this discourse in ways distinctive from other media.

The discussion in this chapter outlines a number of features of television as a medium which provide ideal conditions for mockumentary discourse. The core argument, briefly outlined here and extended in the following chapters, is that mockumentary discourse has become naturalised within the televisual medium. Although it is not the intention to provide a comprehensive genealogy of television mockumentary, the key examples discussed in these chapters collectively provide an outline of its historical development. Initially serving as a key site for early experimentation, the more recent emergence of mockumentary in serial format, within a number of national contexts, can be read as evidence of the increasing sophistication of producers in employing the discourse toward a variety of ends. In a broader sense, these series also reflect the significance of both non-fiction television programming in general and an expansion of the televisual fact-fiction continuum, particularly since the 1990s.

This chapter does not offer a comprehensive overview of the features which distinguish television from other media. Corner usefully identifies five different aspects which have been the focus of historiographic studies of the medium: television 'as an institution, an industry and its organisations' within wider policy regimes and management structures; the professional practices of television programme making; criticism of television at a textual level;

explorations of 'television as sociocultural phenomenon, deeply interconnected with high politics, with the shifting circumstances of the public sphere and civil society, with popular culture and with the changing character of the home and of domestic values'; and discussions of the nature and implications of the medium's field of production, distribution and reception technologies (Corner, 2003: 275–6). There is not the space here to address such complex theoretical terrain. Instead this chapter touches on a number of specific qualities of television aesthetics, representational structures and issues of reception.

Televisual space

I want in particular to draw from the notion of 'televisual space', of conceiving of aspects of the medium in a number of spatial ways. I am using the term 'space' here to deliberately move away from well-trodden paths of television criticism, toward a perspective of the medium which highlights the interrelation between televisual forms and locations of production, distribution and reception. The term can be used to emphasise the specificities of production sites (both geographically and historically), detailing the construction and representation of narrative spaces within texts, highlighting the cultural implications of linking sites of broadcast transmissions and individual sites for reception, and even to conceptualise the spectrum of television programming available to viewers as a 'space' to be navigated. Different kinds of 'places' within this space are determined by varying degrees of scale; a place could refer to a specific social context, a region or even a nation. The concept of space, in other words, also offers a means to discuss the linkages between the local and global, defined in relation to each other (McCarthy, 2001: 10). For Hay, 'the televisual refers both to sites and to mechanisms for linking sites, for producing spaces'. He insists that 'television is not a self-contained site or network but installed at sites and through environments that define (in spatial terms) the meanings, uses, value, authority, and mattering of television' (Hay, 2001: 213).

Given an unlimited amount of resources, the attempt to analyse the nature and significance of a specific televisual text would detail the intersections of social, institutional and technological contexts that mark its production, and trace the myriad possibilities for its distribution and reception. And such sites for reception are not simply within the domestic sphere. For McCarthy, television 'did not simply bring public space into the private space of the home; rather, it reshaped the ways in which the boundary between public and private was conceived in domestic discourse' (McCarthy, 2001: 21). She argues for the need to move away from a sense of television purely as a domestic medium, to instead acknowledge how ubiquitous the televisual screen is in public and semi-public spaces, and the implications of this for the reproduction of social, political and cultural discourses.

The notion of televisual space thus involves a particular acknowledgement of the key role played by the viewing practices of audiences within specific sites. Even if we assume an overwhelmingly domestic site for reception, and pretend the sustained concentration of audiences, we still need to consider the social nature of any specific viewing context and acknowledge the agency of viewers. Ethnographic studies of television audiences have demonstrated the variety of social practices which may intersect within the space in which a television screen is present, complicating the task of assessing the discursive impact of televisual messages. Viewers have always been more 'active' than the stereotype of the coach potato suggested, not least with the gradual incorporation of technologies that allow us to 'graze' over channels using a television remote control or to use video and DVD recorders (and other devices) that allow for easier control of time-delayed viewing. The transformation of television from a mass medium, perhaps the dominant medium of the last century, into a matrix of more diffuse engagements between producers and viewers is the result of any number of such changes in the technological base of the medium at all levels of production, distrbution and reception. A full accounting of these changes is beyond the scope of this book, but they imply profound changes in the manner of televisual address and the nature and complexity of televisual messages.

For Ellis, the fracturing of television's mass audience is reflected in the nature of television programming itself, for example through an increasingly fragmented perspective dominating news discourse (Ellis, 2000: 75) and a preoccupation with the expression of social and cultural anxieties associated with specific sites of production and reception. Consequently, there is an absence of either a strong institutional voice or authoritative perspective on national social and political developments which have traditionally been key to television's dominance within the mediascape (Ellis, 2000: 86–7). Such patterns within contemporary television programming derive in part from underlying tensions between national broadcasters' attempts to continue playing some semblance of a public service role while adapting to a commercial environment that continually erodes the conditions for television to remain a mass medium.

Television to a large extent remains, as Corner suggests, 'the principal source for public information and the chief arena for political expression and for political theatre' (Corner, 1999: 14). It still features programming aimed at 'creating and sustaining an informed public' (ibid.: 19), but the sense of a singular public is perhaps only revived around isolated events (such as the terrorist attacks on the US World Trade Centre and Pentagon on 11 September 2001). At other times it is possible to talk of television as one source among many offering competing forms of information and entertainment, a site for the commercialisation of more collaborative forms of image gathering (especially camcorder and mobile phone videography) or even simply as a teaser and entry point for bringing viewers to a wider array of online information and entertainment cultures. Such wider transformations in the nature of televisual space, and its complex relationship to social and political practices, necessarily frame any efforts to also provide general statements about the nature of television aesthetics, including those that are directly implicated in mockumentary discourse.

I want here to provide a detailing of some of the prominent patterns within televisual programming, particularly the often distinctive look of television content, and how it is packaged into segmented streams of programming. It is easy to dismiss the complexity of televisual content, to miss the visual and ideological density of television programming as a whole. This is not always apparent at a given point in a particular programme, but it is obvious if we consider the accumulation of messages over a period of viewing. It is this potential to impart information in layered form over time which is understood and exploited to full effect by the most proficient television producers.

Some general qualities of television aesthetics

The televisual image has been key to its distinction from other media, even other audio-visual media. Television developed within the constraints of an electronic image on a relatively small screen, with a consequently lower resolution than the cinematic screen. Together with an assumed domestic audience, such factors governed the emergence of familiar configurations of image and sound. Visually, television has tended to be marked by tight framing, especially the dominance of close-ups and an emphasis on foreground action in the frame. These factors shaped the nature of much of the content of television programming; as Ellis notes, the '[d]evelopment of television is partly an extension of technologies to facilitate opportunities to degrees of liveness and intimacy' (Ellis, 2000: 35).

From initial studio-bound productions to the development of satellite linkages allowing outside broadcasts, television has consistently emphasised the potential for 'liveness' as a defining marker. Ellis, building from Jane Feuer's similar critique, has discussed what he terms the 'myth of liveness': 'a charged sense of immediacy, presence, and direct representation that emerges from TV's technological capacity to transmit and receive signals simultaneously, regardless of whether the broadcast in question is "literally" live or not' (McCarthy, 2001: 16).

In sum, the televisual image aims for a degree of immediacy and intimacy, enhanced by editing techniques that emphasise a spontaneous or 'raw' look that in pre-recorded broadcasts could translate to a domestic audience as a kind of 'liveness'. For example, there may be fast cuts between different perspectives on the same scene, particularly using close-ups, while maintaining a strict sense of real-time continuity. This sense of spontaneity may occur through the direct participation of the audience or their proxies, through studio audiences responding to stage events on a sound stage ('live' to tape productions). These patterns predominate across a temporal complexity of types of productions; live, delayed live, replayed coverage; scripted productions; and potentially, syndicated repeats.

In contrast to the myth of liveness, Ellis proposes the term 'witnessing' to denote the rhetorical emphasis on the televisual lens playing witness to events and people in the world (Ellis, 2000). Peters argues that this provides the basis of television's social and political significance by facilitating different forms of witnessing. Television is preoccupied with 'being there', with capturing things 'as they happen', with cameras being present at the unfolding of every intimate aspect of an event. At the centre of televisual space, in other words, is the rhetorical insistence on providing a link from the (domestically situated) audience to other sites in the world. One result is the prominence of non-fiction programming within the medium, both as live broadcast and as looped actuality footage. As Peters notes, there is a powerful sense of authenticity to the act of witnessing: 'An event requires witnesses, a story only needs tellers and listeners. A fiction can be heard or told, but a fact is witnessed' (Peters, 2001: 720). Audiences are positioned as accomplices to the act of witnessing, which is recorded mechanically but presented within tightly bound frames of commentary (Ellis, 2000: 11). As viewers, we are encouraged to be intimate with the 'live' image, to allow it at times to substitute for direct experience. We are encouraged to feel that we are in some sense present ourselves at televised sites.

> Of four basic types of relations to an event, three can sustain the attitude of a witness. To be there, present at the event in space and time is the paradigm case. To be present in time but removed in space is the condition of liveness, simultaneity across space. To be present in space but removed in time is the conditional of historical representations: here is the possibility of a simultaneity across time, a witness that laps the ages. To be absent in both space and time but still have access to an event via its traces is the condition of recording: the profane zone in which the attitude of witnessing is hardest to sustain. (Peters, 2001: 720)

This suggests the importance especially of forms of commentary and other direct address to television viewers that are integral to the act of witnessing. Corner has discussed the 'relaxed sociality' (Corner, 1999: 26) which results from television's direct address to an assumed domestic audience, and other forms of indirect address such as interviews. Ellis has argued that television is characterised in fact by the dominance of sound over image (Ellis, 1992), that forms of narration and commentary dominate non-fiction, while dialogue dominates over action in television fiction. This is not uniformly the case, and is perhaps increasingly less so, as the televisual image becomes more cinematic. Perhaps the best examples of the continued dominance of dialogue over image are still from soap opera. In part, this is because the small screen often cannot reveal the details that the larger cinematic screen can. It is typically less cluttered, more intimate, a 'cleaner' image that is more immediately accessible than the cinematic image – but necessarily paired with forms of narration or other forms of sound (such as music) to convey narrative structure and continuity. In non-fiction programming we are never given just the image, we are always provided with a frame of reference: 'With few exceptions, indirect address is read *within* the image rather than as a commentary *upon* it (Corner, 1999: 42, original emphasis).

Television talk regulates our interpretation of images in a variety of often formulaic ways, such as with the expositional mode of documentary representation, which governs much of news and current affairs programming (Corner, 1999: 41). This is not to suggest that televisual narration is always effective. Ellis argues that to be witness also involves other desires, 'our need for explanation and context; our sense of impotence in relation to the events we witness; and, nowadays, our growing sense of the relative unimportance of television compared to the power we once thought it had' (Ellis, 2000: 36). It is often the act of narration itself which reveals national context; television news footage, for example, is repackaged for local audiences not through a re-editing of the image, but through the substitution of narration into the local language.

Another distinctive aspect of television is a layering of the television image, as television has increasingly incorporated graphic forms of presenting information (and in turn informs more graphic-centred media such as the World Wide Web). These range from sophisticated graphic sequences used in the opening titles to programmes, to captions for interviews and the use of text, symbolic and iconic images and other graphics superimposed over the televisual image. These may occur in familiar, even formulaic ways, drawing especially from well-established traditions of information design,[1] but also look to exploit the possibilities of the metalanguage of motion graphics (Manovich, 2006). Ellis goes so far as to argue that television is a graphic medium rather than a photographic medium (Ellis, 2000: 92), where graphic layers have become naturalised within the frame as a key means of attaching meaning to images. Such graphic forms are used to condense information, providing shorthand forms of narration, an easily accessible overview of an event or issue within a single frame. In non-fiction programming they enable often complex natural and social phenomena to be introduced and explained in easily digested ways and are increasingly an immediate option for producers looking to offer simplistic 3-D modular reconstructions of events where no actual footage exists (such as plane crashes, or battle scenes).

These graphic layers are typically constructed into a sense of hierarchy, conveying information through the composition of components in relation to each other and their timing of appearance on screen (Ellis, 2000: 100). Often different graphic forms are used to present different kinds of knowledge. A familiar example is the use of a scrolling 'news bar' at the base of the screen, which has become a means of introducing competing layers of news content simultaneously on screen. As with other aspects of the televisual images, the more important layers are in the foreground, with, paradoxically, the variety of layers producing a both dense and flattened image. The graphic layering of televisual image, in fact, is key to the sense of stability and ordering at the centre of the medium's address to audiences. This is often a dialectic between the chaotic 'rawness' or immediacy of live images and their packaging within this graphic hierarchy. The intersection and packaging of such content, in fact, is a defining characteristic of much television news reporting, even that which does not claim to be 'live'.

Collectively these features of televisual aesthetics help to provide a rich, symbolic field that is appropriated by mockumentary producers and which often serves to distinguish television mockumentary as a whole from other examples of the discourse. Caldwell has used the notion of 'televisuality' to describe the increasing emphasis by American television institutions on the visual aspects of televisual content. By this he means not only the increasingly dense, graphics-dominated nature of the flattened televisual image but its use within broader discourses of intertextuality, and a tendency to the foregrounding of conventions of parody and pastiche which have always been integral to the medium (Caldwell, 1995: 23). Caldwell's argument notes a number of factors in the creation of 'televisuality' as a governing aesthetic in American television, including an intensification of competition between television channels and with other media, which fosters more frenetic and technologically dependent attempts to maintain its position as a mass medium (Caldwell, 1995: 5). In one sense, television mockumentary simply contributes to these broader concerns by highlighting the distinctive nature of televisual aesthetics, although generally with different agendas in mind.

Mockumentary and television programming

The wider structures of television programming are of interest here, as they are also central to explaining the distinctiveness of television mockumentary. There are a variety of levels to the structures of televisual content, from the organisation of texts into segmented narratives to the manner in which these are presented to viewers within network-branded streams. Televisual narratives must adhere to the demands of a space necessarily saturated by advertising. Programmes are designed to be presented in the form of segments between advertising breaks and are typically expected to adhere to half-hour and hourly timeslots. Such constraints place significant demands on the creativity of the collaborative teams that produce television content. That is, narratives not only need to be broken into the bite-sized forms that operate within such timeslots, but increasingly need to factor in cliff-hangers and teasers before each advertising break, to entice viewers to return. The cumulative result is often repetitive and formulaic narrative forms, relying on relatively compressed forms of storytelling and presentation (usually using immediately accessible generic codes and conventions). This is a pattern repeated across both fiction and non-fiction to varying effects. Within news broadcasting, for example, such constraints enforce a mode of news presentation broken into updates of different subgenres of news, and often content lacking a sense of closure or even overarching coherence of explanation (outside of that repeated from authoritative sources).

Within fictional narrative, the patterns can be more complex, as this basic constraint of segmentation has favoured both high degrees of closure and open-ended narratives. Outside of stand-alone productions (such as televisions dramas, documentary specials and televised events) the dominant pattern in television narratives could be mapped onto a continuum between series and serials. A series might be an anthology of unrelated programmes, but more typically relies on building a sense of continuity across individually screened episodes, especially through recurring characters and setting. There may be continuity through some storylines, but the dominant pattern is towards self-contained stories, with closure at the end of each daily or weekly episode. Most sitcoms still adhere to this narrative pattern, as do most action-centred series such as police and medical dramas. Serials, at the opposite end of this spectrum, develop more complex markers of continuity, typically through introducing a large cast of characters who interact through multiple storylines that reappear and intersect across episodes and across seasons without definite closure. The archetypal serial format is soap opera, designed to accumulate a narrative complexity that encourages regular, habitual viewing.

If we understand the (audio-visual) serial form as operating within this broader spectrum, it becomes obvious that this is a key marker of televisual space. Most fictional television programming operates somewhere between these poles; in fact, despite some generic patterns, as suggested above, any distinction between series and serials has tended to become eroded in the last 20 years. For example, police and medical dramas have become more like soap operas, while long-term sitcoms such as *The Simpsons* and *Seinfeld* (1990–98) have proved capable of generating complex fictional worlds. Differentiation between different series can often centre less on narrative structures and more on stylistic patterns, including particular editing strategies favoured by each genre. While increasingly varied in their narrative structures, television genres in these terms are still generally easily differentiated in their appeals to gender, age, ethnicity and occasionally class. These narrative structures are crucial to the distinctiveness of television mockumentary. Producers have learned to exploit a serial structure that provides a narrative density rarely matched by, for example, cinematic mockumentary (as in the examples discussed in the third part of this book).

Television serials necessarily pose a unique challenge for academic analysis. What is the 'television text' in these circumstances: an individual episode, an entire season, or the entire narrative arc of a serial over multiple seasons? In the more interesting cases, an individual episode of a long-running serial may resonate only with committed, regular viewers as it makes subtle references to narrative points in much earlier episodes or features characters that make irregular occurrences through the life of a serial. This level of narrative complexity is an important aspect of the natural tendency of televisual texts toward intertextuality, a term which encompasses references to other episodes in a series, other television programmes or other aspects of mediated culture. The more complex examples of intertextuality (and again, *The Simpsons* is an obvious example here) tend to assume audiences' awareness of an extremely dense collective media history that can be drawn upon, generating often layered forms of references for audiences that require repeated viewings to catch them all. In a broader sense this field of potential intertextual references is also available to be exploited by mockumentary producers.

Scheduling as a frame

There is one further aspect of television programming which needs a mention here. Corner usefully reminds us of the wider sense of production, which 'extends beyond the completion of the programme itself to include the carrying through of distribution and scheduling, increasingly strategic within multi-channel systems and requiring pre-publicity and final decisions as to target audiences, transmission times, and perhaps levels of advertising support' (Corner, 1999: 71). Any television text appears on screen framed by other forms of programming, within a schedule which is geared towards the attraction and retention of specific demographic groups, typically those that are most prized by advertisers. It is a schedule generally shaped by a keen awareness of competition for viewers' attention from other channels, other media and possibly other social activities within the sites of reception (which are primarily assumed to be domestic).

In terms of televisual space, broadcast schedules operate as a kind of architecture, with individual networks using series and serials as key basic building blocks. For broadcasters, the production, commissioning and acquisition of programming is motivated by the need to develop a core audience that can easily be differentiated through the use of demographic and psychographic forms of measurement (the favoured language of advertisers). The art of scheduling is editing on a massive scale, aimed at the retention of audience's attention over long periods of time and toward regulating those audiences into everyday, habitual viewing.

Television theorists have employed the notion of 'flow' to characterise television programming at this level, but this tends to overemphasise the uniformity of what are still quite disparate textual constructions, not least in the manner in which they may be received by specific viewers (Corner, 1999: 62). As noted above, one of the challenges for television networks is adjusting to a more digitally enhanced set of viewing possibilities where the traditions of programme scheduling often become irrelevant (if we assume an eventual drift toward online databases of all television programmes that can be surfed at will). Network broadcasters have attempted to compensate for the gradual and inevitable erosion of viewing control to viewers through the provision of multiple channels aimed at offering comprehensive viewing options (including staggered times for the same programming across different channels), and through more generally increasing the intensity of forms of address to viewers.

As any regular television viewer knows, among the range of possibilities within television schedules are mixtures of live and recorded content, localised and global forms of programming, and programmes from different historical contexts (reruns and syndicated series). Again, these all serve as both frame and source for mockumentary programmes, providing rich and specific fields of potential intertextual references that are immediately accessible to localised audiences.

The fact-fiction continuum within televisual space

In more specific terms, these characteristics of television programming determine the non-fiction templates that mockumentary more directly appropriates. Television has been a significant site for commercially motivated experimentation of the practices that define non-fiction genres such as documentary. Innovations within a range of reality-based and hybridised television formats have impacted upon the wider documentary culture. The next chapter considers documentary and hybrid forms in more detail, but some introductory comments are useful here.

Firstly, all reality-based television formats draw upon the quest for 'liveness' and immediacy that is still core to televisual aesthetics. News and current affairs, as noted above, place a high premium on the currency of information, prioritising live broadcasts, location footage (especially through satellite links) and the foregrounding of visually spectacular footage that can be exhaustively repackaged and replayed. There is a clear dependency upon visual forms of information, which are nonetheless heavily narrativised and bordered within familiar frames of reference. The result is a tension between constant repetition and frequent updates of a stream of information invariably presented in segmented and highly narrativised forms. Considerations of the wider context, and in particular any deeper political and historical implications of the information being broadcast, tend to be relatively neglected or marginalised.

Such tendencies have attracted numerous critical responses. Writing in 1995, in reference to developments in American television that have since become more widespread, Caldwell critiqued the agenda that often accompanies the demand for such imagery. He identified the development of a tabloid style focused on 'the endless elaboration, dramatization, reiteration, and re-creation of some aberrant event or sensational hook' (Caldwell, 1995: 224), and the emergence of programming preoccupied with 'the exotic, the kinky, the violent, and the voyeuristic' (Caldwell, 1995: 226). In broader terms we can see that such statements identify both the prominence of photographic forms of evidence at the centre of televisual culture and the comparatively formulaic and limited ways in which these tend to be exhibited within factually based formats. The distinctions between news and documentary within these broader characteristics can often rest on differences in the length (and hence narrative complexity) of programmes, and on particular stylistic features, such as documentary's frequent effort to generate a sense of authenticity by relying on images shorn of the graphic layering which is so typical of everyday news presentation.[2]

The segmentation at the heart of television narrative form provides a basic structure for news and current affairs broadcasts, but also inevitably shapes the production of the more complex and longer-form narratives of television documentary. Perhaps the key innovation that television has added to documentary culture is the documentary series, which has the potential to develop a richly layered complexity of people and events across a number of episodes. Most non-fiction television series, however, are still constructed from the basic building blocks required for segmented timeslots. While stretching the narrative time-span, or allowing for the inclusion of multiple social actors, these series still present information using familiar and formulaic modes of representation (the longest-running, and atypical, example could be the astonishing narrative arc at the heart of the *Seven Up* series of documentaries, which have covered the lives of a diminishing number of British participants at 7-year intervals). Although it is difficult to make useful generalisations, it is often the case that any social and political depth to such series tends to come from the accumulation of layers of information across episodes, rather than from more avant-garde or experimental forms of narrative that move away from generic norms. A segmented structure prompts a reliance on accumulating narrative detail, which also often entails a preoccupation with the presentation of real-time chronologies of events and an overall coherence through voice-over narration.

Writing of television serial form more generally, Ellis argues that 'fundamentally the series implies the form of the dilemma rather than that of resolution and closure. This is perhaps the central contribution that broadcast TV has made to the long history of narrative forms and narrativised perception of the world' (Ellis, 1992: 154). Certainly the dominant ideology of short forms of television non-fiction is a focus on the abnormal, the deviant, those social and natural phenomena which can be seen to disrupt some notion of everyday normality (Ericson et al, 1987; 1991) and there is also a flavour of this within television documentary. Following the pattern of other television genres, television documentary series also focus overwhelmingly on the everyday, relying on personalised narratives based on displaying intimate and emotional content. The distinctiveness of television documentary, then, is partly due to the closeness in narrative structure between non-fiction and other television genres. Ellis in fact has insisted that 'there is no real difference in narrational form between news and soap opera. The distinction is at another level: that of source of material' (Ellis, 1992: 159). Documentary segments are designed around narrative climaxes, while serial episodes tend to exploit the open-ended nature of everyday life by avoiding a sense of narrative closure and developing narrative tension that will retain viewers for the following episode.

The emergence of series such as *An American Family*, and its British equivalent *The Family* (1974) and similar examples in other national contexts, follows this broad pattern, and not coincidentally served as the foundation for the later development of hybridised formats such as docusoaps. These formats are discussed in more detail in chapter 4, but it is important to note here the extent to which their emergence built upon wider patterns of aesthetics and narrative inherent in television programming as a whole.

The critique of such patterns often leads to the claim that television has helped to 'dumb down' the collective television public, encouraging a lapsing of critical skills, a reduction in attention spans and a preoccupation with pleasures other than those of knowledge (Postman, 1985). Ellis argues that television 'can be seen as a vast mechanism for processing the material of the witnessed world into more narrativized, explained forms' (Ellis, 2000: 78), which he insists are characterised by speculation rather than definitive knowledge. Instead of providing explanation, televisual space 'renders familiar, integrates and provides a place for the difficult material that it brings to our witness. It exhausts an area of concern, smothering it in explanations from almost every angle. This process of non-totalizing speculation is a crucial activity in an information-rich environment' (Ellis, 2000: 79–80). Instead of a space for the provision of socially and politically applicable knowledge, a reinforcement and expansion of documentary's call to action, television is seen as little more than a forum for the expression of emotional responses to events and people that are central to the act of witnessing.

In one sense, many of the producers of television mockumentary appear to share such concerns, judging by the forms of commentary that are generated particularly by series which reference television news (see chapter 8). Ultimately, however, television mockumentary operates with a more complex appreciation of the possibilities of audience engagement than these commentators acknowledge. Although often highly critical of the contemporary televisual fact-fiction continuum, television mockumentary also typically assumes that its viewers come to their programmes with deeply historical experiences with televisual content, and some sophistication in reading televisual representations.

Viewers and televisual space

Audience engagement with televisual space is the most speculative and least researched aspect of the medium. In part this reflects practical constraints (audience research is time consuming and expensive), but it is also the result of widespread assumptions about viewing practice often largely derived from textual analysis. Both television producers and television critics have tended to view television as an exclusively domestic technology, operating in competition with other social practices in the domestic sphere, including other media technologies. Many of the critiques of the commercialised, formulaic complexity of televisual aesthetics and programming structures tend to assume modes of viewing that are uniquely associated with the medium.

Ellis, for example, writing in 1992, consequently insists that television 'engages the look and the glance rather than the gaze' (Ellis, 1992: 128). Unlike cinema, which 'captures' its audience's attention by encouraging a concerted gaze within a darkened social space designed for just one activity, television must fight to attract and retain the attention of potentially easily distracted viewers. Viewers have immediate access to media devices and other activities that help to define and constitute domestic space. The intensity of such competition helps to drive television's inevitable appeal in the form of a cacophony of sound and visual designed to appeal to the more transient, impulsive and irresistible episodes of domestic activity. The emphasis on qualities such as immediacy and practices such as 'witnessing', the prioritising of discourses focused on nuclear families, packaged as highly segmented narratives within the broader structures of scheduling, are thus ultimately partly founded on a narrow conception of (televisual) spectatorship. Viewers, ultimately, are assumed to oscillate between distraction and periods of (perhaps intense, often emotional) engagement. It is easy to add further complexities to such a picture. Viewers are typically addressed as members of an assumed national unity, geographically isolated in households but linked discursively, in part through the act of witnessing events in the public, global sphere. Their viewing is distracted but also ritualised within everyday practices.

Corner notes the implications of the linking of domestic space and other spaces through television:

> Television reworks the meanings of home life in modernity by developing new modes of linkage and separation between world and home, between public and private, often taking its cue from those established by radio. [...] Within the new system of culturally formative alignments, home space becomes permeable to the public world and the wider popular culture in ways which effect a radical change in both. (Corner, 1999: 87–8)

Dayan in turn characterises the implications for public discourse that appear to follow from television interweaving of public and private spheres. He defines a 'public' as a form of performance characterised by an inherent instability:

> a public does not form around a medium (or a text) but in relation
> to a problem and with respect to other public, existing or potential,
> mainstream or minority. These publics possess an (internal) sociabil-
> ity and an (external) performance. This performance consists of
> taking up a public position, with reference to an agenda. What is
> involved here is the formation of public opinion, a process that
> depends on interventions by differentiated publics. (Dayan, 2001:
> 756)

Dayan suggests that there are four types of publics: an assumed
public that forms the basis of a participative frame, the public that
adopts certain forms of television but is not determined by them,
and two which can be described as publics of television. There is
the public of fans that is social but operates in a make-believe
world, and the public of major events, which 'is very serious, deferential, even reverential. It demonstrates all the characteristics
required to form a public save one: stability. It is an elusive public:
a public for one or several days; sometimes a public for an hour or
two' (Dayan, 2001: 761). This instability matches the transient
nature of live television transmissions, as publics coalesce around a
media event, then dissipate once it is over. The publics formed by
television, Dayan argues, are imperfect ones, neither fixed and continuous outside of their media watching, nor sober and rational, but
instead involved in transient acts of political play.

Such a model of audience social and political engagement is
easily stretched to cover new sites of reception, as noted above.
McCarthy's notion of 'ambient television' highlights how television
has become more prevalent in sites such as bars, waiting rooms,
train stations, offices, airports and stores. She argues for a more
'site-specific' discussion of the medium, as what television actually
means in each of these contexts can be quite distinctive (McCarthy,
2001: 2). Television researchers need to incorporate this understanding as a complement to studies focusing on the domestic
sphere:

> the site-specific nature of many institutional and personal uses of TV
> means that it is impossible to single out one mode of spectatorship
> to define the relationship between screen and environment, regard-
> less of the latter's particular features. Rather, the diffuse network of
> gazes and institutions, subjects and bodies, screens and physical struc-
> tures that constitute the televisual place sustains quite particular
> effects in each place. (McCarthy, 2001: 3)

These aspects of televisual space need to be put in relation to the insights from the range of audience-research traditions (Jensen and Rosengren, 1990) which have emerged, particularly from post-structuralist paradigms within sociological theory. Briefly, these suggest that the meanings associated with any form of text can be assumed to be generated through interaction with an audience (Philo, 1990; Ang, 1991; 1996; Fiske, 1992; Jancovich, 1992; Morley, 1992). Here the interpretations which viewers make of television texts are a product of the interplay between the complexities of social experiences which viewers bring to their encounter with a text, bounded by the specifics of the 'preferred reading' intended by television producers. Each viewer makes interpretations, both consciously and consciously, of the discourses operating in the text, often shaped by their gender, age, class and ethnicity, or more specific aspects of a viewing context, including the physical space for reception itself. As both individual and social acts, such interpretations are necessarily fluid and dynamic (Fiske, 1989; Ang, 1989; 1991; Hoijer, 1990; Dahlgren, 1992; Roscoe et al, 1995). They may change for each viewer during an instance of viewing and over time, prompted by other people's talk about a text or other social experiences. Each viewer can be assumed to be 'active' to the extent that she/he draws upon pre-existing frames of reference initially in making interpretations, or readings, of a text. All such readings are active in the sense that these are activities that necessarily involve continually negotiating or contesting the meanings provided by a text (Roscoe et al, 1995). There is always the potential, either during or subsequent to engaging with a text, for a viewer to develop a 'critical' interpretation (in the case of documentary, for example, this might be prompted by the varieties of stylistic and political reflexivity outlined by Nichols). These assumptions are central to the discussion of audience engagement of mockumentary discourse outlined in chapter 1.

The addition of new technologies that transform television reception practices adds further complexities to any model of television spectatorship. In the case of video cassette recorders and digital recorders, as Corner suggests, 'suddenly, the television set was no longer simply the front end of a service to be switched in and out of, it was an apparatus for exercising audio-visual choice, sometimes for options well outside of the range of television's homely aesthetic' (Corner, 1999: 89). One of the implications of using a concept of televisual space is that we can begin to increasingly conceive of viewers in the digital sense as 'users' navigating their way through programming structures. The use of such a digital lexicon will become more appropriate as television increasingly seeks to converge with the interactive possibilities of digital media that seem to forecast partly the remediation of television programming by online and other digital media, and partly an expansion of the televisual into 'on demand' and downloadable forms of programming. Television in these terms becomes a more directly navigable space entailing much broader site-specific practices that are not necessarily dependent on one technology of reception. Here what constitutes the television screen is as easily refashioned for personal computers and personal mobile devices such as iPods and mobile phones as it is for varieties of widescreen and/or high-definition display.

The assumed mass audiences of the early decades of the development of television broadcasting, in other words, have increasingly fractured in the face of a proliferating of channels, competing media activities (including multiple screens in the same space, accessing different media), diversity of sites, and new technologies of reception. The impact on the set of representational strategies traditionally employed by television producers is difficult to predict in detail but potentially could entail the emergence of completely new televisual forms. There are various trajectories that can be assumed from the emergence of just the technologies noted above, such as aesthetic and narrative forms appropriate to the smaller screens and download capabilities of mobile devices (such as webisodes, and the variety of practices that could be referred to as adhering to a 'YouTube aesthetic').

Other possibilities include more fundamental changes to television programming itself. As noted in chapter 1, Johnson's observations on the nature of contemporary media include arguments that the rise of DVD as a medium prompted the emergence of denser but more nuanced forms of television narrative, characterised by increasingly layered intertextual references and more complex narrative structures involving wider networks of characters (S. Johnson, 2005). For Johnson, such traits follow directly from DVD's emergence as a medium; when the probability of repeated viewings of television texts is accepted as a given by producers. A transformed production practice also follows from the need to design for more collaborative viewing practices, such as providing supplementary online materials.

Television, then, can no longer be easily defined as a 'mass medium' in terms of the scale of simultaneous viewings of a single text by geographically dispersed audiences. Instead, it is a medium which facilitates access to a range of programming forms, helping to constitute the nature of social and political space at the myriad points of reception. For its audiences, television is increasingly encountered as a dense field of normatively fractured, hybridised generic formats, a symbolic space ready to be navigated by remote control and other devices that allow time-shifted and repeated viewings. Television mockumentary is following these patterns, mapping and reflecting broader changes in programming and anticipating the move to more directly playful forms of audience engagement.

Television mockumentary hoaxes

Television mockumentary has always been sensitive to changes in the medium. The discourse has served as a site for commentary on the nature and significance of the changing technological base of televisual space, as much as the social, economic and political relationships which this space helps to facilitate. A brief discussion of the corpus of television mockumentary hoaxes can serve as an introduction to the rich possibilities of the intersection of mockumentary discourse and televisual space. Television mockumentary hoaxes are fictional texts which both play with audiences' assumptions of documentary modes of representation and involve the direct complicity of a host broadcaster. As an extended form of April Fool's Day jokes, most of these are intended to be recognised at some stage by the audience, even if there are concerted efforts to frame an initial viewing as an engagement with a 'documentary' or 'live' broadcast. A brief analysis of some examples here can suggest how we can locate individual mockumentaries within their historical context, at the intersection between aesthetic traditions, generic conventions and national contexts, as well as within the wider development of television as a set of technologies.

Alternative 3 is an early example of a mockumentary hoax. Screening in 1977 on the UK channel ITV, it was intended as an elaborate April Fool's Day joke (although, ironically, scheduling

3. Presenter Tim Brinton introduces an investigative report into an apparent global conspiracy with implications for the future of humanity, in the classic television mockumentary hoax *Alternative 3* (1973).

difficulties meant that it did not screen until 20 June). It was written and directed by David Ambrose and Christopher Miles, with Ambrose having consulted with Orson Welles about his own *War of the Worlds* radio hoax. Fronted by Shaw Taylor (from the public service police programme *Police Five* (1962–92)) within a television news studio and using former *World in Action* (1963–98) presenter Tim Brinton as an on-screen narrator (Figure 3), the programme is constructed as a conventional investigative documentary. It builds from various documents, including newspaper reports and photographs, interviews with experts, 8 mm film clips from various locations (including 'ambush' interviews with hostile interviewees) and hidden-camera segments which apparently 'capture' admissions from unwitting interview subjects. There are also a host of other archival elements used to reference global narratives of then current political and environmental concerns – for example, there is an effective use of current news footage of natural disasters, integrating them into a persuasive narrative of emerging global chaos (that interestingly foreshadows the much later Al Gore lecture documentary *An Inconvenient Truth*). The programme's overall argument that these fragments serve as evidence of an explanation for a global 'brain drain' is linked to a global conspiracy aiming to take the best minds on the planet and move them to a new colony established on Mars.

Viewers are taken step by step through persuasive speculations from such evidence. There is a sense of an unfolding mystery, with the small group of reporters accidentally stumbling upon and gradually uncovering the edges of a wider conspiracy. The character of 'Professor Karl Gerstein' of Cambridge University (Richard Marner) serves as a key revelatory figure as he outlines three possible policy initiatives for the survival of the human race in the face of global environmental collapse: cut the global population, cut human consumption of earth's resources, or (alternative three) leave the planet altogether. Although couched within the sober discourses of television journalism, the programme draws upon wider discourses of environmental disaster that had recently entered the popular mainstream with the publication of seminal environmental texts such as Rachel Carson's *Silent Spring* (1962) – for example, there are rudimentary diagrammatic animations of the newly discovered 'greenhouse effect'. The programme also makes key references to the wider Cold War climate, suggesting that the conflict between the Soviet Union and the United States operated as a colossal public relations exercise to cover up their collaboration in the building of a space colony (likewise the 1969 Apollo moon landing is reframed as a diversionary media event for the world's populations). The programme culminates in the screening of an apparently top secret 1962 film that purports to cover early lunar astronauts' accidental discovery of an existing human colony on the moon.

Perhaps crucially, the programme does not attempt to provide a complete picture of the supposed conspiracy, or a sense of its full disclosure, but only works to suggest the conspiracy's local effects within the UK, through the tantalisingly limited pieces of evidence that its reporters seem to have been able to uncover. Couched within key national discourses of the historical context of its production and referenced closely to the dominant style of television current affairs presentation of this period (even to the extent of using presenters who would be immediately familiar to local audiences), the programme derived its effectiveness from its challenge to viewers to develop a critical reading of its argument. Apart from the scope of the programme's fantastic narrative, there is little to flag its status as a work of fiction. Consequently, and mirroring the initial response to radio mockumentary *War of the Worlds*, the programme prompted some panicked telephone calls to ITV and to newspapers such as the *Daily Mirror* and *Evening News*, and has since developed minor cult status.[3]

Another mockumentary hoax that was extremely effective in its initial broadcast context is the BBC1 programme *Ghostwatch*. Billed as a Screen One Special, it aired at 9.25, on Halloween night, 31 October 1992. Constructed as a 'live' media event, it purported to cover the monitoring, surveillance and exploring of a house in Foxhill Drive, Northolt, whose residents ('Mrs Pamela Early' and her two young daughters) insist is haunted. This programme also employs presenters who would have been familiar to British audiences at the time, in this case high-profile interviewer Michael Parkinson, children's presenter Sarah Greene, sports presenter Mike Smith and comedian Craig Charles. Parkinson hosts the in-studio segments, where he conducts interviews with a British paranormal expert, examines video and physical artefacts from paranormal cases that she has brought and accesses an array of television screens on one wall of the studio. These screens provide the central 'live' feeds from inside and directly outside the haunted house. Greene plays the role of an intrepid reporter entering the house with a small, two-person camera crew, while a jokey Charles captures vox-pop segments from the locals and gathers local folklore of the house. Meanwhile, Smith monitors a number of in-studio telephone operators waiting for viewers to call with information about the house or their own supernatural encounters. (According to Kim Newman's DVD notes, the phone number which flashed on the screen during the programme was 'manned by volunteers who explained the show was a fiction but listened to any ghost stories contributed').

The television special makes full use of the array of then available media technologies, all carefully introduced at the beginning of its narrative. There is a view inside the production's outside broadcast vans, an explanation of various temperature sensors and surveillance cameras installed in the house, and of the crew's hand-held cameras (with their capability for capturing footage in the dark using infrared technology). Parkinson pieces together the historical narrative of the house, with the help of the in-studio expert and information gleaned from local vox-pop and phone callers, who appear to fill in gaps in its violent and traumatic history. In other words, the programme is constructed as a textbook example of an unfolding real-time narrative, using all of the familiar tropes of live television broadcasting (for British television in the 1990s). Parkinson plays the role of a rational journalist whose scepticism is gradually overwhelmed by the apparently unexpected revelations of events in the house itself. He engages in a dialogue with his in-studio paranormal expert and mediates a discussion between her and a New York expert, using a 'live' satellite feed, in the process serving as a proxy for the audience by articulating all of the expected sceptical responses to what appears to be unfolding. The other cast members play varying roles in relation to their expectations of what they might find. Smith (the real-life partner of Greene) offers an initially non-committal 'wait-and-see' attitude, but provides a key focal point for concerns about her safety, while Charles serves as an on-location cynic.

The role of the featured media technologies is crucial to the unfolding of the film's narrative in more than one sense, both helping to build dramatic tension toward the horrific climax and unexpectedly moving centre stage at the end of the programme. All of the attempts to conclusively document supernatural activities in the house are frustrated, with each technology failing in apparent response to the intervention of a hostile entity in the house. Tension builds as we are given less and less information from the house itself, except that Greene and her crew are caught inside as events become more chaotic and dangerous, while we are simultaneously presented with further alarming facts about the location's violent history. Cameras fail, the effort to use infrared footage as a backup obscures our perspective still further, the 'live' feed to the studio is interrupted and finally the apparent live transmission from the studio to viewers' living rooms (as it would have appeared at the time) is broken, then briefly repaired.

Throughout the programme there are warnings about the role that television itself is playing as a causal factor in the 'haunting'. The medium is initially blamed for a rise in claimed encounters by celebrity seekers, then there is the suggestion that the presence of the variety of technologies in the house is provoking the entity there, and finally it appears that the house's supernatural presence has been able to use the television apparatus to escape from the house and enter first the studio and then the homes of viewers. The final scenes appear to suggest that television itself is operating as a massive medium to channel the aggressive poltergeist through a kind of mass electronic seance to spark similar events across the nation. There are panicked calls into the studio from viewers who say the broadcast is causing odd activities in their households and the final scenes appear to show a disorientated and possibly possessed Parkinson wandering around a suddenly panicked and chaotic studio environment. This is an intriguing, horrific premise for viewers; by viewing the 'live' programme not only do they themselves contribute to the escalating events inside the house but their own domestic spaces become transformed in the process (*The Blair Witch Project* offers a safer and more conventional position for viewers, in comparison). It is a narrative that also neatly exploits a host of assumptions about the power of television to construct moments of apparent national unity.

The programme provoked a huge public response, in part because of the hour at which it was broadcast and the consequent potential for children to be watching. Newspapers reported that many child viewers were frightened by the programme, convinced that it was real, and some callers rang the police in panic, while the BBC's switchboard was overloaded with calls. A BBC spokesperson later defended the programme, insisting that it was billed as a drama (noting that a cast list was included in the programme's listing in the *Radio Times*) and, just as with *War of the Worlds*, there was a clear disclaimer prior to the broadcast. There was subsequent wide news media coverage of a family claiming that their son's suicide five days after the broadcast was related to the programme (the BBC was later censured over the case). A later report in a British medical journal even claimed to have evidence that children had suffered the first recorded post-traumatic stress disorder caused by television (*Times*, 11 March 1994).

Other examples of television mockumentary hoaxes have had varying impacts on viewers in the localised contexts of their initial broadcast, demonstrating that their effectiveness depends upon a complex set of factors, including the sophistication of the techniques they use, and a variety of extra-textual factors that are necessary for viewers to suspend disbelief sufficiently to be convinced of the possibility for the claims made in a programme to be true. The case of the New Zealand mockumentary *Forgotten Silver*, which heralded the discovery of a forgotten local cinematic pioneer, suggests the importance of localised discourses as a key factor in shaping viewers' responses to such programmes (Hight and Roscoe, 2006). And there is the *Blair Witch* television trilogy (*Curse of the Blair Witch*, *The Burkittsville 7* and *Shadow of the Blair Witch*, discussed in the previous chapter), which was quickly revealed to be a hoax but which sought to provide viewers with different pleasures by engaging them in multiple layers of a wider, cross-platform fiction.

There are other, lesser examples of such hoaxes, some partly of interest for their use of aesthetics tied to specific technologies and their articulation of tensions within documentary culture over the presentation of different forms of evidence. *Alien Abduction: Incident in Lake County* constructs an apparent series of debates between various forms of experts over the legitimacy of a video tape that seems to offer evidence of the abduction of an American family by aliens. The premise of the programme is built upon the ubiquity of digital camcorders. The narrative of the videotape centres on a family occasion being filmed by the family's teenaged son, who continues to film as their gathering is disrupted by forces largely unseen (until the final shot) (Roscoe and Hight, 2001: 151–5). And *The Buried Secret of M. Night Shyamalan* (2004) is a promotional programme associated with the release of the director Shyamalan's feature film *The Village* (2004). Screened on the US Sci Fi channel, as with the *Blair Witch* texts, it was similarly intended as the centrepiece of a guerrilla marketing campaign. Constructed as an investigative expose of the director, using a familiar template in which the 'journalist' places himself into the frame, it builds a narrative around his frustrated attempts to secure a revelatory interview with his main subject. The programme attempts to generate a sense of mystery and eventual revelation around Shyamalan's background, and especially a near-death childhood drowning incident which supposedly left him with the ability to commune with the supernatural world. The journalist gains the 'revelation' that the inspiration for his films (including *The Sixth Sense* (1999) and *Unbreakable* (2000)) is autobiographic. The programme ultimately hints at its fictional status through the teasing words of the director's final interviews.

A 2002 television mockumentary hoax *Opération Lune* (*Dark Side of the Moon*), draws upon the same popular conspiracy theory regarding a possible 'faked' 1969 Apollo moon landing that features in *Alternative 3*. Here the narrative centres on speculations of the possible role played by then recently deceased director Stanley Kubrick. The premise is that Kubrick was compelled to help stage the moon landing in a film studio as payment for the use of NASA resources, including a unique high-tech camera, on *2001: A Space Odyssey* (1968) and *Barry Lyndon* (1975). Using this as a starting point, the programme outlines a wider narrative, involving key members of the Richard Nixon administration, of the morale-boosting media stunt of a moon landing and their involvement in a violent cover-up of their hoax (in other words, the programme pretends to be a 'documentary' about a supposedly real 'hoax'). The majority of the programme is a reasonably sophisticated editing exercise, moving quickly from expositional sequences which use a great deal of archival footage to construct a plausible narrative, then rapid intercuts between a series of interviews between apparent players of the moon landing hoax who seem to confirm suspicions of their involvement in a hoax. The programme makers managed to gain the participation of actual members of the administration of the deceased Nixon, as well as colleagues of Kubrick – but then deliberately let the audience in on the fiction by including outtakes from their scripted interviews during the end credits, as each breaks into laughter at the absurdity of the tale or fluffs their scripted lines.

These mockumentary hoaxes are all playful exercises in teasing audience expectations associated with forms of authoritative televisual address. They are all examples of a stunt (and promotional) mockumentary agenda that seeks the status of media events rather than looking to combine mockumentary form with more conventional narrative concerns of attracting and retaining audiences. They serve as a useful starting point for discussing the craft involved in mockumentary production but do not suggest its wider significance as a mode of storytelling. The central argument of this book is that mockumentary discourse is naturalised within televisual space, to the extent that it has become a set of familiar styles employed within texts ranging from advertising, to one-off dramatic and comedic texts, to entire series. To some extent mockumentary has been incorporated into the hegemony of televisual address; it has become part of the wider lexicon of television programming. This chapter has sought to outline some of the factors, both stylistic and structural, which govern televisual space and provide such a natural forum for mockumentary forms of appropriation and play.

Mockumentary intersects within other discourses within this televisual space. It draws upon the rich symbolic density that characterises televisual space, including as it does texts that are produced from a variety of geographic and temporal sites, aimed at a myriad of assumed audiences, structured into streams of programming available for navigation by television users. It interacts with a variety of existing traditions, in particular, satiric and other comedic traditions, but also generic traditions of social realist drama, documentary and emerging hybrid documentary forms.

All of these key generic traditions (non-fiction, dramatic and comedic – outlined in the chapters which follow) have, at points, offered quite radical departures from dominant televisual patterns of programming. Television has been quite aggressive in appropriating and refashioning such emerging traditions from other media and incorporating their stylistic innovations, in particular, into the mainstream of programming formats. The question remains to what extent the energising and 'subversive' intent of such innovations lingers within generic textual strategies, and whether audiences are able to recognise these. This not indirectly also relates to the nature of the reflexivity or commentary that can be read into a television mockumentary by its audiences.

Any approach to this issue must in turn incorporate an appropriately complex awareness of the possibilities inherent to television spectatorship. As suggested above, viewers can respond to the preferred readings of texts in ways that are heavily shaped by a myriad of social and political factors that partly constitute local contexts. Viewers demonstrate varying levels of awareness of the possibilities of media producers appropriating documentary aesthetics for fictional purposes. Some are prepared to engage with these texts in a playful way, while others are challenged by the basic premise of mockumentary.

Examples of television mockumentary in turn provide insights into the nature of the complexity of these forms of television programming within the contemporary context. It is possible to argue, further, that the emergence of mockumentary discourse is symptomatic of wider changes within visual culture, of which television remains a significant part. This does not suggest that the study of mockumentary can offer insights not available to other analytical approaches, but television mockumentary is certainly capable of articulating issues at the centre of the medium's constructions of reality, as covered in the following chapter.

Notes

1 See especially the classic texts by Edward Tufte (Tufte, 1990; 1997; 2001; 2006), which cover well-established techniques of graphic representation in both print and audio-visual media. His books cover conventions for representing 'pictures of numbers', 'pictures of nouns', and 'pictures of verbs'.
2 This was certainly the case with the introduction of video technology, with documentaries such as *The Police Tapes* (1977), which in turn provided such an inspiration for television dramatic aesthetics – see chapter 5.
3 The programme's fantastical story has developed a life of its own. I initially tracked down a pirated copy in Melbourne, from a small shop where the woman behind the counter obviously felt she was performing a public service in getting more information to the public on this conspiracy.

4

Television and the real: documentary traditions and hybrid forms

Non-fiction is at the core of television programming. The staple non-fiction format is the daily news bulletins which still serve as flagship programmes within the schedules of network (free-to-air) broadcasters, but the televisual fact-fiction continuum includes current affairs programmes, documentary and the variety of reality-based formats which dominate prime time. It is difficult to suggest what these forms all share, apart from an effort to mediate aspects of the socio-historical world according to varying agendas, ethics and representational styles that typically incorporate a direct address to their assumed domestic audiences. These are texts which range from short (1- to 3-minute) news items, collated into news broadcasts, through to the magazine-style segments of current affairs programmes, to half-hour and hour-long, one-off and serial, forms of documentary programming. All these forms are subject to the broader constraints of a segmented schedule. There are often rigid limitations in terms of documentary length and structure, with programmes required to fill the 22 or so minutes between advertising per half hour or 42 minutes per hour, and producers need to anticipate clear opportunities to break for these advertisements.

Television, certainly more than any other audio-visual medium, is defined through its reliance on non-fiction programming, and changes in these parts of its schedules are invariably symptomatic of more fundamental changes within television broadcasting as a whole. Above all, the televisual non-fiction and related forms of programming reveal the overwhelmingly commercial basis of the medium globally. The apparent division between public service and commercial models which often defined early television history is increasingly decided in favour of corporate agendas centred on competitive appeals for audiences (and hence advertising revenue).

This environment inevitably determines patterns in the production, commissioning, scheduling and sales of non-fiction programming.

Within these constraints it is important to reiterate that national broadcasting concerns continue to play a distinctive role in global television non-fiction. Local television schedules are invariably characterised by combinations of local and global programming content. Local production environments, in terms of their blend of available technologies of production, distribution and reception, anchor television development. Socio-cultural factors such as dominant languages and local values and norms, expressed particularly through formal and informal censorship regimes, continue to govern programming decisions at local sites. All of these factors shape the nature of the mixture of information, education and entertainment that characterises the factual-based programming received by audiences in specific sites.

The intention in this chapter is to outline some of the key formats and their discourses, aesthetics and issues that characterise the televisual fact-fiction continuum at a global level. These suggest the variety of factual-related 'templates' which mockumentary can call upon, reference and appropriate. The discussion below is not looking to replicate the diversity of debates over these forms, including the now considerable body of literature on documentary hybrids produced since the early 1990s.[1] Documentary hybrids have certainly helped to inspire the emergence of key television mockumentary texts, including exemplars of mockumentary series, but collectively they are derived from an enormously complicated history.

Television documentary production

The scale of television documentary production dwarfs that within other media, but it is highly differentiated through its content, as this typically forms the basis of its position within television schedules. Both producers and audiences are familiar with the expectations raised by labels such as 'nature documentary', 'history documentary', 'science documentary', 'sport documentary', 'arts documentary' and so on. Some of these expectations form around a distinctive production style, such as nature documentary's dependence upon observational footage, invariably packaged and presented in the form of anthropomorphic narratives (Bousé, 2000).

Others are focused more on the recycling of similar forms of content – such as the seemingly inexhaustible supply of history documentaries centred on the Second World War, and especially the exploration of any and all aspects of Nazi Germany.

These content-based divisions have implications for individual television documentary texts in terms of their global distribution. Many documentaries either have limited appeal to global audiences, because they focus purely on local concerns, or date quickly, because they are focused upon specific socio-political issues that require the immediate historical context for their resonance (or would require costly post-production to incorporate more up-to-date material). For example, as I write this, the United States occupation of Iraq is winding down and will quickly take on the status of historical narrative, meaning that television productions of the conflict will increasingly need to add more historical information as explanatory context for new audiences. Others forms of documentary content are more 'timeless', such as nature documentaries, which can be continually recycled both within the same local schedule over a number of years and easily refashioned for foreign markets through the simple addition of alternative-language voice-overs. And there are other variations between these examples: one reason for the proliferation of twentieth-century history documentaries is arguably the relative ease with which a number of closely related history documentaries can be produced, as a one-off or series, out of a set of archival materials. In a broader sense, similar dynamics inform distinctions between many other forms in the televisual fact-fiction continuum. At one end of this spectrum are news bulletins, which date almost immediately despite their dependence upon a repackaging of the familiar social, political and historical narratives that constitute national cultures.

Despite such wider structures operating as constraints on television production, this does not mean that television documentary is not also a site for often intense experimentation. The extremely competitive commercial environment within television broadcasting provides a constant tension between innovation and repetition (a tension that underlies the development of all genres). Such competition works to foster generic innovation, but also means that any successful format also tends to be quickly adopted and exhausted by competitors. Television has consequently been the site of the popularising and proliferating of new reality forms, particularly through their hybridity with existing (fictional-based) television genres. Precisely because of its intense commercial environment, then, television has been the site of the transformation of fundamental production practices, aesthetics and ethics associated with documentary culture as a whole.

Central to broadcasters' concerns within this broad competitive environment is the need to attract, build and retain the 'loyalty' of a core constituency of viewers who can then be used as the basis of attracting advertising revenue. One distinctive pattern that emerges is sometimes called a 'brands and strands' approach. Each network attempts to develop a particular brand appeal, generating expectations and assumptions from its potential audiences of the kinds of content and experiences that it offers. Within the constraints of their overall brand, network programmers are seeking to determine the mixture of genres that will help to define their channel(s) yet still appeal to as wide an audience as possible. They will often create particular generically-based strands within their schedules which will be made available for documentary content.

Such institutional demands obviously have major implications for the production and commissioning of television documentary, as it is geared to satisfy the expectations of an overall network brand, or the specific strand within a schedule. A key requirement for broadcasters is to satisfy audience expectations around particular timeslots, which can mean demands for a certain predictability in terms of content, and certainly a consistency in production standards and quality. This can mean one-off documentaries collated and presented together as a particular documentary strand, united around anything from the familiarity of directors' names, to kinds of participants, to an overall politics (for example a common focus on disenfranchised or marginalised groups within society, or a focus on globalised topics of environmentalism or poverty, or simply the presentation of iconic national figures).

It can also mean a significant preference on the part of broadcasters for documentary *series*, which can allow for some sense of stability with a schedule and consequently provide the possibility for a weekly audience to be retained and built over a number weeks, around their expectations of essentially similar content. In the case of documentary series, broadcasters naturally favour above all those which offer strong dramatic possibilities or are focused on distinctive or articulate participants with a compelling story to tell. These are the series that often make for the most captivating television.

For documentary producers, accommodating to the demands of television (often their best chance of reaching a wide audience) can mean everything from producing a much shorter, television-ready cut of a feature-length documentary, to tailoring their approach to a subject in a way that will appeal to a particular television brand (or strand), to considering chasing only those stories which can be easily structured and packaged as either a one-off programme or a series. Such broader dynamics shape relationships within television documentary production, particularly independent documentary producers, and television networks. There are natural tensions here, often based around the often quite contrasting expectations of individual producers and broadcasters over what their audience will and will not find accessible and compelling.

It is noticeable that documentary producers who have been able to achieve a high public profile and who are consequently able to achieve relatively more freedom and certainty in attracting funding for their future projects tend to be those who also have a keen sense of their audience. Examples in this vein could include David Attenborough, who built a career largely out of an innate enthusiasm for the natural world that he was able to use as the basis of an instantly identifiable, accessible-but-authoritative on-screen persona. Attenborough's intimate, conversational narratives about the natural world, easily segmented for broadcast schedules and typically tied to spectacular visual photography, have been enormously influential in defining popular expectations of nature documentaries as a subgenre. Similarly Ken Burns has effectively created his own brand of historical documentaries since the success of *The Civil War* (1990) series, which reintroduced a generation of local audiences to the American Civil War. Designed for broadcast especially on the American PBS channel, his series are based around short, episodic narratives, composed and refined overwhelmingly in post-production through carefully crafted sound design, a distinctive use of archival photography and extensive use of actors as narrators. Despite contrasting styles and approaches to their subject matter, both Attenborough and Burns have excelled in producing television-friendly formats based around high production standards and accessible forms of narrative aimed at the engagement of mass audiences.

Patterns in global documentary production and distribution

These patterns remain, even if refashioned across a broader plateau of scheduling possibilities, within the specialist documentary channels that have proliferated within digital broadcasting environments. There are a number of factors at play here, including the deregulation of global media industries and increased competition between an often smaller number of media conglomerates looking to exploit the opportunities for niche casting within digital television broadcasting (Fürsich, 2003: 134). The attractiveness of reality-based programming for many networks operating in such an environment tends to lie with its cost-effective production in comparison with dramatic fiction or comedy (the production of a hybrid format may cost up to a third less than a drama series or sitcom, although not for higher-profile examples such as *Big Brother* (1999–2006)). Since the early 1990s an acceleration of the commodification of documentary production has tended to move television documentary quite clearly away from exclusively public service objectives. While one result has been the growth of independent producers, rather than filmmakers as elite groups working within the confines of national broadcasting institutions, they are often grouped around the creation of narrow niches of programming content (Hogarth, 2006: 83).

There are also interesting dynamics between the local and global nature of documentary programming. Particularly in the case of documentary hybrids, formats are often produced, promoted and tested in multiple markets, forming the basis of the globalisation of 'popular factual programming' (Hogarth, 2006). While television documentary is often grounded very much within local (national) markets, in terms of its content and initial audience, the broader expectations of production and distribution are also increasingly geared to a more global context (Hogarth, 2006: 15).

The emergence of channels grouped under brands such as National Geographic and Discovery demonstrate these patterns of documentary production on a global scale. Discovery Networks International (DNI) is the largest documentary producer in the world, following an aggressive period of global expansion in the 1990s (Fürsich, 2003: 136), and as of 2006 was 'responsible for about 20 percent of output worldwide and reaching more than 1.2 billion people in 147 countries' (Hogarth, 2006: 50). Within the stable of

Discovery brands are The Discovery Channel, Animal Planet, The Learning Channel, Discovery Health, Science, and Travel and Kids. It would be misleading to think of Discovery as simply an example of a monolithic, homogenised distributor of globalised culture.

An interesting comparison can be made with another high-profile provider of globalised programming, MTV, which has itself discovered the potential of documentary hybrids, having transformed itself from a largely music-based global brand into one dominated by hybrid formats (derived from the need to capture audiences for longer periods than music videos would allow (Jones, 2005: 87)). Owned by Viacom, MTV Networks is a collection of cable and satellite channels with variations in Brazil, Canada, China, various European countries, India and other Asian countries as well as Britain and the United States. The key to MTV's success has been to localise its programming, with schedules based on up to 70 per cent of local content.

> What MTV Networks did was to incorporate into its programming the imagined global thereby naturalizing discourses of struggle between the global and local through an overlay of globalization. To put it another way, by re-organizing its programming to provide local hooks into global culture, MTV Networks was able to co-opt the local imagination of its place within the global. (Jones, 2005: 86)

The same strategy underlies production associated with the stable of Discovery channels; flexible, customised programming for local markets that adapts globalised formats for national and other localised audiences. What is understood as 'The Discovery Channel' changes when viewed around the globe, whether in terms of the mixture of programmes available, or even of different versions of the same text, which are re-edited to suit assumed local tastes or local programming timeslots (Hogarth, 2006: 64).

Ultimately, as Fürsich argues, Discovery should be seen as a 'content provider', looking to exploit broadcasting opportunities across different media platforms and operating across national territories with an adaptable global product (Fürsich, 2003: 148). As with similar forms of globalised production, there is sharp disagreement within commentators over whether this environment supports or subverts the free and open expression of ideas within nationally based documentary cultures. Fürsich argues that the result is a narrowing and marginalising of political content which might be deemed too controversial for a variety of local markets. Discovery's brand of non-fiction entertainment

> touches on the educational and informational functions of television that traditionally have been covered by public television in categories such as science, nature and health. These areas all have global appeal and can be distributed across countries with a minimum of local adaptation (e.g. animals don't have to be dubbed). To make this genre work across cultures, it has to focus on celebratory accounts and be non-offensive, non-political, non-investigative or culturally constrained. This strategy explains why Discovery connects the term 'entertainment' to its genre of nonfiction or factual programs. (Fürsich, 2003: 144–5)

In contrast, Hogarth insists that this environment for the production and distribution of popular television programming is 'neither inherently hostile nor naturally conducive to free expression in the documentary genre. Instead [these political economies] seem to create fleeting public spaces that deserve careful scrutiny and conditional support' (Hogarth, 2006: 81).

A basic television documentary style: vérité aesthetic and intimate narratives

There are other qualities to the television fact-fiction continuum that relate to the distinctive aesthetics and narrative potential of the medium. For this discussion of mockumentary a key historical point was the emergence of the new documentary filmmaking practices of cinéma vérité and direct cinema. These are broadly similar movements; the distinctions between their practices partly derive from their origins within different national contexts, and especially from the particular concerns of key filmmakers. Saunders argues, in fact, that the direct cinema movement could not have emerged outside of the specific intersection of factors operating within the United States during the 1960s, being 'predicated as much on a philosophical reawakening as on the portability of equipment: roving camera-sound systems, developed at first to assist orthodox journalistic or anthropological endeavour, eventually became totems of a new-found cinematic transcendence' (Saunders, 2007: 189).

Direct cinema derived especially from the agenda of *Life* magazine's photo-essays (Saunders, 2007: 6–7) and involved documentarists such as Richard Leacock, brothers David and Albert Maysles, and D. A. Pennebaker, all originally working on television under the supervision of Robert Drew at Time, Inc. All were committed to the possibilities of observational documentary using portable film equipment which they partly built themselves. Instead of preparing a story before filming, they allowed a coherence of narrative rhythm and structure to emerge through the editing process (Saunders, 2007: 10). They produced key films in the 1960s which re-energised their contemporaries, such as the seminal direct cinema film *Primary* (1960), which covered the emergence of John F. Kennedy as a Democratic presidential candidate. They popularised a particular aesthetic and eventually their innovations were adopted in more muted and formulaic fashion within television documentary.

In France, key figures included Jean Rouch, especially for his *Chronique d'un été* (*Chronicle of a Summer*) (1960), which pioneered and helped to popularise the conventions of cinéma vérité with a new generation of French filmmakers, especially the use of hand-held camerawork and synchronous sound. Together with the American Frederick Wiseman (who eschewed the label of cinéma vérité for the looser one of 'reality fictions' (Saunders, 2007: 145)), Rouch pioneered a more interactive and provocative approach toward their subjects than the strictly non-interventionist, 'fly on-the-wall' direct cinema approach.

Both direct cinema (the United States) and cinéma vérité (France) helped in creating a distinctive aesthetic; shaky, hand-held cameras, often long takes, and naturalistic sound. With direct cinema this was married with a comparatively non-interventionist approach toward social reality and an insistence on allowing the camera to serve as a 'window on reality'. The sense of immediacy and 'truth' which this aesthetic seemed to epitomise obviously draws upon wider beliefs in the indexical quality of photographic images, with the development of portable camera and sound equipment seemingly allowing for a more 'grounded' perspective on reality than that offered by more institutional forms of documentary. Instead of a 'voice of god' narration or on-screen presenter providing an apparently authoritative commentary, the images themselves would tell the story. A documentary crew, then, could be merely a 'fly on the wall', present to document the unfolding rhythms of everyday reality that would have occurred exactly the same without their presence. The later emergence of video cameras reinforced the same assumptions and promoted an aesthetic that allowed for a grainy 'roughness' to the quality of the image itself in the pursuit of authenticity.

At times, direct cinema seemed to mean an explicit denial of the role of the filmmakers themselves in effectively constructing, through shot selection and editing control, the 'reality' that emerged from each film text. The rhetoric of early direct cinema filmmakers also often denied the increasing awareness of participants themselves of the partial and selective nature of their representations. The people in front of the lens realised early on the potential of the medium to define their public personas, and looked to control aspects of their own performance. Critics and commentators quickly punctured such aspects of direct cinema's rhetoric, hence the vigorous debates with filmmakers over seminal documentaries such as Pennebaker's *Don't Look Back*, which claimed to offer a 'behind-the-scenes' look at Bob Dylan.

Although shorn of its initial rhetorical claims, the aesthetic of direct cinema and cinéma vérité proved perfectly suited to televisual space, allowing for the exploration of intimate portraits of both public figures and everyday people. The eventual development of television series derived from these approaches is arguably a key moment within the history of documentary culture as whole, as everyday reality became the raw material for intimate dramatic narratives tailored to suit national audiences. As noted in the previous chapter, *An American Family* was a key milestone here, an observational television documentary series focusing on a single 'typical' American family (the Louds of California), which exploited the potential to create dramatic narratives out of everyday familial tensions and issues. The popular success of *An American Family* in the United States, *The Family* in the United Kingdom, and the later Australian-based *Sylvania Waters* (1992) not only inspired audiences but also encouraged television broadcasters to recognise the potential for documentary to be a form of programming that could compete with the appeal of dramatic fiction in prime time.

There are other key trends within the development of the look and feel of television documentary which are worthy of discussion, but which are outside of the scope of this book. For example, television has readily incorporated reality footage from video cameras, digital camcorders, surveillance cameras and phone cameras. The appeal of capturing the unfolding of everyday life has proved irresistible for a medium that aims at attracting domestic audiences and has allowed television to provide a sense of connecting different localities – each viewer's household and that of a series' participants – through a kind of intimate, sympathetic surveillance. In fact, image-capturing technologies that seem to enhance the sense of truly capturing a subject unaware of the presence of a camera have become the most highly prized. Hence the reliance upon surveillance footage within investigative journalism, where it can be exploited as revealing the 'real story'; and within hybrid reality forms, where such footage can be replayed and examined for evidence of supposedly authentic forms of social and political behaviour. These are key dynamics of a proliferating surveillance culture or, more accurately, a convergent surveillance culture (to adapt Jenkins), as it involves the active participation of significant sections of television and online audiences (Andrejevic, 2004).

There are other, equally important but contrasting developments within digital documentary culture, not least the integration of the 'hybrid, intricate, complex and rich visual language' (Manovich, 2006: 11) of motion graphics, which is becoming more accessible to amateur media producers. One result is the emerging field of documentary digital animation, which to date has been used only in limited, typically formulaic ways within television documentary[2] but already suggests the potential to dramatically expand the modes of documentary representation. The *Walking with Dinosaurs* (1999) series and its successors suggest one possible pathway here (Scott and White, 2003; Darley, 2003). These series are drama-documentaries that hybridise the familiar narratives of nature documentary with digital techniques of photorealism.

All of these trends are reflected in varying degrees within the range of television mockumentary programmes. The key inspiration for mockumentary series, however, and a significant instigator of changes within broader documentary culture, is television documentary hybrids. The specific ways in which mockumentary series appropriate and comment upon television hybrid forms are the subject of the chapters in the final part of this book. The discussion here offers an overview of the nature and significance of these types of television programmes, to set up some basic ideas about the key patterns that mockumentary appropriates.

Television documentary hybrids

An initial definition of documentary hybrids is that these are television programmes, both one-offs and series, which incorporate key elements of both documentary discourses and those associated with fictional television genres. These programmes draw on genres as diverse as talk shows, tabloid journalism, gameshows, variety programmes, soap opera and music videos. These have often been grouped under the label of 'reality TV', and although this was a useful label when applied to some initial formats it has rapidly become a catch-all phrase that does not suggest their true variety. Corner argues that these forms should be grouped under the label of 'documentary as diversion', as they represent a new function for the genre as a whole, adding to earlier non-fiction traditions which focused more on exposition, inquiry and interrogation (Corner, 2001a; 2002a). Where documentary fits in relation to such forms within an expanded fact-fiction continuum is a matter of debate. With the proliferation of different reality-based formats and the incorporation of production and presentation techniques more associated with fiction, perhaps what truly distinguishes documentary from hybrid forms is, above all, the types of ethical practices employed by their producers.

Hybrids collectively represent a variety of aesthetic styles, narrative structures, thematics and socio-political agendas, but there is little doubt that their impact on the wider documentary genre itself has been significant. Corner notes an increased focus on three aspects which have always been a part of documentary itself, but not foregrounded to the same extent as they are in hybrid formats: 'the intensity of events, the pull of story and the attractions of character' (Corner, 2006: 90). In some formats this is achieved through selective presentation of aspects of the everyday (a distilled or distorted form of observational documentary), while in other examples producers more actively craft a situation or environment in which everyday players can be cast (in more than one sense). This material places 'a new premium on material strong in kinetic or other forms of affective impact' (Corner, 2006: 90). Some hybrid formats place the highest premium on an 'authentic' vérité aesthetic, particularly variations on a degraded video image, and an emphasis on hand-held cameras and close-ups to capture emotional intensity. Such footage is packaged in ways that diverge from

conventional documentary. Hybrids build, and cater to, expectations of dramatic intensity, with a greater emphasis on aspects of
storytelling such as the building of anticipation and episodic development, paired with suspensions of resolution and similar devices
typical of fictional television genres.

Many formats place emphasis on post-production practices
which focus on generating condensed forms of montage – for credit
sequences, the recycling of spectacular or particularly emotionally
intense footage and the regular teasers of upcoming content –
making some documentary hybrids among the most visually layered
reality-based texts. Corner notes that these hybrids are 'symboli-
cally denser, more playful, less centred and sometimes deliberately
facetious' in comparison with documentary proper (Corner, 2006:
96). They often have a tenuous relationship with conventional documentary concerns, but nevertheless still explicitly draw upon the
variety of assumptions and expectations underlying factual forms.
Chief among such assumptions are those associated with the indexical quality of photographic images, however paradoxical these
assumptions are in the digital era. In fact, Fetveit argues that there
is a direct link between these parallel developments, that in 'a
deeper psychological sense, the proliferation of reality TV could be
understood as an euphoric effort to reclaim what seems to be lost
after digitisation' (Fetveit, 1999: 798).

Hybrid forms favour emotional experience over sober information. At their core are the exploration, discovery and presentation
of forms of 'emotional truth', those revelatory moments which can
claim a sense of raw authenticity in that they resonate strongly with
an audience (Dovey, 2000). This has governed the favouring of
specific techniques, again linked to the potential of specific image-
gathering technologies. Video diaries, for example, have progressed
from their use in docusoaps to more deliberately constructed situations centred on heightened dramatic tension. Audience participation operates at various levels here, both through emotional
engagement with the 'reality' which is presented, and also at times
more directly through involvement in studio audiences, voting on
participants' actions or even successful auditions to become featured participants themselves. Within these frameworks, aspects of
performance are acknowledged, commented upon, recirculated and
celebrated as both markers of everyday reality and responses to
dramatic stimuli.

Bourdon argues that central to hybrid formats is a focus on 'live programming', with a foregrounding on the live spectacle of ordinary viewers telling or revealing to the camera their problems and experiences (Bourdon, 2000: 532). They draw selectively upon the premium which television more generally places on live feeds to reporters on location, varieties of direct address and familiar devices such as vox-pop to emphasise forms of individual confession, either in studio or more commonly through carefully edited video diaries.

In summary, hybrids differ from documentary in terms of content, style and issues of knowledge (emotional truth), as well as offering different configurations of performance, simulation and participation. Above all, they are characterised by a sense of playfulness, and reflexivity toward their own constructions (more on this below). They provide a set of distinct constructions of the socio-historical world; more selective, less adhered to sober forms of presentation than televisual non-fiction, clearly emphasising entertainment over information or education. These are all characteristics which have generated concern and even alarm from television commentators, media academics and social theorists.

Documentary theorists have engaged in an intense debate over the nature and significance of these hybrids, particularly whether they suggest changes in the nature of contemporary social and political communication. There is no doubt that these hybrid forms have broadened the televisual fact-fiction continuum, but much debate centres on whether they have also fundamentally weakened and subverted the distinctive socio-political role that documentary has sought to perform within democratic societies (as championed by John Grierson as documentary emerged as a clear genre in the 1930s). Corner, again:

> Having been variously framed within the terms of 'authoritarian', 'radical' and 'public' models of communicative action, documentary practices have now, in the newer forms of realist diversion, become a commercially successful ingredient of the 'popular'. Notoriously imprecise since its coinage, documentary will undoubtedly weaken further as a defining category at a time when electronic mediations of real life have never been so extensively enjoyed. Saying anything interesting about it in the future is likely to require close attention to this paradox (Corner, 2000: 688)

Corner uses the term 'post-documentary' (Corner, 2001a; 2002a) as a deliberate means of promoting debate over the cultural significance of the proliferation of documentary hybrid forms and the new relationships between filmmakers and audiences that they signify (rather than to suggest an explicit break from previous traditions of documentary filmmaking). Corner has suggested that the significance of hybrids lies in their fostering of demands that documentary itself adapt to new forms of representation:

> Neither postmodern scepticism nor the techniques of digital manipulation present documentary with its biggest future challenge. This will undoubtedly come from the requirement to reorient and refashion itself in an audio-visual culture where the dynamics of diversion and the aesthetics of performance dominate a greatly expanded range of popular images of the real. (Corner, 2002a: 267)

As summarised by Dovey (Dovey, 2000: 83–91), the more common critiques of hybrids includes a 'trash TV' argument which insists that hybrids are symptomatic of a collapse of standards within commercial television. A second perspective views hybrids as forms of 'empowerment', insisting that they represent a democratisation of the documentary genre as everyday voices are favoured over those of authoritative institutions. Finally, there is the group of post-modernist critiques which paradoxically suggest that hybrid forms are central to the emergence of a surveillance society even as they drift away from any direct link to reality. Dovey critiques all three positions, offering instead an argument that hybrids are essentially playing to the fears and anxieties of their audience and are symptomatic of a transformed public sphere resulting from the neo-liberalist transformation of globalised capitalism.

Each of the detailed theoretical positions on documentary hybrids has tended to concentrate on a small number of formats within the broader proliferation of documentary hybrids, often insisting on these as definitive examples of 'reality TV'. Consequently, each tends to offers a useful but inevitably partial perspective on the role and significance of hybrid transformations of documentary as a whole. (As noted above, such trends with the wider documentary culture also need to be understood in relation to more fundamental changes within social and cultural patterns of engagement with mediations of the 'real', not least an accelerating interaction between socio-political discourses of surveillance, autobiography and creative expression.) Many of these concerns are played out in mockumentary appropriations of hybrid formats. The high-profile key formats, and hence audiences' familiarity with them, have provided both inspiration and ready templates for television mockumentary producers.

Key reference points within television documentary hybrids

There is no one representative reality format, no example which can be pointed to as the exemplar of what 'reality TV' represents. In fact there is little consensus between industry practitioners, academic commentators and apparently even audiences (see later in this chapter) over how to classify such formats. Each has its localised variations, even as the key elements of formats have been exhaustively replicated globally. Part of the distinctiveness of television mockumentary derives from how closely individual programmes and series reflect national inflections of documentary hybrids, even as their commentaries remain accessible to broader audiences.

The intention here is to outline some key formats within the proliferation of documentary hybrids which have been a dominant feature of prime-time television schedules since the 1990s. The origins of 'reality TV' formats date from the late 1980s, but hybrid forms of one kind or another have been a part of the development of documentary since its emergence as a genre. Early documentaries, in part because of technical constraints imposed by the state of the film technology, often incorporated dramatic reconstructions (the forerunners of drama-documentary). The result is that early 'documentary' often seamlessly blended the archival, dramatic and indexical in the service of a persuasive argument. An archetypal film such as Robert Flaherty's popular and critically celebrated *Nanook of the North* (1922) maintains an uneasy position as an early exemplar of documentary in part because its scenes were all 're-enacted' by the subjects of the film, in ways that were designed to appeal to Western audiences.

Both drama-documentary (a distinctive fictional form closely aligned with documentary) and nature documentary (constructing anthropomorphic perspectives of the natural world) can be viewed as documentary hybrids. Drama-documentary has a special relationship with mockumentary and is discussed in more depth in chapter 5. Nature documentary has been marginalised within documentary theory, in part because it has flourished especially on the critically neglected medium of television, and also because of this subgenre's early reputation for fictionalised content, its practice of generating condensed and manipulated constructions of the natural world. Bousé insists on referring to this subgenre as 'wildlife films', in order both to position these texts outside of documentary and to highlight the degree of construction and manipulation of footage at the heart of their production (Bousé, 2000: 9–10).

In these terms, nature documentary can be seen as a precursor of more recent documentary hybrids in its transformation of reality for narrative purposes, in the practice of crafting narrativised perspectives that will appeal to mainstream television audiences. Not surprisingly, nature documentary has itself responded to the rise of 'reality TV' by refashioning its own aesthetics to focus more heavily on emotionally dramatic narratives and/or even more spectacular perspectives of the animal world (Cottle, 2004; Kilborn, 2006). In common with broader television aesthetics, it has incorporated a greater reliance on digital practices such as animation based on computer-generated imaging (CGI) and computer-mediated imaging (CMI) techniques (Hight, 2008a).

The current wave of television hybrids has a number of overlapping histories, usefully summarised by Corner (Corner, 2000: 687). First there were initial forays into popular factual forms which centred on law enforcement and emergency services, the first to attract the dismissive label of 'reality TV' from commentators. The key American formats here included the archetypal and long-running *Cops* (1989–) series and *America's Most Wanted* (1988–), both of which generally retained at least lip service to a public service agenda. Both are still produced today, as are formats such as *America's Funniest Home Videos* – which helped to popularise camcorder-based programming, although within a narrow commercialist frame rather than what initially appeared to be its great socio-political promise (Fore, 1993; Raphael, 1997). Ouellette argues that 'a powerful matrix of media discourses has worked quickly to construct and contain camcorder practices within a variety of boundaries (domesticity, spot news, accidentalism, sensationalism), blunting the camcorder's potential for democratic empowerment' (Ouellette, 1995: 42).

A second phase saw the emergence of video diaries, docusoaps, including successful British series such as *Driving School* (1997), *Airline* (1998), *The Cruise* (1998), and other programmes which centred on following groups of everyday people over a series. The third phase saw the emergence of reality gameshows or 'gamedocs', most significantly the key formats of *Big Brother* and *Survivor* (2000–).

Reality TV

For the purposes of this discussion the key format in the history of 'reality TV' series is the long running *Cops*. The series has remained remarkably consistent in the three decades since it first premiered in March 1989 as one of the earliest reality TV formats.[3] Its basic premise, to observe inner-city police officers in the course of duty, has remained the same; as has its signature style and packaging, centred on editing footage captured from everyday police activities into short, punchy narratives that follow the police officer's eye view. Digital camcorders are used to document preparations for the day's law enforcement, ride along with officers in their vehicles as they survey a neighbourhood and explain their procedures (Figure 4) and follow close behind as they encounter petty criminals and

4. A digital camera rides along with an on-duty police officer, a familiar scene from the long running prototypical American reality programme *Cops* (1989–).

often hunt and capture possible offenders. This formulaic structure, and the theme song 'Bad Boys' by Inner Circle, is immediately identifiable to audiences and have inspired numerous parodies which often need only a few bars of the theme song and the use of a shaky, hand-held camera to suggest their reference.

Somewhat less apparent to audiences have been the tightly pre-scribed production practices adhered to by the series' producers, resulting in an arguably highly selective portrayal of both urban American police enforcement and the range of criminal activity that it targets. Commentators on the series have long noted its partial and selective portrayal of law enforcement, together with its tendency to present a relatively narrow selection of forms of crime, focusing on 'burglaries, robberies, less serious assaults, street-level drug busts, domestic disturbances, and incidents involving intoxica-tion' (Doyle, 1998: 104). Such representations of crime, from both *Cops* and similar reality formats based on urban law enforcement, unfortunately tend to reinforce class and ethnic stereotypes associ-ated with petty and violent urban incidents (Kooistra et al, 1998). Writing of the representation of criminal activity typical of these shows, Palmer summarises their overall construction of the urban criminal:

> In the vast majority of cases he is male and seen acting in a hostile manner. His natural habitat is the city where he is apprehended by grainy CCTV cameras whose inability to render him in anything but black and white only serves to make him more alien. He is usually silent, but if he does sound it is to issue instructions or to make threats. This frightening, disconnected figure is made into a signifier of urban *angst*. It is only be reconnecting him to us, the watching community, that we can both control and humanise him. It is only by establishing connections that he, and the world of crime he repre-sents, will be brought within the circuit of the law, to be governed, and we can avoid becoming victims. (Palmer, 2003: 84)

Cops does not focus on white-collar criminals, or the specialised police units which hunt them, if only for the simple reason that these police actions tend not to provide television fare as riveting as the shots of cameras running with police officers as they chase suspects down alleys or burst, heavily armed, into the houses and apartments of criminal suspects. Despite the disclaimer at the beginning of each episode ('*Cops* is filmed on location with the men and women of law enforcement. All suspects are innocent until proven guilty in a court of law'), the effect is to brand as 'guilty' anyone who appears as a suspect (typically with their face electronically blurred).

Among the reasons for the programme's longevity is the fact that it meshes with the public relations objectives of law enforcement agencies, serving to humanise institutions which are often regarded with suspicion and fear by inner-city populations, while still presenting a largely positive perspective of the professionalism of police officers. No incidents involving police violence are included within the broadcast cut of *Cops* (remember the 1991 Rodney King incident?), nor any detailed social and political discussion on the part of officers. Commentators have argued that the show's producers have accommodated to such an agenda in order to retain access to police institutions (Doyle, 1998: 105). The result is a disturbing and simplistic portrayal of the inner-city landscape as an alien environment characterised by random, sporadic and often incoherent violence (Rapping, 2004: 222).

Video diaries

A staple within television hybrid programming, video diaries involve participants being given camcorders and encouraged to present an emotional confession to the lens. The more commercial variations derive from earlier experiments with camcorder-based formats. The key United Kingdom reference points here are *Video Nation* (1993)[4] and the related *Video Nation Shorts* (1998), which popularised the video diary as a short-form format within British television broadcasting. These series adhered to the original promise of (digital) camcorder technology, which was to open the television sphere to more voices, to democratise the television mainstream. Kilborn provides a useful history of the emergence of video diaries in the United Kingdom (Kilborn, 1998a), while Dovey discusses *Video Nation* in detail (Dovey, 2000: 103–32), placing the series within a wider discussion on the development of the proliferation of 'first person media':

> An enormous proportion of the output of factual TV is now based on an incessant performance of identity structured through first person speaking about feelings, sentiments and, most powerfully, intimate relationships. (Dovey, 2000: 104)

Distinctive among first person television formats, *Video Nation* consists of a kind of self-surveillance by camcorders, incorporating parts of both performance and confession which link to wider social relations in often quite open and contradictory ways. As Dovey notes, the key debates for these forms centre on 'how far this public participation in the discussion of everyday personal and public problems represents a democratisation of televisual space and how far they represent a reinscription of moral and political hegemonies' (Dovey, 2000: 116). Similarly, Kilborn notes that although BBC2 producers allowed diarists full editorial control over their programmes, they still retained an overall institutional frame through the selection of participants (Kilborn, 1998a: 205–6).

Unlike talk shows, which quite clearly operate to both judge participants and prescribe corrective actions for their assumed deviant behaviour, the video diary model works to suggest a sense of dialogue with the viewer. This derives partly from the low-grade aesthetic of amateur home movies, which reinforces the authenticity of participants' direct address to the audience. In other words, this is a form which immediately conveys a sense of intimacy with participants and raises expectations of greater emotional openness. This also tends to convey a degree of instability to the form as a whole, with unpredictable and perceptive socio-political insights from participants paired with the banal observations of everyday experience (a pattern which is replicated on a far greater scale through user-produced short videos uploaded to sites such as YouTube). When positioned within docusoaps and reality game-shows, however, video diaries are reduced to one part of more heavily post-produced dramatic narratives, with the result that their apparent authenticity is framed in more exploitative ways.

Docusoaps

Docusoaps are 'a form of nosy sociability' which draws from the narrative conventions of soap opera and the emotional intimacy of daytime talk shows (Corner, 2000: 687). Centred on a small ensemble of subjects linked through interpersonal relationships or simply through a common location, these series closely follow participants through everyday activities. The aim of producers is typically to construct a number of interweaving dramatic narratives extracted from the minutiae of real life. These formats have been especially influential in Britain, where they have enjoyed a higher profile and popularity than in other national contexts. Initial series focused more on institutional settings such as an airline, hospital or cruise ship, or similar locations where producers could expect a 'cast' of regular subjects who must deal with a variety of often challenging situations and characters each week. Docusoaps have since broadened to include a focus on domestic and other settings, but all typically look to fashion emotionally engaging drama from everyday events and situations (Kilborn, 2003).

The British model of docusoap included some series which derived drama from following dysfunctional individuals (such as Maureen from *Driving School* repeatedly failing her driver's licence exam), who were implicitly presented as either life's losers or local eccentrics. As producers grew more confident of the potential of the format, more everyday personal triumphs and ambitions became the centre of often complex narrative structures over the course of a series. Consequently, the process of selecting participants and environments with the potential for emotionally engaging drama is central to these formats' pre-production. The American model of docusoaps, in comparison, has always tended to be more geared toward explicit acts of casting unconnected individuals as a means to positioning a series as engaging with debates over social and political change within American society (Kraszewski, 2004: 184). The archetypal American docusoap, for example, has been MTV's *The Real World* (1992–). Initially set in New York, each subsequent season has featured a different city but employed the same formula of bringing together a diverse group of young and attractive strangers who live together while seeking to make a living and discovering their own identities.

Reality gameshows/gamedocs

Reality gameshows are among the most intensively debated and researched of documentary hybrids.[5] The basic premise of these formats is, in a sense, an inversion of that of docusoaps. Instead of observing everyday people in their social environments, these hybrids take everyday people (or occasionally celebrities) and put them in a completely foreign game environment, either chosen because it will be exotic and challenging to participants (*Survivor*) or deliberately constructed as a closed system to maximise dramatic potential (*Big Brother*). The unexpected popular success of *Survivor* encouraged American television to accept similar international programming concepts (Rose, 2003: 2), while the Dutch-originated *Big Brother* (from Endemol productions) has rapidly proliferated as a globalised format appearing as national variations across an unlikely assortment of countries. Participants are now volunteer 'players', cast through an extensive audition process that allows producers not only to test their response to stressful situations, but also to gather together a set of complementary character types. Players are invariably divided at least along gender, sexuality, class and ethnic lines, and often also in terms of lifestyle attributes such as occupation and fitness. The resulting gameshow format is explicitly intended to be a media event (in the case of *Big Brother*, a multi-platform media event), played out over the course of a series in which audiences are encouraged to engage and identify with dramatic conflicts created through weekly staged competitive activities, and to even participate directly in the overall competition for a single prize winner.

Dovey refers to reality gameshows as 'simulations', in the sense that they resemble experiments in which environments are constructed and manipulated in order to coerce particular kinds of human behaviour. Some variables and factors are set, while others are left open to see how things play out. In Dovey's words,

> The attempt to record social reality has been completely swallowed by the impulse to simulate social reality in performative models. Factual television practices have by and large abandoned empirical observations that rested upon the lack of relationship between observer and observed and replaced it with the observation of simulated situations that only exist because of the intervention of the TV production. (Dovey, 2008: 245)

As Dovey notes, the 'simulation' approach has seeped into conventional documentary television production, resulting in series which are difficult to easily categorise. What could be termed 'situation documentaries' are hybrid formats where participants are taken out of their 'natural' social environment or an element of disruption is introduced, and then this artificial situation is filmed as an observational documentary. In a programme such as *Wife Swap* (2003–), for example, two families are selected for each episode, invariably with markedly different politics or lifestyles (especially based on class and/or ethnicity). They are required to swap their wife/mother with each other and any ensuing dramatic tension over the following couple of weeks is distilled into a narrative for broadcast. The fact that the situation is artificial and that participants are taken out of their everyday living patterns and placed under stress, paradoxically, becomes the basis of viewers' assumption that what they are watching is emotionally authentic. The assumption is that the participants are unable to settle into their normal patterns of role-playing and therefore unintentionally reveal their true natures. Producers put families together who would never normally associate with one another, expecting that the clash of sensibilities creates an environment in which there will be emotional revelations based on differences in politics and social position that offer broad insights into cultural discourses. A similar approach has informed the strand of more sober historical documentary programmes which look to re-enact or simulate historical events and periods using everyday people, such as *1900 House* (1999) in Britain, *Frontier House* (2002) in the United States and other national variants.[6]

Each key format within the development of documentary hybrids has had its own complex history, a result not only of the shifting possibilities of hybridity between existing fiction and non-fiction genres, but also of the manner in which different producers within national production contexts have tended to reshape each format to the needs of their assumed audience within the wider demands of television competition and shifting audience tastes. The formats listed here, then, are intended to serve simply as common reference points for the broader complexity of documentary hybrids rather than as a comprehensive taxonomy. We could easily work from a much wider definition of contemporary hybrids that includes talk shows, from the in-studio confessionals central to *The Oprah Winfrey Show* (1986–) through to the more explicitly constructed forms of contestation and combat that characterise *The Jerry Springer Show* (1991–).

And there is a significant corpus of programmes that, grouped under the label of 'makeover' or lifestyle programmes, centre explicitly on the construction (or re-construction) of individual identity. Derived from informational programmes such as those on tourism and similar consumer guide programming, these are episodic series, featuring a different set of participants each week. These series range from the relatively benign and often playful fashion and home decoration focus of *Queer Eye for the Straight*

Guy (2003–), to the more traumatic and permanent transformations of *Extreme Makeover* (2002–5). This latter programme draws upon and helps to generate anxieties centred on body image, offering radical forms of cosmetic surgery that are constructed as integral to personal fulfilment. A key part of these types of programme is the careful documentation of 'before' and 'after' versions of an individual, generally accompanied by comments from friends and family expressing their approval of the individual's cosmetic transformation.

A more innovative and little-known hybrid form is the documentary musical or 'documusical'. They are included here to suggest the varieties of fact-fiction forms that are still to be explored in detail within globalised formats. The key reference points here are a number of television programmes from British director Brian Hill (Paget and Roscoe, 2006; Baker, 2006: 150–76). Hill's distinctive production technique for documusicals involved using Yorkshire poet and novelist Simon Armitage to refashion interview material into verse which was then taken back to interviewees to be performed to camera as either spoken verse or song. The resulting acts of performance are most effective when framed by conventional documentary material such as interviews that clearly position the programme as a collaboration between a documentary filmmaker and his subject. Hill's early documusicals (*Drinking for England* (1998), *Feltham Sings* (2002)) looked to create and capture performance in their own surroundings. Later programmes have been more ambitious in staging performances and have tended to lose their charge of the real (*Pornography the Musical* (2003)).

Documusicals are a good illustration of how innovations in production techniques within hybrids can open new territory for documentary itself. The key to this form is that performance can suddenly be evidential in a new way to that conventionally considered. Deliberate performance unexpectedly functions as a form of direct address. In other words, participants can be revealing in the nature, style and relative success of their performances. This has always been a feature of documentary itself, although typically critically neglected outside of those documentaries which look to capture professional performers.[7]

Reality TV, video diary, docusoap, reality gameshow, situation documentary, makeover programming and documusicals are formats that collectively demonstrate some of the distinctiveness of the televisual fact-fiction continuum. The extent to which these formats and others will survive another 5, 10 or more years is debateable (there are regular claims by industry figures that they are a fad whose time is ending). Not all of these have been directly appropriated by mockumentary producers (and it is clearly docu-soaps which have been the dominant inspiration for comedians). However, they do serve as an important part of the broader realm of reality-based programming that mockumentary producers assume audiences are familiar with and perhaps directly engaged with.

Audiences and reflexive readings
of the fact-fiction continuum

Ultimately, it is the audience that determine the success and even the validity of documentary hybrids within television's fact-fiction continuum. The collective forms of play within hybrid formats entail various forms of participation on the part of viewers, but they also demand new, potentially more critical, modes of reading. Hill's audience research into popular factual programming, although largely based on audiences within the United Kingdom and Sweden, offers valuable lessons in the demands which such programming place on viewers (Hill, 2005; 2007; 2008). Her research suggests that viewers adopt multiple 'modes of engagement' when approaching the complexity of forms within the televisual fact-fiction continuum. These modes appear to be heavily framed by viewers' existing understandings of non-fiction content, in particular based on news and documentary as generic forms.

> Perhaps one of the most important points to make about documentary viewers is that they change their modes of engagement, depending upon their expectations about the documentary they are watching and the contexts of documentary production and reception practices. (Hill, 2008: 223)

What also seems clear from Hill's ethnographic studies is that audiences to some extent have always made distinctions between forms of factual material that can be inconsistent or at odds with the expectations of documentary theorists and documentary film-makers themselves. For example, viewers tend to assume that performance is a central aspect of observational documentary (taking the common-sense approach that people inevitably 'act up' in the presence of a camera), or that the early hybrids of nature documentary are essentially factual (Hill, 2008: 222–3). The context of viewing can be decisive here, as differently situated audiences draw upon their previous social experience, including with non-fiction forms, and their understanding of factual discourses to make assessments of specific television programmes.

Among the most intriguing implications of Hill's research is that audiences have tended to have a complicated and often contradictory basis for judging programmes, and hence the appropriate mode of engagement they need to employ. Viewers assumed the authenticity of incidents and behaviour that was apparently accidentally or unwittingly caught on camera, and tended to assume and immediately judge the performances of everyday people and appreciated texts which exhibited strong stories and dramatic content. There are layers to viewers' assessment of content here, common-sense expectations of performance in reality formats (Hill, 2005: 57) coexisting with a faith in the ability of the camera to accurately record participants and provide insights into their behaviour.

Again, such interpretations are inevitably contingent on the types of social and political knowledge that viewers bring to an encounter with a text. Hill concludes that viewers have tended to have a default critical stance toward programmes which they can identify as 'reality TV', including a defensiveness in admissions to watching such programmes, and invariably positioning themselves as more knowing than they assume other viewers to be (Hill, 2005: 186). Viewers were keenly aware of the shift towards entertainment which hybrids represent, and they seem to have internalised the stigma constructed by the wider critical discourses outlined above. Yet there are obvious issues of the relativity of viewers' experience and media literacies in relation to such content – it is not necessarily the case that all viewers have developed a detailed critique of the construction of such forms of programming and access to wider critical discourses centred on the social politics of voyeurism and exploitation. Ultimately, it is viewers who are also implicitly assessing the ethical practices employed by a text's producers, making sense of the forms of exploitation, performance and collaboration at the centre of particular documentary hybrids and interpreting the manipulations and constructions inherent in the textual strategies of a hybrid text.

The fact that audiences of documentary hybrids can easily access critical modes of reading when approaching such forms of television programming is perhaps also closely related to the naturalisation of forms of reflexivity within these texts. Roscoe has suggested the phrase 'flickers of authenticity' to account for one dynamic in audience readings of reality gameshows.

> The centrality of performance has constructed a new position for the audience, a viewing position that acknowledges performance as a two-way process. The form may be described as voyeuristic, but given that both parties are aware of the shared gaze [...] it implies a different type of looking. Audiences play the game of evaluating how well participants perform their role. If, as an audience, we play it well enough, we may be rewarded with a 'flicker of authenticity' – moments when the performance breaks down. (Roscoe, 2001b: 14)

Where seeing real people involved in a performance is confusing in an evidentiary sense, involving a deliberate blurring of the assumed dichotomy between acting and actual behaviour, these 'flickers' provide moments of satisfaction and reassurance where we think we see the 'real' person behind the performance required by the series' producers. These moments can be reflexive, but often in only a limited sense, reminding viewers of both the constructed nature of the situation being filmed and also, conversely, the ability of the camera to capture the 'reality' behind the performance.

Roscoe notes the varieties of kinds of performance that are inherent in reality gameshows, requiring a variety of ways to engage with them. There can be role-play demanded by the constructed game environment itself, that is, the roles that participants play for each other. There can also be performances that are played to camera in more intimate moments, designed specifically to gain the sympathy of the viewers. As Roscoe notes, this is especially the case with gameshows where viewers are given control over who leaves and who remains to continue playing (Roscoe, 2001b: 13–14).

In broad terms, hybrids 'teach' viewers to appreciate aspects of performance they are already familiar with, as well as to recognise the role-playing that occurs through 'flickers of authenticity' and to ultimately acknowledge the constructed nature of entertainment-centred reality formats. Hybrid texts are often saturated with other kinds of reflexive moments in their encounters between camera and participants, such as where a docusoap subject makes asides to the camera or reality gameshow contestants try to avoid the camera's gaze. And, as Andrejevic notes,

> As a media event, *Big Brother* assumes its audience to be highly media-literate. It is assumed that viewers know the show is constructed for television, that they are able to engage with it as a hybrid format, and that they are able to acknowledge it as a performance of the real. There are many moments of self-reflexivity built into the event, from the behind the scenes studio tours, through to the insider gossip on the Saturday show, and the on-screen discussions between the housemates about their experiences of being in front of the camera 24 hours a day. (Andrejevic, 2004: 485)

It is impossible to avoid the fact that all activities and behaviour seen on the hybrid screen are highly mediated, and especially that no one, least of all participants, is an 'innocent' captured unawares by the camera. As suggested above, viewers appear keenly aware of the efforts made by producers to construct dramatic pleasures using the tightly structured narratives that build toward climactic scenes focused on emotional conflicts (even as they appreciate those pleasures on another level).

The example of *The Joe Schmo Show* (2003) illustrates some of the possibilities for hybrid formats to provide quite layered forms of engagement for viewers. This was a hybrid series constructed around the production of a fake reality gameshow called 'The Lap of Luxury'. Only one participant, Matt Kennedy Gould, is unaware of the ruse. Everyone else on set plays a role expected of reality gameshows; actors play the smarmy host and other contestants, each portraying a pre-arranged character type familiar from other reality gameshows ('virgin', 'veteran', 'schemer', the 'gay guy', the 'buddy', 'rich bitch', 'asshole'). Constructed as a real-life *Truman Show* (1998), the objective of *The Joe Schmo Show* was to perform an entire series of the fake gameshow without Gould recognising the simulation built specifically to prompt authentic responses from him alone. Among the layers to this programme were scenes of preparation for the fake gameshow, including interviews with the actors playing its cast, and behind-the-scenes footage of the real production team attempting to orchestrate the performance in a way that would appear seamless to Gould. Both viewers and the production team were constantly making assessments of different kinds of performance, including Gould's role-play in 'The Lap of

Luxury', and whether he had in fact recognised that there was a deeper level of construction being conducted around him and had decided to play along. In other words, *The Joe Schmo Show* was a programme about the production practice of creating a reality gameshow, in which viewers were required to make constant readjustments to deal with the type of reality status featured in each sequence, from fake gameshow activities, to actors' video diaries, to Gould's video diary, to the production team performing their anxiety over Gould's exploitation and possible trauma during both the fake gameshow and its ultimate revelation.

A similar hybrid gameshow hoax was at the centre of the British series *Space Cadets* (2005), involving three contestants who believed they had beaten other contestants at a Russian cosmonaut training camp and had been launched into a low orbit around Earth. While viewers knew the ruse from the beginning, the players remained ignorant until the final episode's revelation. A very different agenda was behind the Dutch production of *De Grote Donorshow* (*The Big Donor Show*) (2007), which faked a contest, between three people who desperately needed a kidney transplant, for the prize of the kidney of a terminally ill woman. Attracting global publicity and debate, mostly condemnatory, the programme eventually revealed itself to the audience to be an innovative attempt to raise the issue of a critical shortage of organ donors.

This naturalised reflexivity at both a textual level, and as an inherent part of audience spectatorship of television hybrids, provides a distinctive environment for the reception of television mockumentary. Inherent within mockumentary is a reflexivity toward the fact-fiction forms that a particular text may appropriate. But this is also such a distinctive feature of the reception of hybrid formats that there is a question here as to whether these aspects of televisual modes of reading in a sense neutralise the more reflexive tendencies of mockumentary. Is mockumentary discourse thus inevitably less 'subversive' within the intertextual and reflexive confines of televisual space?

Some hybrid series raise issues of identification and definition, as they appear to operate within overlapping territory between mockumentary, documentary comedy and reflexive documentary. Where, for example, should we position so-called 'reality sitcoms' such as *The Osbournes* (2002–5) and *The Simple Life* (2003–7), where entire series are constructed around the apparent everyday lives of celebrities, but developed along the lines of sitcoms? *The Osbournes*, centred on the family of heavy metal veteran Ozzy Osbourne, is a quite deliberately staged and acted sitcom, with the family members playing themselves within their own home (Morreale, 2003; Kompare, 2004). The first series of *The Simple Life*, featuring socialites Paris Hilton and Nicole Ritchie, has them performing a road trip through rural life and abusing the hospitality of farming families who do not always appear to be in on the joke. Each of these series deliberately constructs a situation for comedic purposes and leaves it up to the audience to decide to what extent anything caught on camera is 'real'. The distinction between playacting and 'being themselves' is blurred here, as the central characters are performers used to constructing public personas for media events.

Juhasz and Lerner argue that 'fake documentaries' (their term for mockumentaries) aim for something more than conventional parody, 'something different, something extra: they *do* manage a "link to the real"' (Juhasz and Lerner, 2006: 2, original emphasis). A similar comment can be made about these documentary television hybrids, even if the balance between parody and reality is deliberately blurred for different agendas. The television fact-fiction continuum accommodates such series, within a broad range of forms that also includes news, tabloid programmes and documentary proper. Collectively, they provide a rich source of symbolic forms for mockumentary's playful referencing and a fluid, dynamic and contested set of mediations of the real which frame and complicate mockumentary as a distinctive discourse within televisual space.

Notes

1 See Nichols, 1994; Bruzzi, 2000; Hight, 2001; Roscoe and Hight, 2001; Dovey, 2000; Corner, 2002a; Friedman, 2002; Holmes and Jermyn, 2003; Palmer, 2003; Kilborn, 2003; Murray and Ouellette, 2004; Andrejevic, 2004.

2 For a discussion of symbolic exposition, graphic vérité and invasive surveillance modes within digital animation, see Hight, 2008.

3 See the official website for links to downloads and episode guides: www. cops.com/.

4 See www.bbc.co.uk/videonation/, which provides information on the series, a brief history, and its progression into an online series of shorts

in which amateurs negotiate the production of their footage to the final edit.

5 See Zoonen, 2001; Roscoe, 2001b; Andrejevic, 2002; Palmer, 2002; Scannell, 2002; Couldry, 2002; Kilborn, 2003; Smith and Wood, 2003; Mathijs and Jones, 2004; Wright, 2006; and the 2002 special edition of *Television New Media*, 3:3.

6 See the 2007 special edition of *Film & History*, 37:1.

7 Or amateurs, Such as the performance of Edie in *Grey Gardens*, as discussed in chapter 1.

5

Television realism, drama-documentary and dramatic vérité

A second set of traditions that we can use to position mockumentary within televisual space is associated with dramatic fiction, although this is an aspect of the discourse relatively neglected by producers. Dramatic television mockumentary currently consists of a small number of texts, either stand-alone programmes or single episodes of an existing series. To date there does not appear to have been a dramatic mockumentary series. However, mockumentary as a whole does draw wider support and inspiration from traditions of both cinematic and television realism that have emerged since the 1960s. These traditions have been particularly important within the development of television drama and have informed distinctive forms of television drama-documentary that themselves inform and intersect with mockumentary in crucial ways. The overlaps here between cinematic and televisual realism are not easily summarised, but both have been heavily influenced by developments in documentary such as cinéma vérité and direct cinema.

Cinematic and televisual realism

The connection of mockumentary discourse with traditions of television realism, especially generic conventions associated with drama-documentary and forms we can call 'dramatic vérité' needs to be seen within a broader historical trajectory. Mockumentary filmmakers, for example, have drawn inspiration variously from the Italian Neo-Realism movement which overlapped with the end of the Second World War, the French New Wave of the early 1960s, and in the last 15 years, developments such as the Dogme 95 movement and other emerging forms of digital filmmaking practice. All of these movements have been influential in challenging expecta-

tions of cinematic realism and in shaping particularly the development of independent filmmaking within countries such as the
United States.[1] Each grew from specific socio-political conditions,
especially the frustrations of a new generation of filmmakers
looking to disrupt existing cinematic practices. Each, particularly
since the 1960s, has exploited advances in portable film and sound
equipment which allowed for more flexible filmmaking practices,
including a greater ease with on-location shooting and, perhaps
most crucially, the ability to record synchronous sound. And each
sought to use distinctive new techniques which eroded conventions
dividing fictional filmmaking from a documentary capturing of
reality.

Italian Neo-Realism was short-lived as a movement of any real
coherence and its exemplars have been endlessly debated in terms
of their specific contribution and position in relation to the declared
tenets of neo-realism. The movement's influence on subsequent
generations of filmmakers has nevertheless been profound. Centred
especially on key works by directors Roberto Rossellini, Vittorio
de Sica and Luchino Visconti in the late 1940s,[2] Neo-Realism
offered a politically motivated departure from the dominant Italian
cinema of pre-Second World War period and the Fascist era.
Prompted in part also by a scarcity of independent filmmaking
resources in Italy in the 1940s, Italian directors relied on shooting
on location with non-actors, using natural lighting and sound, and
favoured stories that portrayed the realities of everyday life in
Fascist and post-war Italy, using apparently naturalistic narratives.
Their films were celebrated (at times more by foreign commentators than by Italians) as a radical departure from the expectations
of global post-war cinema and as evidence of the emergence of a
truly Italian artistic cinematic expression.

The French New Wave drew inspiration from Italian Neo-
Realism, especially the work of Rossellini and Sica. The move-
ment's peak as a creative force is generally assumed to have been
from 1958 to 1962, epitomised by the work of French directors such
as Jean-Luc Godard, François Truffaut, Eric Rohmer, Jacques
Rivette and Claude Chabrol, and associated filmmakers such as
Agnés Varda, Alain Resnais and Chris Marker (Greene, 2007: 3).
The movement's key filmmakers developed a manifesto for a new
approach to cinema in reaction against the prevailing aesthetic of
French post-war cinema, inspired by theorists such as Andre Bazin,

which they articulated through their writings in the journal *Les cahiers du cinéma* (*Notebooks on Cinema*[3]). Their key contribution to film debate is arguably *auteur* theory, based on an argument that in the films of directors produced within the Hollywood studio system, such as Alfred Hitchcock and Howard Hawks, could be discerned the work of an 'author' in the Romantic sense.

Most of the key New Wave filmmakers shared an internship in short films that included documentary practice, where they encountered the possibilities for the just-emerging practices of cinéma vérité. Claiming themselves to be already self-conscious '*auteurs*' they shared a common approach to film praxis, despite often wide differences in their signature styles. Partly derived from limited production resources, this included an emphasis on location shooting, natural lighting and highly mobile, hand-held camerawork which explored the possibilities of portable filmmaking equipment (Greene, 2007: 9). Their films tended to play with the possibilities of editing, particularly through juxtaposing sound and image in new ways, but also through highly self-reflexive sequences. Filmmakers such as Godard were particularly interested in breaking down audiences' expectations of escapist entertainment and sought to continually violate narrative conventions in order to keep drawing viewers back to politically charged reality.

A similar, although stricter, agenda informs the more recent movement instigated by the Dogme 95 group of Danish filmmakers, named after their 1995 manifesto and formed around filmmakers Lars von Trier, Kristian Levring, Thomas Vinterberg and Søren Kragh-Jacobsen. Drawing from the possibilities of low-budget digital filmmaking practices, as well as the much earlier precedents of French New Wave and British Free Cinema (MacKenzie, 2003: 51), the Dogme 95 manifesto insists on an unvarnished cinematic aesthetic as part of an effort to revitalise a global cinema which, they argue, is dominated and creatively stifled by large-budget Hollywood filmmaking practice (Hjort, 2003). Titled 'A Vow of Chastity', the Dogme (anti-auteurist) practice involves adhering to specific constraints such as location shooting, naturalistic lighting and acting, hand-held camerawork and an absence of special effects and post-production sound[4] as a means of encouraging improvisation (Gaut, 2003: 93).

Other contemporary filmmakers draw direct inspiration from the exemplars of French New Wave cinema, such as the Iranian filmmaker Abbas Kiarostami. His *Ten* (2002), for example, shot entirely with digital video and set in a car as it travels through the streets of Tehran, blurs the line between drama, documentary and home video (Andrew, 2005). And the films of British director Michael Winterbottom suggest other trajectories through fact-fiction hybridity using digital filmmaking practice. Winterbottom's *In This World* (2002), for example, is a drama-documentary which achieves a distinctive edge of authenticity through filming with DV cameras and employing amateur actors to retrace the path of Afghani refugees attempting to smuggle themselves into Britain.

The experience in Britain demonstrates some of the complexities of the ways in which all of these post-war innovations in dramatic fiction were articulated by specific production practices. In British television, vérité practice eventually began to transform news and current affairs, although somewhat delayed because 16mm film stock was initially considered to have too low a resolution for television, and hence to look too amateurish. Sexton notes, for example, that the BBC did not establish a 16mm film unit until 1964, about the time that the key documentary series *World in Action* began using portable film and sound technology (Sexton, 2003: 433–6).

The adoption of such technologies was eventually to transform British television documentary practice, allowing for more intimate observational footage that did not need to be combined with post-production sound. The result was a broadening of documentary aesthetics, although not always away from a traditional reliance on 'voice of god' narration combined with various forms of archival and other footage as the basis of documentary texts. In turn, such new documentary practices influenced a new generation of television writers, directors and producers who revitalised television drama, including drama-documentary. The overlapping and mutually reinforcing traditions of documentary vérité, television drama and drama-documentary created a compelling mix of fact-fiction hybridity in 1960s British television. Creative personnel often worked within both documentary and dramatic divisions at television institutions such as the BBC, while there were also significant linkages between television and British cinema during the period.

A key milestone in this history was the formation of the Free Cinema group by Tony Richardson, Karel Reisz, Lindsay Anderson and Lorenza Mazzetti, partly sparked by the example of Italian Neo-Realist and French New Wave movements. Focused on the production of short films and documentaries, leading members of this group later formed the core of what was subsequently identified by critics as the much looser and more difficult to identify 'British New Wave' (Lay, 2002: 11). This movement tends to be identified with a combination of independent spirit and left-wing politics which closely informed its production practices. Typically employing unknown, or little-known, local actors and emphasising location shooting, British social realism tended to deal with the 'gritty reality' of everyday lives (and in fact their films were initially identified by critics as 'kitchen sink' dramas). Most British filmmakers of this ilk favoured an unvarnished aesthetic style, to highlight their deliberate divergence from the polish of American cinematic realism from Hollywood studios (Lay, 2002: 8).

The British New Wave was another movement heavily influenced by cinéma vérité, which inspired experimentation with camera angles, composition and montage. However, while many of the films of this movement have drawn from vérité aesthetics it is difficult to reduce the movement to a particular representational approach. Its filmmakers tended to diverge along a number of individual styles, with each filmmaker developing different forms of representation appropriate to their particular thematic concerns. The field of British social realism consequently encompasses both the near-documentary style of Ken Loach and the more conventional dramatic style used by Mike Leigh.

Television played a key role in the emergence of the British New Wave as social realism attained a high profile during the late 1960s through a number of key television texts. The medium became a key site for aesthetic exploration, helping to shape the emergence of a distinctive and hugely influential dramatic style that overlapped with and informed that of soap opera (such as *Coronation Street* (1960–)), dramatic series (especially police dramas), documentary series and, eventually, hybrid formats such as docusoaps.

In its thematics, social realism focused on everyday social inequalities based on ethnic, gender and especially class divisions. In the 1960s, the concern of producers was also to move away from a conventional dramatic three-act structure, to allow open-ended, episodic or non-linear and often real-time narratives that did not always focus simply on a central character (Lay, 2002: 20). Programmes emphasised naturalism in terms of dialogue, lighting and distinctive editing styles ('fades equal a long lapse of time, dissolves a short time and cuts immediate time' (Caughie, 2000: 94). The vérité aesthetic of hand-held 16 mm cameras, flash pans and occasional out-of-focus shots was used to reinforce the sense of an opening up of space for new forms of content and issues relevant to everyday British life (Sexton, 2003: 444), as one means of signifying a sense of authenticity for a dramatic production.

There is an important intersection here with the history of British television drama-documentary, a form which needs a quick introduction.

The overlap between drama-documentary and mockumentary

Drama-documentary is itself a complex fact-fiction genre (Corner, 1996; Paget, 1998; Rosenthal, 1999; Lipkin, 2002) which combines the accessibility of mainstream film and television melodrama with the factual discourse that underpins the documentary genre (Paget, 1998: 35). A simple definition of drama-documentary is that it offers dramatised versions of actual events and is a form often chosen from a motivation to reach a wider audience than the documentary genre has traditionally attracted. Biographical films in this form tend to be centred on historical, political or cultural figures already well known to the public. The figure is re-introduced to the audience with a suggestion that the film represents their 'real story', containing an emotional truth less easily portrayed through the representational constraints of documentary.

Lipkin talks of drama-documentary as dealing with 'quasi-indexical narrative' (Lipkin, 2002: 2). Rather than an indexical representation of the real (as with documentary), the genre offers iconic representations couched within the narrative forms of melodrama. The logic of socio-political arguments that are prioritised within documentary is present in the dramatic text but tends to be articulated more implicitly, at the level of thematics, the overall agenda of the text and within the specific nature of its narrative constructions. Although largely reliant on iconic reconstruction, drama-documentary often directly integrates actual and re-created material, either in succession or together within a scene.[5] In terms of melodramatic narrative structure, drama-documentary employs techniques such as the telescoping of complex events and histories, creating a narrative arc out of an everyday story and 'editing out' aspects of a story that are repetitive, confusing or simply extraneous to the main narrative thrust. And there are, typically, elements of a realistic dramatic style, such as key lighting, naturalistic sound, continuity editing, the use of actual locations for settings, (often unknown) actors that resemble the actual figures they portray and a low-key or naturalistic style of acting.

These are often combined with documentary conventions, including the use of captions to identify dates and locations, original footage, photographic stills, news extracts or other archival footage and voice-overs from actors or a real person featured in the text (Paget, 1998: 61–89). At other times there will be acted reconstructions, simulations of documentary material or a mix of archive and library material. Typically, both factual and fictional sequences appear in ways that deny any tension or contradictions between these competing forms. Instead, these serve to reinforce each other; any documentary materials serve to authenticate the narrative, while the dramatic elements work to add emotional weight to the rational discourses underlying a drama-documentary text. All of these forms of representation are used to increase the sense of a text's 'proximity' (Lipkin, 2002: 53–4) to actual social actors and historical events, and in fact the balance between these elements is often crucial to the persuasive effect of a particular text. As Lipkin notes, the more complex sequences, those that particularly blur the boundaries between what is real and what is fictionalised, are often the most effective in this sense.

There are also, however, drama-documentaries which are deliberately reflexive towards themselves as narrativised constructions, in sequences that are often closer to the agenda of mockumentary. There is the playful mixture of narration and direct address by Steve Coogan as the lead character in Michael Winterbottom's *24 Hour Party People* (2002), which includes repeated references to the selective and partial perspective on historical events created through dramatic reconstruction. In *American Splendor* (2003) the fluid shifts between dramatic narrative, documentary, animation and openly reflexive studio sequences (featuring both actor Paul Giamatti and the real person he plays in the film, Harvey Pekar) match the film's commentary on representation and everyday life in Pekar's autobiographical comics (Hight, 2007). This potential for tension between fictional and documentary elements of drama-documentary suggests where it intersects with mockumentary.

Key British television programmes in the 1960s within the social realist mould included Peter Watkins' *Culloden* (1964) and *The War Game* (1965), and two of Ken Loach's episodes from *The Wednesday Play* (1964–70) series, *Up the Junction* (1965) and, especially, *Cathy Come Home* (1966). *Cathy Come Home* offered a harrowing portrayal of a young family's descent into poverty, homelessness and disintegration, filmed in such a way that audiences accepted it as if it was in fact a drama-documentary (that is, as if Cathy was based on a real person) (Caughie, 2000). And *Culloden* and *The War Game* are key early examples of television programmes that clearly sit at the overlap between drama-documentary and mockumentary.[6] Watkins himself is an interesting filmmaker to consider in relation to mockumentary, as his work has often entailed incorporating conventional modes for conveying reality both as innovative dramatic technique and as a means to explore a wider critique of social and political communication (with films such as *The Gladiators* (1969) and *Punishment Park* (1971)). *Culloden* and *The War Game* share these concerns, but derive more specifically from a drama-documentary agenda.

Culloden offers a dramatic reconstruction of the 1746 battle between Scottish Jacobite forces and the English armies of King George II, but filmed as if it were being covered by a documentary crew. There are 'interviews' with military commanders and soldiers from both sides, revealing the fears of the Scottish Highlanders drafted through their clans into a battle with better-prepared English troops, and coverage of the battle that demonstrates the military incompetence of the Scottish leaders such as Bonnie Prince Charlie. The programme was actually made within the documentary department at the BBC and deliberately drew upon the non-fiction template constructed by the documentary series *Panorama* (1953–) and *World in Action*.

The War Game, in turn, provides the template for a 'what if' drama-documentary, taking available information on the impact of a nuclear war in the United Kingdom to present an entirely rational, carefully detailed but horrific accounting of the events that could be expected to unfold for much of the British population. Many of its sequences have the raw authenticity of cinéma vérité, as cameras explore scenes of social disintegration and desperate social and political decisions for survival, all while a voice-over explains the inevitability of such extreme triage measures as the shooting of sick people in the wake of the collapse of an over-whelmed health system. This raw authenticity partly explains why it was apparently banned by the BBC.

Of these two innovative drama-documentaries, *The War Game* has the most descendants, as numerous subsequent 'what if' televi-sion programmes have sought to prompt debates over social and political issues by carrying forward a specific trajectory from a contemporary issue to its logical conclusion some time in the near future. Some of these texts are particular kinds of drama-documentaries that draw heavily upon the codes and conventions of documentary. *Smallpox 2002: Silent Weapon* (2002), for example, was constructed as a future 'documentary' investigation of the global spread of a lethal smallpox virus, looking back to the present day to trace its emergence, exploring the views of experts and the video diaries of a British family encountering the virus. *The Day Britain Stopped* (2003) used documentary form to speculate on the possible social chaos if the British transport system became overwhelmed. Such texts can be positioned within drama-documentary on the basis of their factual intent, but can also be seen to overlap with mockumentary for their simulation of documentary construction.[7]

Television programmes which use the same approach, but aimed at constructing more explicitly fictional entertainment, are more clearly drawing on mockumentary discourse. Two examples here could be *Special Bulletin* (1983) and *Without Warning* (1994), both American television movies that drew upon the example of Welles' *War of the Worlds* in presenting completely fictional narratives in the form of live news reports which interrupt regular programming. Mockumentary stunts which draw upon the conventions of live television, they operate in similar territory to the mockumentary television hoax *Ghostwatch* (see chapter 3) and likewise now appear somewhat dated through their close efforts to mimic local practices of news presentation.

Special Bulletin, broadcast by the NBC network on 20 March 1983, was constructed as a condensed narrative of breaking news reports, occurring over several days from the fictional 'RBS network', on an unfolding threat of nuclear terrorism by a group of anti-nuclear campaigners demanding American nuclear disarma-ment in Charleston, South Carolina. A local television crew becomes central to a hostage drama, allowing the group to broadcast its demands on 'live television'. Two news anchors in the New York studio provide links to press conferences, vox-pop with panicked locals and interviews with experts who explain the psychology of the terrorists and detail the possible effects of a nuclear explosion. The narrative operates as a series of fragments, as information is repeated and interviews and story segments are interrupted, with the studio continually cutting to yet another 'live' feed.

A strong component of the programme is a repeated argument, from both anchors and interviewees, that the presence of the television cameras and possibilities for massive media coverage helped to create the crisis. The programme ends with a nuclear explosion as a Delta Force military response to the terrorists goes wrong. As with *Ghostwatch*, the programme provoked confusion among audiences over its ontological status. NBC reportedly received thousands of phone calls from viewers wanting to find out whether the nuclear disaster it featured was real (El-Miskin, 1989: 72), despite the posting of thirty-one messages during the broadcast proclaiming its fictionality (in the case of at least one network affiliate the word 'fiction' was superimposed over the entire broadcast (El-Miskin, 1989: 74)).

The dramatic mockumentary *Without Warning*, broadcast by CBS on Halloween Eve 1994, is much closer to *War of the Worlds* in that it develops from a science fiction premise, with aliens making initial contact through asteroids precisely targeting locations on Earth. Also covering events over a series of days, this broadcast sought to suggest the relative incoherence and lack of wider perspective inherent in news reporting. Studio anchors attempt to present, and widely speculate on, fragments of information presented through familiar means of news reporting such as satellite feeds to reporters scattered around the globe, interviews with experts and emotional vox-pop with eyewitnesses. Key characters, including one of the anchors and a central reporter, were actual news professionals essentially playing themselves. As the narrative culminates in the imminent destruction of the Earth, the programme implicitly assumed that all viewers would eventually gradually recognise its fictional status.

Dramatic vérité: *Hill Street Blues* and *Tanner '88*

The key point being made here is that although the 1960s drama-documentaries, speculative drama-documentaries of the 1990s and dramatic mockumentaries discussed above can all be tentatively identified within specific representational traditions, they also obviously serve as reference points for a wider spectrum of hybridised forms of television dramatic fiction. In broad terms we could refer to such a corpus of texts as sharing in common a tendency toward a 'dramatic vérité' which is distinctive to and exploits the representational possibilities of televisual space, even as it points to more general patterns within visual culture. The term 'dramatic vérité' is broad enough to refer to the construction of a sense of immediacy, dramatic urgency and even a sense of 'virtual liveness' (Sexton, 2003: 432) through employing codes and conventions taken from the televisual fact-fiction continuum.[8] The examples discussed above look to use such techniques to generate a sense of spontaneity, unpredictability or restlessness that enhances an overall sense of verisimilitude. In Caughie's terms, they look to generate 'the rush of the real', 'the sense of it happening now' (Caughie, 2000: 100) for viewers watching the television screen at home. Such dramas look to generate an aura of authenticity, especially in the case of drama-documentaries, or simply an enhanced intimacy that accords to a vérité aesthetic played on the small screen, while still offering to viewers the more conventional pleasures of an omnipotent perspective on characters and action.

Dramatic vérité, in broad terms, involves an effort to exploit fundamental tensions between the aesthetics of drama and documentary. Caughie, for example, has discussed the distinctions between what he terms the 'documentary gaze' and the 'dramatic look' as they appear within televisual space.

> The dramatic look, that is to say, is the look which is familiar from theories of cinematic narrative, the rhetoric of the realist film: point of view, field, reverse field, eyeline match. [...] in the classic paradox, the dramatic look creates its 'reality effect' by a process of mediation so conventionalized as to become invisible. (Caughie, 2000: 111)

The documentary gaze, in contrast, 'depends on systems of mediation (hand-held camera, loss of focus, awkward frame) so visible as to be immediate, apparently unrehearsed, and hence authentic', relying on an impression that actions are unrehearsed and hence more authentic (Caughie, 2000: 111). In essence, there is a fundamental tension between the desire to maintain liveness and immediacy which is so central to televisual narratives and the quest for a more cinematic narrative form (Caughie, 2000: 101).

Dramatic vérité, then, refers to a broad arc of representational strategies demonstrated across television dramatic traditions that are still largely determined by generic conventions (and in more nuanced ways by the variety of social and political factors which constitute national broadcasting contexts). Dramatic forms of television mockumentary often operate within the broader arc of dramatic vérité, drawing from the naturalisation of this aesthetic within a range of prime-time television series. The precedents for dramatic vérité within specific national contexts can help to explain the frame which is consequently constructed for the possibilities for dramatic television mockumentary. Again, the differences between the British and American experiences are suggestive of wider patterns. In Britain the exploration of key dramatic television programmes was heavily informed by social realist agendas (as outlined above), especially the effort to create public debate around pressing social issues through the use of drama-documentary. In contrast, North American television production has always been couched in production models that tend to shy away from political agendas which might challenge mainstream audiences. Here the political implications of television drama tend to be cumulative and diffused, with experiments in dramatic vérité focused more on their immediate possibilities for revitalising dramatic production in order to make it more relevant and attractive to mainstream viewers. Two key reference points for dramatic vérité in the United States are the police drama series *Hill Street Blues* and the Robert Altman political satire *Tanner '88* (1988).

Hill Street Blues debuted on American television on 15 January 1981 (Gitlin, 2000: 302) and was immediately celebrated for its distinctive approach to police drama. Series co-creator and producer Steven Bochco drew inspiration particularly from a PBS documentary called *The Police Tapes* (1977), by filmmakers Alan and Susan Raymond (the same filmmakers behind the innovative documentary series *An American Family*), which covered the everyday frustrations and alienation in the ranks of police officers within the Fort Apache precinct in South Bronx. Experimenting with videotape, which had until that point been disparaged by television broadcasters as providing too low an image resolution, the filmmakers produced a programme that became a virtual template

5. The morning roll-call sequence from *The Police Tapes* (1977), the raw
and compelling video documentary that inspired the creators of
Hill Street Blues (1981–87).

for the visual style of later police-centred reality formats such as
Cops. The *Police Tapes'* black and white, hand-held, grainy footage
of police officers captured in their duties inside the police station
and in ride-alongs in police vehicles (filming through the windscreen from the back seat) provided the same charge of authenticity
as direct cinema's initial arrival within cinematic documentary
(Figure 5). Significantly, the disturbing political subtext to *The
Police Tapes*, which offered a compelling vision of an institution in
disarray, was not taken up by documentary hybrids. Interviews with
weary, disillusioned and unexpectedly honest and articulate senior
officers provided a detailed socio-political critique of law enforcement in the poorer areas of South Bronx (one officer even com-
pares his police force to an occupying army).

   The initial intention of *Hill Street Blues'* producers was to match
the *Police Tapes* by also constructing this police drama in black and
white.[9] While this was later abandoned, Bochco did replicate some
aspects of a vérité style to create a completely distinctive approach
to American television drama. These were not adhered to through-

out each episode, but were particularly in evidence in opening sequences featuring the police station roll-call and daily briefing – scenes directly inspired by those within *The Police Tapes* (Thompson, 1997: 67–70). These scenes aimed for the look of low-budget documentary, using hand-held cameras and shots that appeared to follow and catch conversations, with some shots incorporating obvious changes in focus. These scenes featured a soundtrack with deliberately overlapping and chaotic conversations between characters and a (then) unusual absence of music. The soundtrack was partly inspired by the aural style used by Robert Altman for his films and produced by an improvisational comedy troupe called Off the Wall to 'improvise everything from squad-room phone murmurs to dispatch calls and crowd noises' (Gitlin, 2000: 294).

The rest of the series conformed to a more conventional style, although with a greater use of hand-held cameras, an increase in the typical pacing for police drama and scenes which incorporated jump cuts or shots in which characters momentarily blocked the sight of the camera. Gitlin notes the effort to provide background action within scenes, and frequent use of tightly composed shots to suggest a claustrophobic atmosphere in internal scenes (Gitlin, 2000: 2–3). The style was developed by director Robert Butler and Bochco over the first five episodes, intended especially to generate a sense of realism by creating the illusion that the events being filmed were random and reflective of a wider social environment that was similarly dense, but fragmented and chaotic. Bochco similarly looked to recreate *The Police Tapes'* overall sense of an institution in decline, recognising the dramatic potential of showing the police precinct and its officers under severe stress. This carefully crafted visual style was married with a soap opera structure, with each episode moving quickly between a number of overlapping narratives focusing on the professional and personal lives of a large ensemble cast which might play out over a number of episodes.

The series was immediately recognised by audiences and critics for its innovatory approach, although it eventually became more formulaic, as NBC executives demanded more structure and conventionality in narrative and style in order not to confuse viewers. The stylistic innovations of the series, however, quickly became established as a familiar aesthetic for dramatic television series, and were extended and superseded by series such as *Homicide: Life on the Street* (1993–99), *NYPD Blue* (1993–2005), *ER, The Practice* (1997–2004) and *The West Wing*, to the extent that the original *Hill Street Blues* now looks tame in comparison. This series, together with the many descendants of dramatic television series which it inspired, was key to the development and popularisation of a dramatic vérité approach characterised by both a kinetic visual style, accepted by audiences as signifying 'realism' and 'immediacy', and soap opera narrative structures.

The other key reference point for the emergence of an American televisual dramatic vérité style, and one which is frequently cited as an inspiration by mockumentary producers themselves, is *Tanner '88*. Although frequently mistakenly described as a mockumentary, it was a direct influence on Tim Robbins' mockumentary *Bob Roberts* as well as a number of subsequent television series that flirt with mockumentary discourse. Written by political cartoonist Garry Trudeau (*Doonesbury*) and directed by Robert Altman, this eleven-part series (a 1-hour pilot followed by 30-minute episodes) focused on the presidential candidacy of 'Jack Tanner' (played by Michael Murphy). Tanner is written as an atypical candidate, an intellectual shaped by the political agendas of the 1960s and struggling to come to terms with a post-Reagan political process that demands a carefully crafted and charismatic media profile rather than a detailed policy platform.

The key to the significance of this series lies in the decision of Altman and Trudeau to produce the series during the actual 1988 Democratic primaries and to position the fictional Tanner as if he was just another candidate. Trudeau later explained that '[f]rom the beginning, our intention was to write as close to the news as possible and shoot it in a loose, documentary style, so as to create the impression for viewers that Jack Tanner really was running against Bob Dole, Gary Hart, Mike Dukakis and the other presidential wannabees of 1988' (Trudeau, 2002: 23). This involved a kind of guerrilla satire approach, with Trudeau scripting vignettes and Altman encouraging the cast to partly improvise within any given situation. Altman employed his distinctive technique for overlapping dialogue and naturalistic narratives and gained the participation of public figures such as Waylon Jennings, local reporters and campaign officials as secondary cast members who pretend to be working with the Tanner campaign. Together with Altman's unusual choice of video instead of film (Jameson, 1988: 74), and a production

6. Fictional candidate Jack Tanner (Michael Murphy, second from right) encounters real candidate Pat Robertson (far right) during the 1988 US presidential elections, in an early episode of Robert Altman and Garry Trudeau's playful satire *Tanner '88* (1988).

process designed to be as last minute as possible to take advantage of weekly developments on the campaign trail, the effect is a construction of a television event that appears to be unfolding within, and responding to, the actual American presidential campaign season.

The most interesting scenes derive from Tanner and his 'documentary crew' playing in the same space as actual political figures, who in the early episodes obviously have no idea that he is fictional (Figure 6). As the series gained the attention of the national political press, Democrats in particular sought to become active participants in the series, offering frank on-camera advice to political innocent Tanner that they would not offer in any other public forum (after his own presidential campaign ended, for example, Bruce Babbitt appeared in a lengthy scene in episode 5 where he counsels Tanner to be honest and open with the public). The blurring of the line between fact and fiction, however, is not always so playful.

Scenes in episodes 8 and 9 play in a Detroit ghetto, at an anti-drug rally set up by the Tanner campaign, with participation from locals who start to express very real political frustrations. As Tanner listens and offers quiet support, Altman captures an unscripted neighbourhood debate over inner-city decline – offering a subtle political critique of his own by including in the series the kind of discussion that does not appear within news coverage of the real campaign.

The series uses hand-held video cameras (which is partly why it is often labelled a mockumentary), but does not seek to maintain the pretence that there is an actual camera crew present. Occasionally, however, the series slips more directly into mockumentary mode. One of the campaign staffers (Deke Connors, played by Matt Molloy) is constructing what he terms a 'neo-realist' film documentary on Tanner, and we see some of the shots from his camera. One of these is a secretly filmed view from under a coffee table of Tanner venting his political frustrations and spontaneously articulating his political ideals. Frustrated by Tanner's inability to simply turn on this political passion when required, his chief of staff, 'T. J. Cavanaugh' (Pamela Reed), uses the footage as the centrepiece of a television campaign centred on a new campaign slogan: 'For Real'. The campaign becomes one part of the series' layered commentary on the centrality of television within the modern American political process, as Altman suggests how any real political energy is immediately packaged and commodified into easily digested political brands.

The sequel to *Tanner '88*, a four-part mini-series entitled *Tanner on Tanner* (2004), centres on Tanner's daughter 'Alex' (Cynthia Nixon). A young, enthusiastic supporter of her divorced father in the first series, in *Tanner on Tanner* Alex has become a somewhat naïve documentary filmmaker looking to understand her father's failed 1988 campaign. Visually more complex than the original series, this interweaves three different perspectives represented by the main narrative's cameras for the series, a DV camera used by Alex for her 'documentary' (often operated by characters themselves), and a third camera used by one of Alex's students who is making his own film using Alex as his subject (Hurwitz, 2004). Altman and Trudeau sought to repeat the same semi-improvised approach as *Tanner '88*, but the series suffers from a comparative lack of focus and appears to meander more than the original series.

Developing a critique of the decline of documentary filmmaking since the 1990s (with frequent references to the work of Michael Moore), the main narrative centres on Alex's failed efforts to construct a documentary on her father's campaign and the eventual sacrifice of her own filmmaking ambitions in favour of her father's revived political career. Meanwhile her student, apparently representing the new generation of documentary filmmakers, documents her failures in a raw, emotionally intrusive portrait which devastates Alex. The series' key message is that, while documentary culture has broadened to saturate every aspect of private and public life, its more politically urgent and critical capacity has effectively been marginalised and superseded by more emotional, exploitative and banal forms of mediated 'truth'.

This series is notable for its number of cameos by public figures, ranging from filmmaker Martin Scorsese to political figures who would be familiar to its American audiences. One scene, featuring Alex's clash with Alexandra Kerry (John Kerry's daughter, a real-life documentary filmmaker) while both are trying to interview the son of Ronald Reagan, suggests how easily the (real) participants were able to slip between different forms of performance.[10] The crew and cast also mingle with actual participants on the floor of the 2004 Democratic Convention, where Tanner himself (that is, Murphy) appears to be recognised as a former fictional political candidate. The result is less of a critique of the political process than a playful blurring of reality and fiction where non-acting members of the cast are all happy to participate in a continuation of the 'Tanner' folklore.

Bruzzi's critique of *Tanner '88* includes speculation that for politicians there is no real distinction between performance and reality, no essential political individual behind their public façade. She suggests that the difference between viewing the John F. Kennedy documentary *Primary* (a direct cinema exemplar) and the same approach employed toward Bill Clinton's campaign in *The War Room* (1993) rests on the increasing sophisticated awareness of political campaigns of exactly how their candidates are represented (Bruzzi, 2000: 136), a transformation of the democratic process instigated by television that is captured and satirised by *Tanner '88*. Trying to incorporate Roscoe's flickers of authenticity (see chapter 4), then, is a pointless exercise for filmmakers; 'to try to enforce the distinction between the "real" person and the performance is futile, the politician is necessarily performative' (Bruzzi, 2000: 152). This might not be quite true of *Tanner '88* itself, produced at a time before the explosion of documentary hybrids, as viewers can easily discern the changes in performance between presidential candidates Pat Robertson or Bob Dole, caught unawares in encounters with Tanner in the early episodes, and that of Kitty Dukakis as she gives heartfelt advice to Tanner's girlfriend in episode 11. However, Bruzzi's observation offers one explanation for the failure of another dramatic vérité series that it directly inspired.

K Street (2003), co-produced by Steven Soderburgh, Henry Bean, Mark Sennet and George Clooney, and conceived as a fact-fiction hybrid, involved setting up a fictional lobbying firm using two actual, high-profile Washington operators, James Carville and Mary Matalin, together with three actors as their associates. The series used the same last-minute production process as *Tanner* in order to generate a similar sense of immediacy and spontaneity and capture a sense of the confusion and dynamism of the everyday Washington political scene. Episodes centred round the involvement of actors in real political situations, interacting with political figures and developing loose narratives linked to topical stories. The series is classic dramatic vérité, with a camera style composed largely of a polished hand-held aesthetic, with quick cuts between multiple perspectives in the same scene (rather than long takes with a single camera), lots of low-angle shots and occasional tracking shots down corridors. Other interesting touches include captions to identify locations and the Altmanesque technique of overlapping conversations.

The series failed both critically and commercially, with commentators suggesting that the blame lay in part with a basic inability to make interesting television out of political processes that are themselves inherently confusing and slow to outsiders (Motavalli, 2003). More interestingly, some critics argued that the series' attempts to develop a satirical edge on Washington politics were undermined by the enthusiastic participation of local insiders, who either wanted to perform in a series associated with Soderburgh and Clooney or who immediately recognised the publicity possibilities of the programme (Siegel, 2003; Lee, 2003). Absent the sense of a spontaneously captured reality, or a particular tension between the fictional and the actual, the series had to rely on an inadequately constructed ensemble narrative and was cancelled after one season.

Mockumentary drama one-off episodes (within series)

While series such as *Tanner '88* and the descendants of *Hill Street Blues* suggest the popularity of dramatic vérité, as noted at the beginning of this chapter there has to date been no dramatic mockumentary series. The few examples of mockumentary television programmes in a dramatic vein include a number of one-off programmes, most notably the television hoaxes already discussed, and a small number of one-off mockumentary episodes of television series.

To some extent, one-off mockumentary episodes of dramatic series are all stunts, intended more as novelty pieces, as none is central to the dominant styles employed by any of its 'host' series. Caldwell, looking at a broader range of television programmes than mockumentary, refers to a group of similarly isolated novelty episodes that he calls 'docu-stunts'. These are instances within fictional television programming which appropriate aspects of documentary aesthetics or discourses and are 'special episodes aimed at eliciting coverage and viewership during sweeps weeks and premieres or critical prestige for Emmy consideration' (Caldwell, 2002: 259). Caldwell explains the background for this kind of experimentation, noting that such strategies have been employed since the 1950s in American television, in series both comedic and dramatic, as varied as *Father Knows Best* (1954–60) and *Leave It to Beaver* (1957–63). Here episodes may use elements of documentary aesthetics such as hand-held camerawork, or incorporate forms of documentary experience and content which directly reference or comment upon documentary practice, or issues specific to reality hybrids (Caldwell, 2002: 259–92). Within this context of docu-real stunts, episodes which can be identified as dramatic mockumentary, or the sustained effort to suggest documentary construction, can be seen as one approach used within a range of techniques intended to create innovative dramatic television content.

Caldwell suggests that the (broader category of) docu-stunt serves a number of ends: highlighting the performance of actors; offering a 'metareflection that elaborates distinctions about casts and characters'; playing at being both episode and 'making of'; or just a novelty style to allow an episode to work through clips of series highlights (Caldwell, 2002: 288). Although ultimately intended as marketing devices, such stunts also offer the potential to open an episode to a wider set of thematics than is typical of a series as a whole.

> The range of critical-theoretical 'framings' in docu-stunts – *on screen*, in front of large television audiences – offer extended mediations on the nature of television; relations between fiction and documentary; tensions among entertainment, art, and reality; phenomenological issues of television experience; and aesthetic questions of program quality. (Caldwell, 2002: 260, original emphasis)

The creation of such 'framings' has particular implications for the nature of audiences' engagement with familiar characters and aesthetics within dramatic series that employ mockumentary for a single episode. In broad terms, the suggestion of an external documentary crew entering the fictional space of the series creates an immediate distancing effect. On the one hand, this allows the series producers to play with the sense that their narrative is grounded in some form of actuality which continues outside the scenes that are seen each week by viewers, an apparent 'reality' that can be explored in different ways through an encounter with a documentary filmmaker and crew. On the other hand, however, this external perspective creates some distinctive challenges for the conventional forms of engagement intrinsic to television realism.

While viewers are typically encouraged to identify with regular characters, and are provided with access to their internal psychology and motivations for their actions, a perspective from a 'documentary camera' renegotiates these forms of intimacy. The result is an episode which typically provides viewers with less narrative information than they are used to receiving, and channelled through the agenda of an apparent documentary filmmaker. A typical dramatic series will also employ a variety of stylistic features, visual effects such as slow motion or filters, or extra-diegetic music added in post-production, used to enhance dramatic tone, atmosphere and pacing. Maintaining the pretence that an episode is a non-fiction construction also means reducing (or translating) such stylistics down to a very different palette of techniques. To some extent the success of one-off mockumentary episodes depends on how producers deal with the complexities of the different layers of narrative that are consequently established: the narrative provided by a 'documentary' encounter and the familiar narratives of the series itself that need to be conveyed through new means. The play between these offers the potential for a reflexivity towards the type of non-fiction which the mockumentary references, as well as reflexivity towards the construction of the host dramatic series itself.

There are a number of examples of one-off dramatic mockumentary episodes, largely produced for American television series. Some are more openly playful, such as an episode of *Xena: Warrior Princess* (1995–2001) where a modern-day tabloid reporter looks for an exposé of the 'real Xena',[11] or a futuristic Earth news broadcast covering debates over recent events at the space station at the centre of the cult science fiction series *Babylon 5* (1994).[12] Others are more sober, such as a documentary crew covering the last-minute attempts of the legal team of *The Practice* to save the life of an inmate on death row.[13] The three examples chosen for discussion below offer a similar variety of agenda but deserve more discussion for their efforts to include more interesting commentaries on the nature of the non-fiction formats which they each reference.

'X-Cops' (The X-Files)

'X-Cops' is an episode from the science-fiction/supernatural series *The X-Files*, produced for the series' seventh season.[14] The episode is constructed entirely as a pastiche of an episode of the reality hybrid *Cops*, including hand-held video cameras in ride-alongs with police officers performing their duties, captions identifying personnel and locations, 'teasers' for upcoming action before advertising breaks and the use of the series' familiar theme music and opening voice-over narrator. Following the action over a night with police officers from the Los Angeles Sheriff's Department, cameras encounter the series' two leads, FBI agents Fox Mulder (David Duchovny) and Dana Scully (Gillian Anderson), as the police investigate apparently supernatural acts of violence in a Los Angeles inner-city neighbourhood. The documentary cameras begin to focus more on Mulder and Scully, as they appear to be most likely to uncover an explanation for what is occurring.

With its use of digital video cameras, the episode is a stylistic anomaly of the *X-Files* series as a whole, which typically aimed for a much more cinematic aesthetic. The result is somewhat jarring for regular viewers of the series, as it provides a quite different 'look' from the expected highly polished production values, not least because Mulder and Scully are somewhat diminished by appearing

within the frame of a low-grade digital video. The narrative structure for the episode is a mixture of elements familiar from both
Cops and the wider *X-Files* series. Scenes centre especially on ride-
alongs in police cars (and here within the FBI agents' cars), with
cameras filming from the back seat through the front windscreen,
and visits to the houses of victims of an apparent supernatural
entity loose in the neighbourhood. There are frequent shots of
Mulder, Scully and police officers running through darkened streets,
alleyways, backyards and corridors. As with *Cops*, the action is
necessarily always focused on key protagonists arriving at a scene
after some event, with officers trying to piece together different
forms of evidence and testimony to construct a plausible narrative
of what has occurred.

While the episode is a novelty for the series, it is one which also
gels with key aspects of the series' dominant narrative patterns.
At its base an unconventional police thriller, the series tended
to oscillate between ongoing encounters with a dense, layered
science-fiction government conspiracy involving an apparently
long-established alien presence on Earth, and more singular episode
narratives featuring entities derived from classical horror, supernatural stories and American folklore. Episodes did not always
offer satisfying resolutions, often leaving elements of a mystery
unsolved and out of the reach of the agents. The series as a whole
played with generic boundaries, gender stereotypes and dichotomies between reason and faith. Mulder and Scully served as a
potent pairing, with Mulder invariably riffing on traditional forms
of knowledge and his own intuition and Scully adhering to the role
of a rational scientist. As Kellner argues, the *X-Files* was distinctive
in that it 'engages in a pastiche of plot-lines, genre, conventions,
iconography, folklore, and bits of history found in the forms of
previous media culture', creating in particular a 'metacommentary'
on television itself, its standard forms, conventions and mythologies
(Kellner, 1999: 161–7).

'X-Cops' plays with the *Cops* format, suggesting what might
occur should a television documentary hybrid crew accidentally
encounter Mulder and Scully during the course of one of their
investigations. True to form, Mulder is intrigued by the prospect
of documenting a supernatural entity in front of a nationwide
(American) audience, while Scully is more cautious about how the
FBI might be represented. As with the *Blair Witch Project*, the

documentary eye is revealed to be inadequate to the task of scientifically uncovering the supernatural. In the final scenes, Mulder and Scully fail to capture the entity, but discover that it has escaped while other members of the crew cowered in a cupboard and consequently also failed to even capture any footage of what they encountered. The programme's narrative is comparatively fractured and episodic, as we see only the agents' encounters with the cameras, including the helpful speculations to camera that Mulder provides and Scully's uneasy sarcasm over the presence of the crew. The real-time unfolding of events which serves as a template for *Cops* episodes here provides a sense of action, but not a wider narrative arc, nor any thematics (apart from the format's underlying pro-police ideology). Another aspect of the series which the episode cannot sustain is the degree of intimacy between Mulder and Scully, especially the unresolved sexual tension that is a key subtext of their relationship (perhaps one reason why this episode does not rate highly with the series' fans). Ultimately, then, the 'X-Cops' episode reinforces the authenticity of camcorder footage of events, but also suggests that such a representation can offer only an incomplete version of the 'truth'; footage from an external camera crew cannot suggest the sense of historical perspective, emotional access, and understanding of personal and professional motivations that viewers expect of a series with a richly layered social or institutional setting. A similar comment could be applied to the next example of a one-off dramatic mockumentary.

'Ambush' (ER)[15]

A mockumentary approach was chosen as the basis of a stunt to mark the opening of the fourth season of the medical drama series *ER*.[16] Constructed as documentary footage captured by a camera crew with a definite tabloid agenda, the episode unfolds as a day in the life of the fictional hospital emergency room. Initially suggested by cast members Anthony Edwards and George Clooney, as a throwback to the spontaneity of television's Golden Age of 'live' broadcasts in the 1950s, it was later suggested by producer and director of the episode, Thomas Schlamme, that the anxiety of live broadcast could in fact approximate the anxiety that actual doctors and nurses might feel on being suddenly confronted with a documentary camera crew (Gilbert, 1997). Performed twice, to cater to the 2-hour time difference between the eastern and western coasts of the United States, the episode operates as a somewhat unique mockumentary stunt. Because of pre-publicity, the broadcast audience were fully aware of the 'live' nature of the staged play and the consequent lack of opportunities to construct the series' normal visual and narrative complexity. For this episode, then, audiences were encouraged not only to engage with the series' fictional premise, but to appreciate the technical and performance achievements by a tightly choreographed ensemble cast and crew within the series' detailed set. The episode was enormously successful, gaining an average of 42.7 million viewers in the United States (Rice, 1997), making it at that stage the third most-watched programme in the history of American television dramas (Butler, 2001).

One of the descendants of the *Hill Street Blues* dramatic vérité template, the series' signature style combines a soap opera complexity in its narrative with a fluid, cinematic aesthetic. A key innovation of the series is that it is filmed within a complex set that replicates the layout of an actual emergency room, but with breakaway walls that allow for the easy access of camera operators and other crew from scene to scene, allowing each episode's cameras to appear to enter and move easily through a coherent space (Butler, 2001: 315). Butler notes the regular use of a Steadicam, which provides for more fluid camera movements (including such stylistic flourishes as a camera rotating rapidly around characters within the set). These visual aspects helped to distinguish the series' aesthetics from the more heavily hand-held-centred camerawork favoured by *Hill Street Blues* and subsequent police dramas such as *NYPD Blue* (Butler, 2001: 317).

The 'Ambush' mockumentary episode was forced to compromise with aspects of this signature style, both for practical reasons in the staging of a live performance and also to retain the consistency of the pretence that the final broadcast operates as a plausible documentary. As Butler notes, 'the irony here is that the live broadcast was presented as if it were *not* live, as if we were viewing videotape that had been shot previously for a documentary about the emergency room' (Butler, 2001: 312) – in other words, the inverse of the mockumentary hoax *Ghostwatch* (discussed in chapter 3). The result is an episode which has a slower pacing than usual, with a relative absence of extra-diegetic music (except where consistent with a documentary production). While the crew used eleven cameras, including five hand-held, a remote and several stationary units (Katz, 1997), the episode is constructed to suggest the presence of a camera crew with only two hand-held cameras and a 'surveillance' camera set up in the fictional doctors' lounge. There is a series of continuous one-shot takes, with the majority of the footage coming from the hand-held cameras. The programme cuts between these, with increasing speed toward the end of the programme, but always consistently with the notion that there are just the three cameras which are realistically able to capture all of the action which is presented.

In terms of its narrative, the central tension within 'Ambush' is between the agenda of the hospital, looking for some positive public relations, and that of the documentary crew, who seem to be looking especially for evidence of bureaucratic mismanagement or medical negligence. Although the episode references a number of the series' continuing narratives, these tend to be used more as a point of reference for regular viewers rather than to be dramatically advanced. The episode feels much more like a playful 'time out' from the regular series, with frequent reflexive moments which remind the audience that the characters are continually aware of the presence of the documentary crew (and, at another level, also serving as reminders that the cast are aware of the live broadcast cameras). Characters continually look at the camera, accidentally bump into it, wave 'Hi mom', ask the cameraman if a line should be repeated, or tell the camera operator to move; all reinforcing the notion that the supposedly real characters are 'acting up' in the presence of a reality TV crew.

This playful, reflexive aspect of the episode is favoured over attempts to sustain the pretence of a completed documentary about the emergency room. Although the episode is not presented as such in its title sequence, it operates more as a rough cut of a documentary than a completed broadcast-worthy production. There are too many scenes featuring direct criticism of the filmmakers, including the director seen in frame negotiating with and directing her subjects, and revealing her motivation directly to her camera operator. The key camera operator is never seen, but his character is constructed through his shot selection and framing. His lens wanders away from characters who do not offer dramatic or emotional material, zooms quickly into the faces of those who do and continually searches for more visually interesting compositions. We gain a marked sense of the crew's absence of real ethical practices: a scene which the director agrees to cut in return for an emotional interview is left in, and pleas for privacy or respect are implicitly ignored (through the inclusion of the very footage that is the focus of characters' complaints). Much of the episode's narrative information is not given willingly by characters, but caught by the surveillance camera, or obtained by the crew filming through windows, or through microphones unintentionally left on. If this is the final edit of an actual documentary, then the filmmakers are either incompetent or willing to casually sacrifice their own reputations for dramatic purposes. Ultimately, then, reflexive moments are broad and clearly flagged to viewers, while the characterisation of the documentary crew is somewhat simplistic and two-dimensional. Their role reveals a scripting for live performance more than for television production; they serve as little more than a dramatic foil to the regular cast rather than as the basis of a detailed or informed commentary on the nature of television documentary itself.

'Access' (The West Wing)

A final example of a mockumentary episode within a dramatic series comes from the fifth season of White House drama *The West Wing*. The episode is titled 'Access',[17] after a PBS programme which has supposedly profiled one of the core members of the series' large ensemble cast. It carefully draws from a specific documentary template for its construction, combining a detailed and sophisticated mixture of expositional narration, real archival footage, faked news broadcasts (usually viewed on television screens by characters) and, especially, interviews and hand-held location footage. The result is a more sober construction than either of the episodes discussed above, but also one which allows for a much broader and detailed set of thematics. The concerns of this episode are centred less on suggesting a commentary on television documentary and more on generating a critique of the dominance of electronic (particularly televisual) media in shaping contemporary political communication.

The West Wing as a series offers a complex, sophisticated perspective on policy making within a White House administration, even as it insists on rendering such complexities within an overall perspective on American presidential politics safely couched within the norms of television mythology. The fictional President Josiah 'Jed' Bartlet (Martin Sheen) is a composite of the better qualities of a variety of American presidents, but also a liberal Democrat modelled on aspects of the Kennedy mystique (most explicitly in the title sequence to the series, which replicates a series of iconic black and white *Life* magazine photographs of John F. Kennedy in the Oval office). Creating a sense of the White House staff as a kind of surrogate family, with Bartlet himself as a wise and knowledge-able father figure, the series follows the professional and personal lives of key decision makers within the Bartlet administration. The content of specific episodes is typically linked to topical issues within the American political scene, although the series invariably presents solutions which are often plausible only within the dictates of television dramatic fiction.

'Ambush' centres on two days in the life of C.J. Cregg (Allison Janney), a cast regular performing, at the time of the episode, as the president's director of communications. Other regular characters play comparatively minor roles, a key departure from the norm of the series as a whole, which aims for a complex narrative structure with characters tending to make consistent appearances across epi-sodes or regularly featuring in one of an episode's interweaving narratives. This mockumentary episode is positioned within the overall narrative arc of the series, but also presented as a documen-tary representation of events broadcast some time after they occur, and crucially after the Bartlet administration leaves office. (This premise allows the fictional documentary crew to plausibly gain a considerable degree of access within the White House while pre-senting itself as removed from, and having a greater historical per-spective than, the wider series itself.)

Aimed at a politically literate audience, *The West Wing* typically incorporates high production values, and employs a signature style similar to that of *ER*, with flowing tracking shots through the detailed reconstruction of the west wing of the White House. The series is particularly known for its fast-paced and witty dialogue, initially developed by creator and writer Aaron Sorkin. These ele-ments, the meshing of fluid movement and rapid dialogue, were paired with multiple plotlines through each episode, with characters generally taking different trajectories through the west wing as they verbally sparred and negotiated over political strategies and per-sonal interactions. The resulting sense of kinetic energy is largely missing from the 'Access' mockumentary episode, only approached at times when the 'documentary' accompanies rapid montage sequences of vérité footage with voice-over narration from either the fictional documentary director, or extracts from an interview with Cregg.

As with the *ER* episode discussed above, the *West Wing* mockumentary episode begins with an extended sequence clearly flagging for viewers the change in mode from the series signature aesthetic and narrative style to that of documentary. Cregg is in her office, first seen through the viewfinder of a digital camera, talking to the director and initially unaware that the crew have started taping. After multiple shots from hand-held cameras as the crew set up lights, the tape suddenly 'rewinds' and the 'documentary' begins more formally with a voice-over introduction to Cregg's interview. The interview forms a core strand for the episode which follows, intercut with vérité footage from Cregg's duties during the apparent two days of filming. The observational scenes are in turn intercut with various archival footage, home movies of Cregg (obviously actor Janney's own childhood home movies) and excerpts from her appearances on television within news coverage of a crisis at the time of the crew's visit. There is a clear distinction between the composed and orderly interview sequences[18] and others where the crew are merely following Cregg and her staff as they coordinate public responses of the Bartlet administration to the crisis. An overall frame is provided by the voice-over exposition of the 'documentary' filmmaker, who argues that presidential politics are now unhealthily dictated by the demands of 24-hour television news coverage, with the information-management role of the communications director inevitably thrust into centre stage. Our sympathies in the episode lie with the White House, specifically with Cregg as her efforts to articulate a broad, national agenda conflict with the simplistic demands of television news media to collapse any complex perspective into the fragmented immediacy of 24-hour news bulletins. The vérité sequences ground the episode's key themes, portraying administration staffers as honourable and working at their best, but also conveying the sense that the crew is gaining access to the construction of history itself (Russo, 2005: 16). While Cregg persuasively articulates a detailed historical perspective on her role and the growth of news media coverage of the White House, the news professionals she must encounter every day have no historical memory except of recent crises, also defined through saturation television coverage.

The production design for the episode works to reinforce these themes more indirectly. The White House offices are saturated with television screens, providing a sense of claustrophobia and tension as Cregg struggles to anticipate where the focus of news coverage will go next; the news coverage feels like a disruptive invasion of the close-knit-community space of the White House. While the documentary crew appear to have full access to the White House, Cregg, her staff and colleagues are frequently captured through the additional frame of office windows (many with blinds or reflections that interfere with our vision) and doorways – which, Russo argues, provide a subtle commentary on the nature of information flow and control between personnel within the buildings (Russo, 2005: 17–18).

This *West Wing* mockumentary episode, as with those discussed above, demonstrates how a documentary treatment involves a reduction in the forms of narrative information typically provided to television drama viewers. It also goes further, however, in generating a thematic which insists that any (non-fiction) representation of a political event is unable to provide a coherent and comprehensive account of its historical complexities. Although occasionally developing reflexive moments towards documentary filmmaking, none of the dramatic mockumentary episodes discussed here moves beyond constructions of documentary texts which are themselves formulaic. Undoubtedly this is to make the mockumentary episodes easily accessible to each of the series' regular television audiences; whether it is the familiar template for *Cops*, which immediately puts into play specific narrative expectations before any appearance by agents Mulder and Scully, or the PBS documentary format, which flags a sober portrayal of events in a presidential administration. These limited frames are deliberate, motivated partly by the need to develop a distanced perspective which interrupts and intervenes in an existing fictional milieu, and partly to not allow this perspective to become too disruptive of audience's engagement with familiar characters and ongoing storylines. The case of *ER*'s 'Ambush' episode is instructive: the complexity of competing perspectives on a familiar fictional setting offers too much potential to reveal the constructed nature of the series itself, so is positioned as a playful stunt.

These one-off episode examples ultimately suggest the difficulty of sustaining mockumentary in terms of drama for an entire series within televisual space. The task of maintaining a number of potential layers of perspective and commentary challenges television producers to become more creative within the narrative constraints of mockumentary form. The dominance of dramatic vérité within the genre of television drama also means that, while there is wider support for the aesthetic approaches employed in dramatic mockumentary programmes, there are also well-established alternatives for developing the sense of immediacy and realism that is also integral to the agenda of dramatic mockumentary.

We have yet to see an effort to create a dramatic mockumentary series that matches the exemplars of dramatic mockumentary within cinema: the playful musing on cinematic truth in *David Holzman's Diary*, the satirical bite inherent in documenting the life of a serial killer in *C'est arrivé près de chez vous* (*Man Bites Dog*),[19] the absurdly extreme version of a *Survivor*-styled reality game at the centre of *Series 7: The Contender*, or *Zero Day*'s disturbingly convincing video diary of two alienated youths planning for a massacre at their high school. Perhaps the time has already passed when a similarly powerful dramatic mockumentary series will appear on mainstream television; perhaps it is the online arena which offers the greatest potential in this direction. This stunted and inconsistent history of dramatic mockumentary stands in direct contrast to the rich veins of mockumentary series that draw upon traditions of television comedy, as discussed in the following chapter.

Notes

1 Greene notes that the French New Wave was influential in sparking similar movements in countries such as Brazil, Germany, Hong Kong, the United States and Japan, in the process ironically attaining a greater profile and influence than in France itself (Greene, 2007: 108).

2 Although there is debate over the wider body of work that constitutes the neo-realist movement, Shiel notes that the critical consensus is that its masterpieces include Roberto Rossellini's *Roma, città aperta* (*Rome, Open City*) (1945), *Paisà* (1946), and *Germania anno zero* (*Germany Year Zero*) (1948); Vittorio de Sica's *Sciuscia* (*Shoeshine*) (1946), *Ladri di biciclette* (*Bicycle Thieves*) (1948) and *Umberto D.* (1952); and Luchino Visconti's *La terra trema* (1948) (Shiel, 2006: 3).

3 *Les cahiers du cinéma* (*Notebooks on Cinema*) (1951–), London, Phaidon Press, available at www.cahiersducinema.com/.

4 See www.dogme95.dk/the_vow/vow.html.

5 Lipkin distinguishes here between the typical drama-documentary strategies of modelling, sequencing and interaction (Lipkin, 2002: 13).

6 This argument is in contrast to chapter 3 from *Faking It* (Roscoe and Hight, 2001), where we insisted that mockumentary and drama-documentary were quite distinct forms, marked by divergent approaches toward factual discourse.

7 Ward in fact argues that both of these texts should be considered mockumentaries rather than speculative drama-documentary because of the ways in which they position the viewer in ways that 'foregrounds the conditional nature of the events depicted' (Ward, 2005b: 272).

8 The term 'dramatic vérité' is deliberately intended to complement Brett Mills' use of the phrase 'comedy vérité' to describe a parallel set of aesthetics operating within television comedy, and especially recent innovative sitcoms (Mills, 2004). See chapter 6.

9 See Gitlin, 2000: 273–324 for a detailed outline of the development of the series, including the long and difficult gestation process for creators Steven Bochco and Michael Kozoll.

10 In an interview included on the DVD for the series, Altman notes that the scene featured both Reagan and Kerry's crews, the *Tanner on Tanner* crew, as well as a PBS crew doing a 'making of' documentary. In such a situation, finding the 'reality' of any event seems beside the point.

11 'You Are There', season 6, episode 125, directed by John Laing, aired 5 February 2001.

12 'And Now For A Word', season 2, episode 15, directed by Mario DiLeo, aired 3 May 1995.

13 'Spirit of America', season 2, episode 16, directed by Michael Schultz, aired 22 November 1997.

14 Episode 151, directed by Michael W. Watkins, first aired 20 February 2000.

15 This discussion is intended to add to that provided in Roscoe and Hight, 2001: 134–8.

16 Episode 70, directed by Thomas Schlamme, broadcast 25 September 1997.

17 Episode 518, directed by Alex Graves, aired 31 March 2004.

18 The archival footage and home movies are presented within a thick black border, reinforcing a sense of these events being removed from the chaotic footage of the present day.

19 Ironically, this Belgian student film was developed as a parody of a local (Belgian) docusoap series.

6

Comedic traditions: satire, sitcom and comedy vérité

The third set of generic traditions within televisual space that frame, support and intersect with mockumentary discourse is those associated with comedy. Mockumentary operates freely within televisual space in part because of the variety of ways in which comedic forms themselves draw upon and constitute key layers to a spectrum of media content which emphasises reflexivity and intertextuality. A broad generalisation is that specific instances of parody and satire necessarily take their cues from other media forms and the wider cultural discourses of their time. There are strains of television comedy which have generated increasingly layered forms of intertextual references, since the early 1990s, to the wider discourses of televisual space itself. Key 1990s sitcoms relied heavily on layered forms of intertextual referencing (*The Simpsons*) or developed their comedic potency through playful subversion of core expectations associated with the sitcom genre itself (*Seinfeld*). As noted previously, televisual space is partly characterised by the normalisation of some forms of reflexivity, although more typically through stylistic rather than politically reflexive elements within televisual texts. This is especially the case with such staple forms of programming as television advertising, which offers an endless stream of cultural riffs, frequently incorporating elements of mockumentary discourse (such as intertextual references to non-fiction related forms).

Within such broad generalisations, however, it is difficult to offer definitive statements about the nature and quality of television humour, as so much of it is couched almost exclusively within the social and cultural discourses of a particular national context. American television draws from the cultural norms, stereotypes and generic concerns that are assumed to be most relevant to local audiences, just as European, Japanese or Indian television humour is flavoured with cultural references that can often be obscure for audiences of other localities. Within this complexity of electronic culture, there are some common patterns, in part because successful forms and genres tend to be either broadcast or replicated outside of their immediate national context.

The foci of discussion here are especially British and American television satire since the 1960s, and innovations within the sitcom genre that began to become dominant in the 1990s. These developments are positioned within the terrain of television comedy in ways that highlight their relevance to mockumentary discourse. Although not intended to offer a genealogy, this chapter does look to suggest the broader role which television has played in the emergence of mockumentary discourse itself, often providing templates which filmmakers have appropriated and expanded upon to create cinematic mockumentary.

In terms of television satire, the three key reference points are the British series *Monty Python's Flying Circus*, the American *Saturday Night Live* (1975–) and North American *SCTV* (1976–81). Episodic and highly segmented sketch-based series, these all tended to employ non-fictional referencing as significant elements of their overall discourses. Collectively they have been important in the gestation of mockumentary discourse by helping to establish and popularise techniques for the appropriation of non-fiction that were later taken up by producers of television and cinematic mockumentary. All three of these series are also historically significant as exemplars of the use of satiric and parodic forms which draw directly upon the complexity of symbolic forms within televisual space. Within this broad frame, however, each series was shaped by quite distinct production and institutional contexts, and was inevitably marked by the different personalities and talents of its key personnel.

Monty Python's Flying Circus

Monty Python's Flying Circus (*MPFC*) has perhaps the highest global profile of these three series. It was centred on the talents of five Britons (John Cleese, Michael Palin, Terry Jones, Graham Chapman, Eric Idle) and one American (Terry Gilliam). Their stated influences included the Marx brothers, vaudeville and, especially, Spike Milligan, one of the members of the ground-breaking radio programme *The Goon Show* (1951–60), which provided the template for *MPFC*'s sense of unpredictability and love of language (Landy, 2005: 33–4). Milligan himself successfully made the transition from *The Goons* to television and developed *A Show Called Fred* (1956) and other series marked by a distinctively surrealist absurdist approach to humour. *MPFC*, however, also clearly built upon forms of British satire in the 1960s that flourished within theatre, print and eventually television, most obviously with the production of the weekly satirical series *That Was The Week That Was* (1964–65).[1]

As has been typical of the British model of television production, the core ensemble of *MPFC* wrote their own material and had full creative control (within the usual dictates of institutional censorship). They relied on personal chemistry and an interplay between their eclectic comedic talents, including a form of internal peer review before something was deemed worthy of the broadcast. All from university backgrounds, with training in university revues, the core members also completed a variety of internships within the British television broadcasting system, developing as writers and performers through programmes such as *The Frost Report* (1966–67), *Do Not Adjust Your Set* (1967–69), *The Complete and Utter History of Britain* (1969) and *At Last the 1948 Show* (1967). These experiences not only gave them insight into the possibilities of television, but crucially also left them with an enduring frustration with institutional forms.

MPFC as a series developed a distinctively playful approach toward comedy, drawing from a wide range of allusions to British culture, including for the first time television forms as a target for parody. Many of its sketches drew from the broad range of established television genres, such as news, reporting, interviews, game shows, sitcoms, children's shows, plays and films (Landy, 2005: 21), but put them together in unexpected ways.

> The style of the *Flying Circus* and its choice of subjects for sketches revealed the potential of television to experiment with programming through format, character, visual image, and sound, outrageously exploiting the temporal nature of television through an appearance of immediacy, liveness, and experimentation with continuity as well as segmentation. (Landy, 2005: 2)

Taking for granted both their audience's familiarity with television codes and conventions and their readiness to see these institutional forms subverted, the series quickly began to exhibit a strong self-reflexive quality, partly through having its own sketches leak into one another, often with characters interrupting and commenting upon a previous sketch. Instead of structured sketches, leading to an ultimate punch-line, many sketches ended abruptly or without resolution. The result was a programme with a stream-of-consciousness feel, a format designed to break out of the constraints of the familiar television formulas, evolving into 'free-association (il)logic' (Sterritt and Rhodes, 2001: 19) and effectively, argues Lewisohn, a new television genre (Lewisohn, 2003: 527).

A primary comedic technique used was to replicate sober discourses of authority, then position them in such a way as to reveal their absurdity. *MPFC* was here able to tap into key aspects of the wider *zeitgeist* of the 1960s, particularly the beginnings of the counterculture and its distrust of and tension with institutional forms of authority (Neale and Krutnik, 1990: 205–7). A key target for the series was the British Broadcasting Corporation (BBC), and the wider culture of public service television that assumed a nation-building role for itself. The series used the visual and aural style of the BBC model of factual discourse, parodying that model in order to undermine the cultural assumptions behind its acceptance with British audiences. Often a BBC-styled presenter (in person or voice-over) attempted to interview completely absurd characters, in effect creating humour out of the collision between the rigidly rational stance adopted by the presenter and the lunacy of the people and activities which the (invariably male) interviewer was attempting to cover. These formats might include presenters sitting at desks in the middle of a field, vox-pop interviews with people 'in the street', or simulations of black and white Pathé Gazette news-reels. Another common comedic device was for authority figures (such as military officers, police, judges, conservative politicians, BBC news announcers and even God) to suddenly start spouting complete nonsense; or experts who would offer perfectly rational-sounding explanations for absurd behaviour or phenomena.

The result was revealing of the construction of conventional forms of presentation, including those of non-fiction. There is a degree of ambivalence here, however, as despite the irreverence and sense of subversion toward such forms, *MPFC* still usefully employed these to enhance its own sense of anarchy. The series was arguably more parodic than satiric toward television non-fiction. One example can serve as illustration: the 'Hell's Grannies' sketch from the first season.[2] The story opens with a BBC announcer (Eric Idle) soberly intoning the outlines of an issue facing an English city, over shots of an English working-class neighbourhood: 'This is a frightened city. Over these houses, over these streets hangs a pall of fear. Fear of a new kind of violence which is terrorizing the city.' The footage cuts to a shot of youths in leather jackets walking in a park, and who are suddenly attacked by a group of elderly woman armed with handbags. The narration continues: 'Yes, gangs of old ladies attacking defenceless, fit young men.' Video footage follows of the delinquent grannies terrorising locals, overlapped with sound-bites from vox-pop with frightened locals. The clip, having started on an absurd premise, keeps within a sober mode, moving between interviews with locals, before starting to lose its structure. Idle attempts to offer a sociological explanation for the granny gangs (Figure 7), then falls through a manhole cover removed by

7. Eric Idle offers a sociological explanation for delinquent grandmothers in a parody of BBC reporting from *Monty Python's Flying Circus* (1969–74).

the grannies, who race to close the hole again, cackling with glee. The grannies race in and out of a shop on motorbikes, and as they escape we see a shot of the backs of their leather jackets with their gang patch 'Hell's Grannies'. The sketch then begins to abandon its coherence, moving to cover the town's 'baby-snatchers' (babies who snatch adults) and 'vicious gangs' of keep-left signs, before being interrupted by an officer who complains that things are just getting silly. The sketch is archetypal *Monty Python*, using a simplistic, formulaic representation of BBC reporting to provide a basic structure before disintegrating into a kind of televisual free association.

MPFC eventually achieved cult status in North America with the compilation film *And Now For Something Completely Different* (1971) and the broadcast of the series on CBC in Canada in 1970, although *MPFC* was not shown on American television until 1974 (Lewisohn, 2003: 676). By this stage the British ensemble had become exhausted with writing and performing the series and began to move on to cinematic and individual projects. Although none of the television writers and producers who professed to be influenced by *Monty Python* sought to replicate its free-flowing collage of the rational and the absurd, there are any number of subsequent series which also sought to develop modes of parodic intertextuality toward television discourses. Among the key North American examples are *SCTV* and *Saturday Night Live*.

SCTV and SNL

Both *SCTV* and *Saturday Night Live* (or *SNL*) gathered together a generation of comic talent who emerged during the early 1970s and introduced it to mainstream television audiences. The two series were produced in parallel during the later 1970s and each focused on sketches which parodied familiar tropes of popular culture, especially the codes and conventions of local television, films and music. *SCTV* never quite achieved the same status or popularity within North America as *SNL*, and was not able to retain its creativity after an exodus of talent that followed its initial success. *SNL*, meanwhile, became something of an American comedic institution, continually re-energising itself with new intakes of fresh comedic talent who tended to see the programme as a stepping stone to a broader comedic career. The two series' similarities and differences are instructive in suggesting the manner in which television productions are decisively shaped by the tenuous mixture of the creative potential of their personnel, the constraints of institutional production practices and an effort to appeal to the discourses of an assumed national audience.

SCTV (originally titled *Second City Television*) was produced over an 8-year period, was largely based in Toronto and claimed to be the first series based entirely on satirising the medium of television itself. The core premise of the programme was that it was the output of a local television station, struggling to survive financially and with a mediocre production cast and crew. Regulars in the ensemble cast included Harold Ramis, John Candy, Joe Flaherty, Eugene Levy, Catharine O'Hara, Martin Short, Andrea Martin and Rick Moranis (a number of whom were eventually recruited into *SNL*).[3] Many *SCTV* segments masqueraded as programmes broadcast by the station, interspersed with behind-the-scenes sequences showing the chaotic nature of its organisation. They drew from the full range of recognisable television formats, including parodies of gameshows, cooking shows, 'live' events, talk shows and a variety of other non-fiction formats such as news bulletins, current affairs and information segments, as well as advertising. The ensemble cast developed and refined a variety of characters who reappeared over the episodes, including not only amateurish on-screen presenters, but producers and even the fictional head of the SCTV Television Network (Guy Caballero played by Flaherty).

In direct contrast to *SNL*, the *SCTV* programmes were carefully scripted, produced and filmed over a number of weeks, providing the completed programmes not only with a consistency in quality but a comparatively greater sense of finesse and control in their comedic structure and timing. *Saturday Night Live*, however, was written in the week before it was performed and drew upon the sense of uncertainty and energy associated with a live event. Despite a shared approach toward the playful appropriation of televisual forms, then, each programme drew from quite different traditions of comedic performance, and the potential of television to frame and showcase those performances. *SNL* was inevitably more uneven from week to week than *SCTV*, but it was nevertheless also capable of bursts of sheer originality and even brilliance that tended to overshadow its lesser moments for its core audience. Initially developed by Canadian Lorne Michaels, a self-confessed fan of *MPFC* who was looking to bring live comedy back to American prime-time television, the programme involved an ever-evolving group of regular players, beginning with key members Chevy Chase, John Belushi, Dan Aykroyd, Laraine Newman, Gilda Radner and Garrett Morris and later including other comic talents such as Bill Murray. As Hall notes, *SNL* has tended toward a consistent structure for its weekly broadcasts since the 1970s.

> Unusually for such a groundbreaking show, *Saturday Night Live* (or *Saturday Night* as it was briefly know when it came on air in 1975) has stuck to a tried and tested formula, lasting ninety minutes, relying on a resident cast, guest host and musical guest, and keeping to a fairly fixed running order mixing gags, routines, spoof commercials, sketches, celebrity impressions, film or TV parodies and music. (Hall, 2006: 207)

Apart from its contribution to traditions of television satire based on the appropriation of television genres and formats, *SNL* serves as a key reference point in the development of television mockumentary through its staple sketch segment titled 'Weekend Update' (WU), a pioneer in television news parody.[4] Initiated in the series' first season with Chevy Chase as its anchor (with the regular catchphrase 'I'm Chevy Chase and you're not'), WU lasted from 5 to 10 minutes and generally tended to present absurd fictional news items using the sober modes of television news presentation (Figure 8). Drawing from the same sense of irreverence as the mock BBC bulletins from *MPFC*, 'Weekend Update' mocked celebrities and other public figures, including politicians (most notably President Gerald Ford, helping to popularise an impression of Ford as a bumbling idiot).

Chase's initial reign helped to establish the segment's approach. Archival photos were paired with incongruous stories, or completely reframed within an absurd narrative, or there might be 'live' feeds to reporter Laraine Newman on location to play with ideas of access to the tentative, speculative nature of information available through breaking new stories. An 'editorial reply' item within the bulletin often featured a performer who spoke while Chase made faces behind their back, including regular Gilda Radner as an elderly viewer named Emily Litella, whose statements are based on her mishearing an issue (for example, 'eagle rights amendment', rather than 'equal rights amendments'). Another regular item

8. Chevy Chase playing anchorperson in the influential fake news segment 'Weekend Update' from the first season of *Saturday Night Live* (1975–).

offered a repeat of the top stories 'for those hard of hearing', with Garret Morris appearing in an iris over Chase's shoulder, shouting out the headlines as Chase reads them. According to Reincheld, the production of the segment was a last-minute affair, designed to be as topical as possible and inadvertently mimicking the production of news itself (Reincheld, 2006: 193).

Despite variations in the consistency of the segment over the years, and the different qualities provided by the lineage of performers playing as anchors, creator Lorne Michaels has argued that it has become increasingly relevant as a response to trends towards an entertainment-dominated agenda within the actual news (Reincheld, 2006: 196). The segment is widely acknowledged as an early template for such successful news satires as *The Daily Show* (discussed in the following chapter).

There are many one-off mockumentary comedy programmes that draw from the satiric and parodic traditions partly established by series such as *MPFC*, *SNL* and *SCTV*. Many of these have emerged within British broadcasting and tend to use mockumentary discourse simply as a novelty frame allowing the targeting of a number of other cultural references. The arrival of Channel 4 in 1982, intended to provide something of an alternative to the mainstream public service agenda of the BBC and ITV, proved to be crucial, as it provided space for the latest emerging generation of comedic talent.

Harry Enfield, for example, surfaced first on Channel 4 and over the course of a long television career developed a number of one-off mockumentaries, taking characters developed on his late 1980s and early 1990s sketch-based series and positioning these within more extended narratives, particularly with long-time collaborators Charlie Higson and Paul Whitehouse. All of Enfield's mockumentaries rely on a formulaic construction of expositional mode, and tend to take this documentary mode simply as a given. *Norbert Smith: A Life* (1989)[5] functions almost as an industry in-joke, with *The South Bank Show* (1978–) host Melvyn Bragg parodying his own arts-programme interviewing style as he presents the life and career of the fictional 'Sir Norbert Smith' (played by Enfield). Smith is presented as a distinguished British actor from the same generation as other knighted luminaries such as John Gielgud and Ralph Richardson, and the programme effectively operates as one long raspberry to this older generation of actors. Following Smith's biography allows the programme to present clips from his fictional theatrical, television and film career, in the process targeting iconic moments from British entertainment history.

Similarly, *Smashey and Nicey: The End of an Era* (1995)[6] parodies commercial radio disc jockeys, with Enfield and Whitehouse as the title characters, two creatively and morally bankrupt radio personalities at the end of their careers and struggling to maintain their credibility. It is loosely based on the career of real-life DJs such as Tony Blackburn and Alan Freeman, who play along with the parody by briefly appearing as themselves. *Normal Ormal: A Very Political Turtle* (1998)[7] presents the political career of the fictional Ormal (Enfield) as a means to target a variety of real-life Conservative political figures and their personal failings during the reign of Prime Minister Margaret Thatcher. Ormal's biography is couched within a historical narrative of British politics from the previous 30 years that would be immediately familiar to local audiences (Lewisohn, 2003: 261).

Thatcher's political domination also proved an inspiration for the satirical output of the ensemble group The Comic Strip, which operated under the title *The Comic Strip Presents . . .* (1982–2005) to produce a series of 39 programmes for Channel 4. Founded by co-writers of Peter Richardson and Pete Richens, the group's core performers also included Robbie Coltrane, Adrian Edmonson, Dawn French, Rik Mayal, Nigel Planer, Jennifer Saunders and Alexei Sayle, with others drafted in over the years. The Richardson-led collective served as the television internship for all of its core players, who subsequently went on to develop individual television comedic careers as writers, actors and director, some with influential television series (such as *The Young Ones* (1982–84), *French and Saunders* (1987–)), while continuing to collaborate under the Comic Strip banner. Eschewing the conventional production template development of a comedy series with a stable ensemble of characters, the *Comic Strip Presents . . .* reinvented themselves for each programme, producing a series of films which referenced an electric range of genres and cinematic styles. Each episode played with audience's expectations of familiar genres and styles such as neo-realism, film noir, children's programmes, gangster films, science-fiction, spaghetti westerns and even Hollywood blockbusters, with varying results but demonstrating increasingly cinematic ambition and professionalism. Three of these short films were mockumentaries: *Bad News Tour* (1983) and its later sequel *More Bad News* (1988),[8] and the disappointing *Eddie Monsoon: A Life?* (1984).[9]

The *Bad News* episodes cover the career of an inept and talentless heavy metal band, covering similar territory to *This is Spinal Tap* (but with the first episode predating that film by a few months). The first episode centres on tensions between the strife-ridden amateur band and a professional BBC-style documentary crew who obviously hold them in little regard, while the second revisits the band, with a documentary crew prompting them to re-form (despite open loathing between key creative members) by offering them a record contract and an appearance at the real heavy metal rock festival 'Monsters of Rock', held at Castle Donington, Leicestershire. Naturally, both narratives result in disaster for the band, with the second episode finding the musicians in hospital after being beaten up by outraged heavy metal fans. Both are layered texts incorporating some superbly crafted reflexive moments which target the constructions of television rockumentaries, and in these terms they tend to occasionally surpass the rockumentary parody of *Spinal Tap* itself.

The second television comedic tradition which serves as a key reference point for mockumentary discourse is a staple of television schedules: the sitcom genre.

The traditions of sitcom

As discussed in chapter 3, at the core of television programme is narrative structures that operate within a continuum between series and serials. At the more episodic end of this continuum are genres such as sitcoms (situation comedies), which for much of their history have tended to offer endless variations within a broadly formulaic approach to programme narrative. Mills notes the comparative neglect of academic research on sitcoms (Mills, 2005: 19), which he suggest is a reflection of both the undervaluing of television in general within academia and the wider lack of critical appreciation of the complexity and significance of comedy itself. The chapters which follow deal with many of the more interesting and more complex examples of mockumentary, those which develop characters across the narrative arcs of entire series and often intersect with the core conventions of sitcoms. Many of the exemplars of mockumentary series draw from and adapt long-established aspects of the genre and are often grouped with other widely discussed series which brought innovations to sitcom conventions dating from the late 1990s. The intention here is to outline these patterns within sitcom more generally, in order to frame the more specific analyses of comedic mockumentary series which follow in later chapters.

The conventional formula for sitcoms has been more or less stable over the decades since the beginnings of television as a mass medium, when the genre solidified its role as a staple of television programming. Certainly, sitcoms have proved valuable terrain for producers, both instantly recognisable to audiences and seemingly offering infinite variation within established patterns. They tend to be half-hour series, typically performed on a brightly lit sound stage, either before a live audience or with a laugh track added in post-production (or with both). Cameras tend to be quite static, with a focus instead on shifting within a typical three-camera set-up in order to capture dialogue and action in long and mid-shot, and occasional close-ups for specific reaction shots. Other familiar patterns include reliance on an ensemble cast, within a consistent situation, performing a core of recurring characters. These characters are often stereotypes who are not intended to develop over the course of a series but instead simply revert to their core characteristics at the beginning of each episode. An ensemble cast will form a family or its surrogate, even when based in workplaces or public spaces. Most sitcom episodes rely on self-contained narratives, frequently a primary and a secondary narrative that often (but not always) coalesce into one, with an emphasis on closure at the end of each episode. All of these traits reveal the origins of sitcom, initially in musical theatre and then in radio comedy. And all are marked by an overriding assumption that its audiences are domestic and typically middle class (Mills, 2005: 40).

Within such generic formulas, however, there have been considerable variations between sitcoms. Even in early exemplar sitcoms, such as the American *I Love Lucy* (1951–57) or the British *Hancock's Half Hour* (1956–60), there were obvious differences based on the comedic talent being showcased, and specific types of comedic performance based on either verbal or physical skills. In the decades since the 1950s so-called Golden Age of television, sitcoms have gradually broadened the possibilities for characters and subject matter, in the process mainstreaming representations of ethnicity (*The Cosby Show* (1984–92)), class (*Roseanne* (1988–97)) and sexuality (*Ellen* (1994–98)) that were unthinkable in television's early years. Despite these changes, sitcoms tend overall to be a conservative form, in the sense that they will follow social trends rather than operating as a site for discourses that may challenge their audiences.

Mills notes the centrality of forms of performance as a marker for sitcom, which tends to highlight and foreground performance styles in ways that other television genres do not. Sitcom performances are self-conscious, and never intended to be bound by the constraints of realism.

> Comedy is often little more than a very obvious set of quotation marks, with performances which are not coded as realistic and which don't contribute towards the psychological realism of the character; instead such acting displays its purpose – to make you laugh – while simultaneously offering those gestures as comic within themselves. (Mills, 2005: 78)

Sitcom characters tend to be constructed through repeated verbal or physical mannerisms, themselves clearly referenced to established forms of comedic acting (Mills, 2005: 80) such as slapstick or more verbal-centred comedy. Different characters within a sitcom may rely on different kinds of performance, or move between performance styles depending on the particular context – there is often not a need for consistency here in the same way that is required for a dramatic series. Many sitcoms, in fact, are designed around specific comedic characters that are already well honed through live performance. Especially in the American tradition of sitcoms, a series may be constructed around a proven comic persona, with the other characters intended more as supporting players, to help showcase the central character's performance style.

The types of pleasures which specific groups of viewers gain from a comedic performance are related to their experience and appreciation of different forms of humour, which includes their recognition of the comic intent of a particular text (its preferred reading), together with the wider knowledge of past episodes and previous series that it may directly or indirectly refer to. A sitcom episode may rely on cues to narrative or character points that were established by previous episodes, or it may engage and play with our wider expectations of specific types of performance that we have seen in other forms of comedy. All of these forms of pleasure are related to the types of cultural knowledge that television producers assume of their audience.

> To understand pleasure, then, is to attempt to make sense of a broad range of complex phenomena, which can be personal and social, momentary and enduring, progressive and reactionary, physical and mental. The precise reasons why audiences seek out comedy, and gain pleasure from it, are inadequately understood. To merely say 'because it is funny' not only ignores a variety of other possibilities, but also downplays the complexity of funniness itself. (Mills, 2005: 142)

The different forms of comedic pleasures favoured by specific cultures are an important factor in accounting for differences in the flavour of sitcom texts from nation to nation. There are other factors, however, and once again the differences between American and British sitcom traditions are instructive of various social, cultural, economic and institutional factors in shaping patterns within the production and reception of television.

There are important differences in the nature of sitcoms purely as products of industrial practices. Sitcoms have never played such a central role within television programming within the British market that they have within the United States; in Britain it is the soap opera which has traditionally occupied this dominant position (Mills, 2005: 5). This is not necessarily because of cultural factors (that is, that Americans are funnier, or like to laugh more), but can be traced to the historical development of television within each nation. For a variety of reasons, American dramatic television did not attract the same level of resources in its early years and did not become cemented as staple domestic entertainment in the same way that occurred in British broadcasting.

As a core focus of the American television industry, sitcoms developed production practices that are often markedly different from those across the Atlantic. The British model is for a single writer to retain some degree of creative control, serving as the central performer on a programme and sometimes also as producer. In the United States it is more typically a producer who initiates a production, selecting other creative personnel, including writers, who are themselves more likely to be operating within teams. If a highly collaborative and industrial product such as television can be seen as sustaining auteurs, then in the British model they will often be the writer, while in the American model they will more likely be serving as executive producer.

These differences inevitably mark other aspects of the production practice. British sitcom incorporates highly idiosyncratic forms of performance, but with a consistency derived from the demands of its core writer(s). A 'Britcom', if it reaches broadcast, may find a particular niche within the mainstream schedule. In comparison, American sitcoms tend to be more definitively designed for a mass prime-time audience. They are generally the product of a much faster production model, having been written, rehearsed and recorded in the week before their broadcast (Mills, 2005: 56), thus retaining the power to be topical when needed. These traditions, however, do not necessarily hold true in the two decades since 1990, as television production itself has broadened across a wider spectrum of networks, with the emergence, for example, of HBO in the United States, BBC3 in Britain, as well as more independent sources of production.

Each model is also inevitably marked by its industry's wider expectations of the comedic possibilities which will be tolerated by

its assumed audience(s), shaped most crucially by previous successful examples of the genre. It is difficult to generalise here, as there
are always exceptions to any attempt at a categorical statement on
the nature of comedy within a national context. But it is notable
that British sitcoms have allowed space for a comparatively rich
vein of social (and occasionally political) satire, while American
sitcoms focus their energies more on the interpersonal and the
familial. While British sitcoms can laugh at differences in class,
American comedy has tended to obscure class issues altogether.

These differences help to explain the lack of a trade in sitcom
formats that is as strong as that for other television genres. It
has always been a source of frustration for television executives on
both sides of the Atlantic that sitcoms have not proved ame-
nable to translation to a more localised production (the British
and American versions of the mockumentary *The Office*, discussed
in chapter 9, are a relatively rare example of successful sitcom
transplantation).

Comedy vérité's refashioning of sitcom: *The Larry Sanders Show* and *Curb Your Enthusiasm*

Despite the relative stability of sitcom as a genre, innovations have
begun to transform key parts of its codes and conventions, particularly since the 1990s. Mills uses the notion of 'comedy vérité' to
discuss a group of innovative sitcoms that attempt to work against
the constraints of the genre and look to reinvigorate sitcom, particularly through experiments with new aesthetics, and also through
playing with other key aspects of the genre. Central to comedy
vérité texts is the adoption of a vérité style for comedic purposes,
a distinct break from traditions of situation comedy performed on
a sound stage in front of a live audience. In many cases this also
means abandoning a laugh track altogether, and consequently a
movement away from any pretence toward 'liveness' in performance. Mills notes that not all sitcoms have had laugh tracks –
M.A.S.H. for example did not consistently use one – however, this
popularising of a more 'natural' soundtrack still marks a significant
moment in sitcom history (Mills, 2005: 50–1).

> Comedy vérité not only represents the logical conclusion to contem-
> porary developments in television forms, whether factual or fictional;

it also suggests that the sitcom, a form forever maligned for its stability, offers a site for subtle, yet powerful, critiques of television media.
(Mills, 2004: 78)

While Mills never uses the term 'mockumentary', among the many
examples he discusses are British mockumentary series such as the
fake news programmes *The Day Today* (1994) and *Brass Eye*
(1997–2001), mock reality programmes *People Like Us* (1999–2001)
and *Human Remains*, and comedic video diary *Marion and Geoff*
(2002–3). The category of 'comedy vérité' clearly overlaps with that
of mockumentary series, as it is broad enough to apply to any
number of television comedy series that do not qualify as mockumentaries, but in which production practices are still marked by
hand-held camera work, naturalistic sound and lighting and the
absence of laugh tracks, and that escape the conventional stage-
bound sitcom. Comedy vérité texts, then, should instead be seen as
providing wider support for mockumentary experimentation by
naturalising the use of vérité aesthetics in relation to sitcoms.

This shift in the genre has been widely commented upon within
television criticism, although there is no clear consensus on the use
of terminology (with many critics mistakenly calling anything with
a hand-held camera a mockumentary). Hall refers to the wider
trend as 'reality comedy' (Hall, 2006: 153), suggesting that the
number of programmes generated in Britain using the format, or
close to it, suggests that this has almost become the mainstream.
The adoption of a vérité style has implications for other aspects of
a programme, such as an effort to include more muted forms of film
acting rather than the more expressive television acting, as well as
a blurring of the distinction between workplace comedy, single
comedy and family comedy (Ostrow, 2004a).

As with dramatic vérité (see chapter 5), there are key reference
points for the emergence of comedy vérité as a significant pattern
within televisual space. The most important of these is the HBO
series *The Larry Sanders Show* (1992–98), which covered the
behind-the-scenes production and broadcast of a talk show by
Larry Sanders (Garry Shandling), the fictional king of American
talk shows. Shandling was responsible for the innovative *It's Garry
Shandling's Show* (1986–90), which was nominally a sitcom but
could more properly be termed a reflexive comedy: the sitcom
format was here a loosely adhered to premise, with characters

repeatedly breaking the fourth wall to talk to the studio audience or commenting on the programme while they were in it. On the *Larry Sanders Show* Shandling played Sanders as a complex and infuriating character: self-absorbed but lacking in confidence, highly intelligent but perpetually shallow, sneering of his colleagues and rivals in private but ingratiating in person (Lewisohn, 2003: 455). Each episode tended to centre on personal and professional tensions surrounding the nightly broadcast of the Sanders Show, with comedic situations typically generated by the complex and dysfunctional relationships between the core players on the talk show's production. Sanders' on-air sidekick Hank Kingsley (Jeffrey Tambor) played a more extreme version of Sanders himself, continually dropping a façade of confidence to reveal a shallow and deeply paranoid man more desperate to retain his television career than his dignity. Kingsley was invariably at the centre of scenes involving cringing embarrassment and humiliation. Rounding out the core trio of the cast was talk show producer Artie (Rip Torn), a ruthless professional who protected Sanders' illusions and carried out his whims.

The Larry Sanders Show oscillated back and forth between the use of hand-held video cameras for behind-the-scenes sequences and a close pastiche of a late-night American show. Episodes typically featured cameos from actual American celebrities, each playing with their public personas by 'revealing' character flaws, petty jealousies and rivalries in behind-the-scenes sequences which directly contrasted with their familiar performances on Sanders' talk show (an immediately classic storyline had David Duchovny apparently becoming attracted to Sanders, to his extreme discomfort). With no laugh track, and muted and realistic performances by the entire cast, the result was a richly layered, biting satire on the American culture industries, suggesting that subtle brutality, manipulation, superficiality and performance, personal humiliation and self-delusion are central to everyone's survival in American film and television production.

A number of comedy vérité series have sought to tread the same path as the *Larry Sanders Show*, contrasting the production of a television programme with revealing behind-the-scenes dramas. The Australian series *Frontline* (1994–97) used similar techniques to present a satire of television news production. Hand-held video cameras provided slightly grainy footage for the behind-the-scenes sequences, contrasting with the higher production values of the mock news bulletins produced by the cast. The series was directly inspired by *This is Spinal Tap* (Giles, 2002: 121) and focused on the battle for ratings between the actual Australian current affairs programmes *A Current Affair* (1971–) and *Real Life* (1992–94). It represented the television news-gathering process as hopelessly compromised by the commercial ethos and questionable ethics of tabloid journalism, characterised by the abandonment of anything but a lip service to public service ideals. Within this frame some characters remained sympathetic as they struggled to survive within the hostile environment of television news, despite being willing collaborators in the manipulation of news events into dramatic and spectacular narratives to attract greater audiences than their rivals.

Another key reference point in comedy vérité is *Curb Your Enthusiasm* (2000–), an HBO sitcom with no laugh track which is filmed on location in Los Angeles using hand-held cameras. The series is a good illustration of the differences between mockumentary and comedy vérité, as the series was inspired by a 1-hour mockumentary special titled *Larry David: Curb Your Enthusiasm* (1999).[10] This original mockumentary was structured as the work of a documentary crew, following Larry David around in the lead-up to an HBO stand-up comedy special (typically, David pulls out at the last moment, unable to deal with the pressure). We see David preparing for his performance, engaged in meetings with television producers who have completely different ideas from David over how he should be promoted and even perform, and in encounters with people in his everyday life. These scenes are interspersed with occasional 'interviews' with celebrities who comment on David's personality. David's comic persona is self-centred and desperate to avoid conflict or any socially awkward situations, but nonetheless continually creates explosive situations because of simple misunderstandings and miscommunications that inevitably escalate. In the mockumentary special, David is openly uneasy with the presence of the camera crew, continually makes sarcastic jokes to other characters at their expense and often looks directly into the camera lens (violating the sense of pure observation that the crew is aiming for).

In the half-hour series which followed, hand-held cameras are again used, but without the suggestion that David is the subject of an actual documentary. Instead, a comedy vérité style is used to play off the edgy quality to David's comic persona and enhance the cringe quality at the heart of the situations he tends to create. Apparently loosely inspired by events in David's own life, the series moves away from the structured feel of a conventional sitcom by providing naturalistic performances and narratives centred on the minutiae of everyday life (in a sense building from the 'show about nothing' premise of the brilliant sitcom *Seinfeld*, which David co-created).[11] Each of the episodes draws from a 5- to 7-page outline that David writes, with dialogue improvised for specific scenes within that outline (Marin, 2000). Regular cameos by fellow comedians playing 'themselves' add to the sense of realism the show references, with some guests kept in the dark about key plot points so as to retain a sense of spontaneity. The wealth of improvised takes are then distilled and crafted into a coherent episode through post-production. As with the *Larry Sanders Show*, the result is a sense of capturing unfolding situations, with nuances typical of real relationships rather than carefully scripted punch lines involving stereotypical characters.

The vérité style has become commonplace within sitcom globally, allowing for greater experimentation with locations and forms of comedic performance. A list of other key vérité sitcoms could include the Britcom *The Royle Family* (1998–2000), which drew heavily from the naturalistic approach of British soap opera but did not rely on a hand-held camera, and the docusoap-inspired American cult series *Arrested Development* (discussed in the next chapter), which is commonly mistakenly labelled a mockumentary. The series *Significant Others* (2004) was a short-lived vérité sitcom that focused on a number of dysfunctional couples. Identifying characters with captions, the series also had the couples directly address the camera in therapy sessions, leaving it ambiguous whether the characters themselves or just the cast were being filmed. The George Clooney and Steven Soderburgh-produced *Unscripted* (2005) was a vérité sitcom covering the lives of a number of young Hollywood actors, playing 'themselves', who were attempting to start their careers. Frank Langella played Goddard Fulton, a somewhat creepy acting coach whose ruminations on the nature of acting provided an overall narration, while local productions (such as *ER*) provided cameo locations and realistic backdrop to the young actors' ambitions.

Flirting with mockumentary discourse:
sporadic use within series

Other sitcoms have experimented more explicitly with mockumentary discourse as an integral part of their approach. In its first season the New York-based sitcom *Sex and the City* (1998–2004) used mock interviews and vox-pop as a means of presenting a variety of attitudes around each episode's take on gender issues, relations and etiquette. The four key members of the cast were captioned with their characters' names, while more occasional characters are more simply identified are 'Toxic Bachelor', 'Hopeless Romantic' and the like to suggest their social standing or defining character trait. This device allowed lead character Carrie Bradshaw (Sarah Jessica Parker), a newspaper columnist, to serve as narrator through using her own interviews as a form of direct address to the audience. These interviews were gradually dropped over the first season, in favour of a voice-over narration that implied Bradshaw was reading aloud her weekly column. The vox-pop from peripheral characters was also dropped, and those with the other lead characters in turn were substituted by lengthier group conversations where they explained their attitudes directly to each other.

The Australian sitcom *Kath and Kim* (2002–) was initially modelled closely on replicating a docusoap, with the lead actors Gina Riley and Jane Turner (playing a mother-and-daughter odd couple) 'interviewed' and their words used as voice-over narration and counterpoint to hand-held footage (the actual interviews were included in a DVD release). The series appeared to be directly parodying the early 1992 BBC docusoap *Sylvania Waters*, filmed in Australia, and co-creator Turner has described the series as a 'sort of reality television situation comedy' (cited in Turnbull, 2004: 102). The style created humour partly through revealing the contradictions between what characters said and what was captured by the cameras. As the series progressed, however, the device was applied inconsistently, with voice-overs becoming more stream-of-consciousness than interview-based and more directly triggered by specific on-screen action. Eventually the voice-overs became simply the overheard thoughts of the characters. What remained of the docusoap aesthetic was a roving hand-held camera, never acknowledged by the cast. *Kath and Kim*, then, moved from mockumentary mode to a more obviously comedy vérité approach.

Other sitcoms have incorporated one-off episodes partially using mockumentary discourse (these serve as the comedic versions of Caldwell's docu-stunts, discussed in the previous chapter). The sitcom *My Name is Earl* (2005–), featuring Jason Lee as the title character seeking karmic redemption from past wrong-doings, offers one example that is perhaps more docu-stunt than a sustained exercise in mockumentary. An episode entitled 'Our *Cops* Is On'[12] has a framing narrative set in a bar frequented by the regulars, who relieve their boredom by tuning in to a repeat of a 2003 *Cops* episode featuring themselves. The majority of the episode is the *Cops* parody itself, which the regulars treat as a home movie (they sing the theme song as it comes on air) and which also functions as an extended flashback sequence. Playing with the familiar *Cops* format, Earl and his friends continually react to the presence of the show's cameras, and eventually Earl steals a police car with a *Cops* cameraman in the back seat begging for his life.[13]

Some one-off comedic mockumentary episodes do not attempt to generate the same kind of reflexivity toward the non-fiction format which they reference. An episode of *Just Shoot Me* (1997–2003) titled 'A&E Biography: Nina Van Horn'[14] simply takes an actual tabloid format (A&E channel's documentary series *Biography* (1987–)) and uses it to provide background material on a key character. Similarly a 1-hour special episode from the final series of *Ellen*, titled 'A Hollywood Tribute',[15] is constructed as a conventional expositional documentary, in this case taking the first openly gay actor/character within a sitcom back into television sitcom history. Ellen Morgan (Ellen DeGeneres) is substituted for famous characters from actual sitcom history in pastiches covering decades of iconic television comedy. In between these sketches, interviews with actual stars attest to the role that the fictional Ellen played in their own careers. The special ultimately works to position clips from the seminal 1997 *Ellen* episode in which Ellen revealed she was gay as being simply a continuation of sitcom traditions dealing with social and political issues.

Such episodes use documentary formats as a stunt vehicle, aiming for nothing more adventurous than the opportunity to invent and play with character biographies that are rarely developed within situation comedies, where, as noted above, the norm is two-dimensional characters reduced to a series of static personality traits. Other comedic mockumentary episodes offer more interesting applications of the discourse. The following two examples of one-off mockumentary episodes, while still promotional stunts in the manner described by Caldwell, are more interesting efforts to exploit their documentary appropriations to add to the overall depth of a series.

Mockumentary comedy one-off episodes (within series): M.A.S.H and The Simpsons

The long-running *M.A.S.H.*, derived from the satirical Robert Altman film of the same name, was set in an American mobile army surgical hospital unit in the Korean War. The series tended to downplay satire in favour of a mixture of mildly anarchic comedy and dramatic pathos. Intended as an anti-war series for the anti-Vietnam War generation, the sitcom was generally conventional in its approach, with an ensemble cast, episodic narrative structure (with primary and secondary narratives, resolved at the end of each episode) and familiar liberal ideology.

The series included an end-of-season episode titled 'The Interview'[16] which was one of the series' more innovative. This episode is constructed as a black and white television documentary reminiscent of the period of the Korean War, with cast members 'interviewed' by actual former war correspondent Clete Roberts. Roberts introduces the report by describing it as a 'behind-the-scenes' look at a M.A.S.H. unit, an attempt to get to know the real people behind their impressive medical performance statistics. Caldwell notes the episode's references to the (pre-vérité) approach associated with reports from the Korean War made by the pioneering American news anchor Edward R. Murrow, including the reliance on static camera set-ups, comparatively rigid compositions and strict adherence to medium shots for interviews (Caldwell, 2002: 264). Each *M.A.S.H.* character appears in the episode in an individual interview, identified by formal captions, with minimal sound effects (such as the occasional sounds of a helicopter overhead or the routine of the camp). There is an overall sense of spontaneity, however, with footage of the camp in operation captured from a hand-held film camera, and an occasional boom microphone dropping into the frame.

The largely static camera and black and white footage provide a distinct visual break from the conventional approach of the series, and the episode similarly works to 'step back' from the everyday concerns of the characters which dominate other episodes. Key members of the main cast (for unknown reasons, only male characters appear) respond to Roberts's questions about their attitudes on the Korean 'police action', their proximity to the front lines and their responses to their medical duties. Their responses are familiar to regular viewers (they accord with information we already know of them from previous episodes) but are used to suggest a humanist response to the horrors of war and a sense of shared dedication and community spirit that characterises the rest of the series. Their performances are more sober than is typical for the series (Figure 9), with leader character Hawkeye (Alan Alda) 'both more brutally honest, jaded, and pessimistic' (Caldwell, 2002: 264) than in a typical episode. Reinforcing the overall anti-war ethos of *M.A.S.H.*, there is a notable absence of patriotism or militaristic discourse, aside from the short, marginalised interview snippets from ultra-patriotic

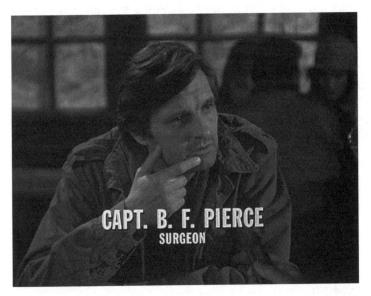

9. An uncharacteristically serious Hawkeye (Alan Alda) interviewed by Clete Roberts for his perspective of the Korean War, from the black and white mockumentary episode that ends the fourth season of *M.A.S.H.* (1972–83).

Major Frank Burns (Larry Linville), who appears absurd next to the others' testimony. The final sequence, as Roberts signs off his report, is a visual and aural montage contrasting the quietness of sound bites from the interviews with a series of jump cuts between footage of the camp in a frenzied operation to cope with a surge of incoming casualties, before ending on a freeze-frame.

As with the dramatic one-off mockumentary episodes from regular series discussed in the previous chapter, the 'television newsreel' approach inevitably establishes a sense of distance from familiar characters. Here, however, rather than the mockumentary stunt offering a competing perspective that disrupts the more familiar aspects of the series narrative arc, it works to reinforce the overall ideology of the series. In Caldwell's words:

> Nonfiction emerges, then, as a direct intervention into the world and lives of the fictional characters by offering psychological back story that deepens the intensity of the depictions. Docu-real back story gives the cynical, jaded and dark humour of the participants even more pathos. (Caldwell, 2002: 265)

A very different effect is aimed for with a mockumentary episode of the classic animated sitcom *The Simpsons*.

The Simpsons' regular complex narrative style arguably incorporates a number of mockumentary elements, including mock news programmes, educational and public relations films and occasional clip programmes presented by 'actor Troy McClure' (Phil Hartman). These are a by-product of the series' referential humour, natural extensions of the layered comedic references to its construction as a sitcom and to wider American popular culture.

> The basic premise of *The Simpsons* is right out of sitcom-land: it's a series about family life in a typically American town. As in many sitcoms, the town is an idealised, somewhat nostalgic American burg [Springfield] from a time that never existed, with just enough contemporary window-dressing to make it resonant. *The Simpsons* focuses, like many sitcoms, on the day-to-day trials and tribulations of a cohesive nuclear family with each episode introducing a new element that throws the family's staid life into disequilibrium and then following the resulting attempt to return to stasis. (Turner, 2004: 30)

Integral to the series is that it is as aware of sitcom history as its audience, and incorporates into its ethos a perpetual commentary on its own construction, including 'the show's own conventions, the standard tropes and formulas of TV shows generally, the way the entertainment and news industries function, the machinations of the mass media, the nature of TV as a medium and the society it has created in its all-pervasive image' (Turner, 2004: 419). Despite its heavily intertextual and reflexive layers, the characters themselves remain blissfully unaware of their existence as cartoons, a premise that serves as the leaping-off point for the mockumentary episode 'Behind the Laughter', from the end of the eleventh season.[17] Although the episode is not among the years of the series' creative peak,[18] it still offers an illustration of the series' richly textured constructions.

Referenced to VH1's format *Behind the Music* (1997–2004), which offered tabloid biographies of musical stars, 'Behind the Laughter' purports to chronicle the 'real life' story of the family that plays the Simpsons on television. Narrated by *Behind the Music*'s regular narrator Jim Forbes, the episode simply decides to ignore the fact that the series is animated. It instead pretends that it is in fact a conventional (filmed) construction, with actors who rely on a formulaic set of character traits in the same manner as any sitcom. The biography of the 'real' Simpsons family, then, plays on a stereotypical musical biography narrative: unexpected popular success, corruption by sudden wealth, followed by individual excesses involving sex, drugs and other vices, group disharmony and disintegration, and eventual recovery to become again the original cohort beloved by its audience.

As Turner notes, the episode is an 'exercise in sustained irony', given that the characters are animated and neither the real actors providing their voice talents nor other members of the cast and crew are known outside of the industry (Turner, 2004: 387–8). There are far too many aspects of the episode to cover in any detail here. The entire series is recast by the episode as a production written and directed by Homer Simpson himself (Dan Castellaneta), who insists that his show was intended to be more 'realistic' than other sitcoms. The wealth of secondary characters in Springfield appear as actors with various kinds of gossip to provide on the family. Classic jokes from previous episodes are reframed as accidental rather than deliberate scripting, while real controversies generated by the programme are positioned as part of the actors' lives (such as the political debate that erupted over slacker Bart Simpson

(Nancy Cartwright) becoming a role model for American youth). Other aspects of the programme are revealed as glossy fictions, contrasting with the ambitions and mediocrity of the talent of the actors themselves and their increasingly sordid private lives (Bart the actor becomes a sleazy alcoholic, while his sister Lisa writes a best-selling expose of the programme). Throughout the episode, Forbes' narration takes the usual tabloid discourse of *Behind the Music* to extremes (a typical line: 'The Simpsons started out on a wing and a prayer. But now the wing was on fire and the prayer was answered by Satan').

In comparison, another *Simpsons* mockumentary episode, 'Springfield Up' from season 18,[19] does not achieve the same density of comedic references, pacing or satiric sharpness. It references the classic *Seven Up* series of British documentaries that revisits a group of participants every 7 years. In the *Simpsons* episode, Declan Desmond (former Monty Python member Eric Idle) revisits Springfield residents every 8 years, allowing for some play with their back stories. This episode falls more clearly within the stunt agenda that Caldwell criticises in his discussion of docu-stunts.

Despite the relative sophistication of 'The Interview' and 'Behind the Laughter', these comedic mockumentary episodes also still function more as novelty pieces than as opportunities to engage with and extend the essential premise of a series itself. Nevertheless, these still demonstrate how mockumentary discourse is couched within, and supported by, a variety of comedic traditions within television space, particularly those that have generated key experimental and innovative programmes within their respective historical periods.

Notes

1 See Carpenter (2000) for a detailed history of the development of 1960s satire in Britain.
2 Episode 8, season 1, directed by Ian MacNaughton, aired 7 December 1969.
3 A number have also served at the core of Christopher Guest's regular ensemble featuring in his mockumentary films *Waiting for Guffman* (1996), *Best in Show* (2000) and *A Mighty Wind* (2003). Guest is part of mockumentary royalty, having played guitarist Nigel Tufnel in the classic *This is Spinal Tap*.

4 *SNL* also screened a Rutland Weekend Television-filmed Rutles sketch parodying Beatles mythology, which led to the 1978 television mocku- mentary special *The Rutles: All You Need is Cash*, produced by Lorne Michaels himself and featuring many of *SNL*'s main cast together with Python members (see Roscoe and Hight, 2001: 101–10 for a discussion of *The Rutles*).

5 Directed by Geoff Posner, broadcast 3 November 1989.

6 Directed by Daniel Kleinman, broadcast 4 April 1994.

7 Directed by Metin Hüseyin, broadcast 1 November 1998.

8 *Bad News Tour*, episode 4, season 1, directed by Sandy Johnson, broad- cast 24 January 1983. *More Bad News*, episode 2, season 4, directed by Adrian Edmonson, broadcast 27 February 1988.

9 Episode 6, season 2, directed by Sandy Johnson, broadcast 4 February 1984.

10 Directed by Robert B. Weide, aired 17 October 1999. Interestingly, Weide is a documentary filmmaker specialising in comedians (Marin, 2000).

11 See Lavery and Dunne (2006) for an excellent overview of this series.

12 Season 2, episode 36, directed by Ken Wittingham, aired 4 January 2007.

13 This episode falls into the same frame as the klutz cops mockumentary series discussed in chapter 8.

14 Season 4, episode 79, directed by Pamela Fryman, aired 9 May 2000.

15 Season 5, episodes 106 and 107 (a two-parter aired as a one-hour special), directed by Gil Junger, aired 13 May 1998.

16 Season 4, episode 96, directed by Larry Gelbart, aired 24 February 1976.

17 Season 11, episode 1122, directed by Mark Kirkland, aired 21 May 2000.

18 Turner argues, convincingly, that *The Simpsons* peak of creativity, its 'Golden Age', lasted from early 1992 to mid-1997, early season 3 to season 8 (Turner, 2004: 37–45).

19 Season 18, episode 1813, directed by Chuck Sheetz, aired 18 February 2007.

Part III
Television mockumentary series

7

Experimenting with mockumentary forms

Mockumentary is one of many discourses within televisual space, one which draws from and intersects with a variety of well-established generic traditions in television production, as suggested by the discussions in the previous chapters. The richness of mockumentary within television stems from the variety of forms which have employed the discourse within dramatic, comedic and occasionally non-fiction series. Mockumentary has consequently served as a site for a variety of agendas, including commentary and reflection on the nature of various modes of representation. One natural consequence has been the inclusion of commentary on a variety of issues more typically played out within wider documentary culture, such as those related to the ethical practices of filmmakers, varieties of forms of performance and the 'construction' of reality itself through its mediation.

The aim of this final part of the book is to explore a variety of case studies in television mockumentary series. The development of television series (rather than simply isolated one-off programmes or episodes within a series) is significant, as it suggests that mockumentary has become naturalised within the television lexicon. Mockumentary, in other words, has become part of the mainstream of globalised television formats. No longer simply a novelty style, used as part of the wider spectrum of docu-stunts (to use Caldwell's term) within established series, mockumentary has become integral to the conception of series themselves. This has meant the sustained use of a mockumentary premise across multiple episodes, a core part of the set of strategies for developing a series' narrative, whether this has been in the form of episodic narratives (with closure at the end of each week's episode) or in more complex serial patterns as part of a developing narrative arc across one or more seasons. As discussed in the previous chapters, there are some self-imposed narrative constraints inherent in using mockumentary discourse. Employing a sustained aesthetic referenced to fact-fiction consequently also involves adhering to non-fiction related conventions in conveying story information to audiences. This requires some skill. The emergence of mockumentary series suggests an increasing experience with mockumentary discourse on the part of television producers and a readiness to explore its possibilities in tandem within a variety of generic forms.

The more interesting mockumentary series, covered in the following chapter, successfully use mockumentary as a central means of developing a complexity of characters within a variety of narrative situations. As noted previously, these currently appear to be exclusively the province of comedy. Although comedic mockumentary is often a deceptively simple story-telling form (see for example the discussion on *Marion and Geoff* below), as with all good comedy, this appearance belies the degree of talent and sophistication involved in series construction.

Within these broader patterns are some key differences in the manner in which mockumentary has been used within different contexts, particularly within national contexts. Once again, the distinctions between the American and British uses of mockumentary are illustrative of wider patterns. Britain has been the base for a significantly greater number of mockumentary series, as compared to the use of mockumentary in the United States more as a novelty style within one-off programmes or isolated episodes of existing series. The reasons for this are necessarily complex. In Britain there has been an extended period of docusoap formats within prime-time broadcasting, itself partly a reflection of distinctively English preoccupations with popular soap opera. This prevalence of docusoap programming both provides comedic producers with a ready-made template for referencing and ensures a degree of familiarity for potential audiences. The high profile of docusoap within schedules since the 1990s also suggests that this is a tradition ready to be parodied. British mockumentary productions also need to be seen within well-established satiric brands of comedy not only in television but within other media such as theatre and radio (radio, in fact, has served as an important site for the gestation of mockumentary concepts). And, not least of all, British broadcasting has provided the means for a gathering together of talented individuals looking to explore this kind of textual territory.

The British mockumentary pattern consequently provides a variety of supports for the development of mockumentary series, and there is now a well-trodden trajectory from radio comedy, through one-off comedic specials or segments of existing comedy skit shows, through to full development as a series. The BBC has historically played a key role here, despite the frustrations of generations of comedic talent with its bureaucratic constraints on experimentation. Hall notes the development of the early sitcom *Hancock's Half Hour* first as a radio series, before moving to television in 1956 (Hall, 2006: 10). This pattern has been a consistent feature of television programme development in the decades that followed, and in the 1980s and 1990s mockumentaries such as *People Like Us* and *The Day Today* were part of this trend. In more recent years, within a digital environment, secondary television channels have begun to perform the same role, such as BBC3, which showcases new series which may move to either BBC2 or BBC1 if they demonstrate promise (Hall, 2006: 10).

Of course, not all mockumentaries that make the transition from radio to television are successful. The British mockumentary mini-series *500 Bus Stops* (1997) features the eccentric singer-songwriter John Shuttleworth (Graham Fellows). Fellows developed Shuttleworth as a character for a series of 15-minute radio shorts on BBC Radio 4 and Radio 1, centring on his odd, keyboard-based songs and a misplaced confidence in his own musical ability, with the radio series supposedly broadcast from his garden shed. In *500 Bus Stops*, constructed as a blend of home movie and road movie, Fellows appears on screen as Shuttleworth and is heard off screen as both Shuttleworth's wife and his neighbour 'Ken'. With Ken supposedly documenting his exploits with his camcorder, Shuttleworth sets off (by bus after his car breaks down) on a 'National Rock Tour' of southern English towns and performs in unlikely locations, such as supermarkets. The migration of this character to television is not entirely successful, both because it lacks the spontaneity of Fellows playing off other actors and because the meandering narrative that works on radio eventually becomes frustrating on video.

The American pattern, in contrast, suggests a much more sporadic exploration of mockumentary, with producers tending to develop a series as a singular experiment before abandoning the form (there does not appear to be the television equivalent of Christopher Guest, or even Woody Allen, who has engaged sporadically with mockumentary over a number of decades). Often applied as simply another style within existing television series and, as previous chapters demonstrated, not always successfully, mockumentary here is more typically seen as a gimmick form, and American series in general consequently tend not to fully exploit its satiric and reflexive potential. *The History of White People in America* (1985–86), for example, was an early television mockumentary series which drew on the template of social documentaries of the American PBS network. Martin Mull presents a series of segments parodying white ethnic stereotypes, focusing particularly on the everyday traumas of a 'typical white family'. Featuring some of the ensemble from *Spinal Tap* this series plays with discourses from American social debates (Mull visits an 'Institute of White Studies') by making white Americans the exotic 'other' subject of a documentary treatment. As with *This is Spinal Tap*, the critique of the non-fiction form which it references is muted, being more playful and almost nostalgic toward the stilted, sober form of early PBS documentaries.

At another level, the American pattern of television mockumentary demonstrates some of the complexity of the ways in which mockumentary style has been used within television globally, for, despite this stunted development, the United States is still the scene of one of the longer-running mockumentary series (the American version of *The Office* (2005–)) and, as we have seen, significant developments in closely related forms such as dramatic vérité and comedy vérité. As discussed in chapter 10, the differences between the British and American versions of *The Office* are in fact suggestive of such wider patterns of the use of mockumentary within these national contexts.

Outside of the British and North American examples, there are a number of other mockumentary series, variously couched within wider satiric patterns.[1] Not all of these are completely original (to date, the British series *The Office* (2001–3) has been recreated in the United States, Canada, Germany and France, with production plans for Chile), but there are distinctive series from Canada (with *Trailer Park Boys* (2001–) being the longest-running mockumentary series globally), Australia (*The Games* (1998–2000), *We Can Be Heroes: Finding the Australian of the Year* (2005) and *Summer*

Heights High (2007)), New Zealand (*Wayne Anderson: Singer of Songs* (2005) and its sequel) and Ireland (*Paths to Freedom* (2000)), all discussed in the following chapters. Each of these illustrates the potential for mockumentary to provide a platform for the exploration of a variety of localised cultural discourses.

Analysing mockumentary

The examples discussed below and in the following chapters differ greatly in the nature of their appropriation of television documentary and hybrid forms, and the extent to which they develop the layered approach toward narrative construction that typifies the more densely constructed mockumentary texts. Those television producers who are able to accommodate mockumentary with other narrative strategies within a series, to more plausibly integrate it into the premise of a series, tend also to be successful in providing space for audiences to appreciate the discourse's inherent reflexivity toward the fact-fiction continuum. Assessing a mockumentary series, in turn, involves interpreting the nature of the various layers of that text's preferred reading. Each mockumentary derives initially from the specifics of the agenda of its producers, whether it is intended as an exercise in cultural parody or dramatic fiction, as an initial hoax playing to the expectations of its audience, or to develop a commentary on the specific non-fiction or fact-fiction texts that it references. There are key questions which arise naturally from this complexity. How is the audience being positioned to read a specific mockumentary text? How is the agenda of the text communicated to its audience and, most crucially, how (and when) is the fictional status of the programme or series conveyed?

At some level, each mockumentary is attempting to present a story, to use the techniques associated with documentary or reality-based texts to present a compelling narrative. Whether this narrative is about its apparent makers, or their encounters with other fictional characters, or intended to serve simply as a means to cue viewers' expectations through intertextual referencing, the specific textual strategies employed by a producer are key. What kinds of techniques are employed to convey information about characters and their roles within a narrative? How are codes and conventions appropriated from another genre or format employed to create a sense of plausibility and realism? How are we given clues as to the personalities and character traits of the central players in a fiction? As we have seen with one-off episodes of existing series, a mockumentary approach can involve constraints in representing those elements of fiction that viewers are accustomed to receiving, such as an omnipotent understanding of events, and especially our understanding of the motivations of characters. Many mockumentaries have difficulty in balancing the demands of conventional television storytelling and maintaining the sense of limited access or perspective that an apparent documentary crew might be able to gain in such a situation.

A key aspect of any interpretation of a mockumentary series involves a series of issues associated with the nature of the film or television makers who play a role within the fiction itself, and how their relationship with other characters is constructed. The specific representation of documentary filmmakers or other media producers is obviously closely related to the nature of the codes and conventions that a mockumentary references. If a mockumentary pretends to be an observational documentary, there is the opportunity to construct the filmmaker(s) through appearing in the same frame as their subjects, or being heard as an interviewer asking questions, or more subtly through the movement of a camera, and what it focuses on. Mockumentaries love to play with the appearance of a fictional crew, such as having them appear unexpectedly in deliberately reflexive moments, as, for example, where a crew might be caught within frame or reflected in a mirrored surface. Outside of these explicit in-frame representations, as viewers we are typically given cues to suggest the nature of the sensibilities of these 'filmmakers', either directly through their actions and words as characters or indirectly through the editing choices that they appear to have used to complete their production.

These are also key parts of a mockumentary series' commentary either on the specific non-fiction or hybrid form which it appropriates or on documentary culture as a whole. Mockumentary contains an inherent reflexivity toward factual discourse and forms, although again much depends on viewers' interpretation of a text's preferred reading, the specific literacies we bring to a text, as to whether such a commentary is a consistent part of readings by audiences. Many of the series discussed in this volume contain a marked critique of the more tabloid and hybrid forms of documentary culture. Some producers are clearly engaging in a thoughtful deconstruction of such forms and a sense of the wider implications which are raised by documentary and documentary hybrids forms (such as a blurring of distinctions between public and private, issues of performance, play and authenticity, the significance of the indexical image within visual culture and the 'sober' discourses within which such images are embedded).

Motivation for such thematics could also be the frustration which television writers and other creative personnel have toward the fact-fiction forms which have supplanted their position within prime-time programming. Certainly there was a negative reaction within many parts of the television industry with the rise of reality-based programmes, with the assumption that they did not need scripting, that they could be a cheap alternative to more expensive dramatic fare. This is not borne out in reality, of course, as productions like *Survivor* and *Big Brother* required enormous production resources in order to provide a rich sense of scale and spectacle and to engender complex forms of viewer interaction. With many mockumentary series, the issue becomes one of the degree and nature of any commentary on such hybrid forms. Representations of the (fictional) producers, their agendas and the ethical practices they have (or have not) followed are all cues given to the viewers of such a commentary.

A key aspect of mockumentary narrative is often the choices made in representing the nature of the fictional filmmakers' relationship with their apparent subjects, including the types of access that have been granted for a camera crew, or the other types of evidence that they appear to have collated in order to construct an impression of their subject. Some mockumentaries construct the presence of a documentary crew as an explicit intrusion upon an existing social reality, creating a tension between their agenda and those of their subjects (the *ER* episode 'Ambush' is a good example here) which forms the basis of the mockumentary's core narrative. Key questions here include asking what impact the presence of a (foreign, external) camera crew has on the existing set of relationships between the characters. Is their presence a trigger for specific narrative events, do they observe events which we assume would have happened 'naturally' (that is, even without the camera's presence)? What can we understand about fictional characters through their responses to the presence of a camera, their awareness of how they are being represented? And what might this suggest about the wider social context which they inhabit, and its acceptance of photographic cultures?

A further narrative issue, and one which tends to be addressed only with series that occur over more than one season, is the question of feedback from the (fictional) audience, or the aftermath of the apparent broadcast on a mockumentary's subjects. Some mockumentaries deal directly with the implications of the public exposure of central characters, with the impact their appearance on national television might have on their lives, while others ignore this possibility altogether (as we shall see, this is a key difference between the British and American versions of *The Office*).

The role of the (real) audience is obviously also crucial to the impact of mockumentary, in a number of ways. As should be obvious from the nature of the questions above, mockumentaries are often directly engaging with core aspects of audiences' familiarity with issues of mediation that are fundamental to documentary culture. As with many other television texts, these series draw from the rich tableau of possibilities for intertextual references over and beyond the obvious references to a specific template from the fact-fiction continuum. Many of those references are specific to the national context of a series' assumed audience: there are cultural references that resonate particularly with a target audience (even if they remain accessible to other audiences). Where a mockumentary series fits in relation to the many possible shades of parody and satire also partly depends on the types of knowledge that specific groups of viewers bring to their reading of these texts. As discussed previously (chapter 1), parody tends to retain an underlying affection for that which is being mocked, while satire is more focused on a political critique which wishes for the replacement of its target. The role of the audience is crucial here. It is possible for some series to be more satirical within a given context, sometimes even outside of the deliberate intention of their makers. The example of the New Zealand mockumentary *Forgotten Silver* demonstrates how flags to a text's fictional status can be overwhelmed by some audiences' preoccupation with a text's satiric possibilities. All of these interrelated questions of aesthetics, representation, discourse, narrative and commentary and how they play with the expectations of localised audiences are available for producers designing a television mockumentary series. The discussions below and in the remaining chapters engage with a number of series which illustrate the implications of a variety of creative decisions made in their respective productions.

Mockumentary series have become part of the mainstream of television programming, no longer an assumed parasitic form in relation to documentary, but accepted as another potential style of storytelling. As series such as *Sex and the City* and the Australian *Kath and Kim* demonstrate, however, there are also many examples where producers decide not to commit to mockumentary discourse, whether out of frustration with its formal and narrative constraints or simply out of confusion over what exactly differentiates mockumentary from patterns of comedy vérité and broader techniques of parody and satire. Before moving to look at full-length mockumentary series, it is useful to consider series which employ elements of the discourse, fragments of an appropriation of non-fiction forms, as a consistent part of a wider set of narrative strategies.

Fragments and segments: a partial use of mockumentary discourse

These series are close to mockumentary, and are often labelled as such by critics, but are typically just flirting with the discourse as a means of setting up specific expectations on the part of their audience. They offer a useful demonstration of what is not sustained mockumentary despite the frequent use of key elements of documentary and hybrid forms. An interesting series here is the American sitcom *Arrested Development* (2003–6), a key example of comedy vérité and the one series under this broad group which is probably the closest to mockumentary. Series creator Michael Hurwitz in fact has acknowledged the vérité *Curb Your Enthusiasm*, the British version of the mockumentary *The Office* and the mockumentary films of Christopher Guest as direct inspirations. The series also draws much from the format of docusoaps for its innovative approach toward sitcom, using voice-overs, a single hand-held camera, captions to introduce characters and natural lighting. These are used together with other unusual devices such as brief flashbacks, archival footage, fake news items, visualisations of characters' fantasies and nightmares, and a fake trailer for upcoming narratives at the end of each episode. The result is a visually dense series, often with sight gags in the background of scenes that are missed on first viewing (Ostrow, 2004b). While the series has no laugh track, there is a heavily scored soundtrack in the fashion of docusoaps.

The central character is Michael Bluth (Jason Bateman), struggling to both transcend and lead a dysfunctional family after his father is jailed. The core voice-over is provided by executive producer Ron Howard, who offers a deadpan explanation of the absurdities of each member of the Bluth family and their troubles. As with docusoap, the voice-over serves as a useful device for economical storytelling, used for quickly and efficiently outlining a situation or characters' motivations for a scene. The result is a sitcom that moves often rapidly and unexpectedly from situation to situation, and between multiple storylines containing often completely disparate character developments, yet manages to retain an overall coherence. While not a popular success, the series was a surprise Emmy award winner, and critical favourite with commentators praising its innovations (Posner, 2004; Gilbert, 2005) and placing it together with other comedy vérité series (Ostrow, 2004a) and experimental sitcoms such as the medical fantasy *Scrubs* (2001–).

In a DVD commentary on the pilot for the series Hurwitz and directors Joe Russo and Anthony Russo describe the careful efforts to draw from docusoap as a template, but not remain constrained by its limitations. Using a two-camera set-up and encouraging the cast to be improvisational in their movements within a scene, the effect was to suggest the camera following the action rather than the typical choreography of a sitcom. Over the course of the first series, the decision was made not to adhere strictly to a documentary format and not to draw too much attention to the camera through extravagant movement. This allowed for angles and shots that would not be plausible for a documentary, but that were necessary to, for example, get reaction shots from characters or include shots that incorporated background action or anticipated the entry of new characters into a scene. As with other comedy vérité series, the commitment to improvisation, together with this series' visual and narrative density, put a great deal of emphasis on the construction of an overall narrative coherence during post-production.

A similar sense of proximity to mockumentary governs the British children's series *Prehistoric Park* (2006). The series is one logical successor to the various *Walking with* series,[2] which all drew inspiration from the science-fiction premise of the Steven Spielberg dinosaur feature film *Jurassic Park* (1993). These earlier series were largely animated drama-documentaries, using CGI animation (graphic vérité) married with the template of nature documentaries to present playful but educational portrayals of palaeontological speculations. *Prehistoric Park* goes one step further in the direction of *Jurassic Park*'s science-fiction fantasy to imagine a wildlife park that is gradually stocked by real-life naturalist Nigel Marven from his time travels into the prehistoric era. The tag line for the series was 'What if extinctions didn't have to be forever?', and its episodes focused on the excitement of saving animals literally on the brink of extinction. The result is a combination of adventure story, nature documentary and zoo soap opera designed for a young audience (the series also screened on Discovery's Animal Planet channel). Marven excitedly identifies dinosaurs, authoritatively explains their behaviour and effortlessly chases and captures the monstrous beasts or lures them through to the present (Marven's convenient but fantastical time portal consists of metallic pegs that he simply plants in the ground to immediately create a vertical fluid wall familiar from science fiction series).

Much of the series was produced using hand-held cameras, including shaky shots as the camera operator appears to come too close in proximity to CGI-generated giant dinosaurs. Marven speaks directly to camera to explain his actions, and there is a conventional anthropological narrative constructed through voice-over narration from actor David Jason, particularly in the park sequences as each new addition is named and accommodated into everyday routines. The series never settles into a mockumentary format, however, as the need to provide visually spectacular shots means that occasionally there are over-the-shoulder shots from the dinosaurs' perspectives, or apparent sweeping crane shots from within a dinosaur herd and elaborate CGI reconstructions of impending meteor showers and exploding volcanoes that Marven escapes by racing back through his time portal. The series never looks to subvert the codes and conventions of nature documentary but instead treats these as a given and uses them as a familiar format for a fantastical approach to educational television.

John Lurie's fake fishing programme, *Fishing with John* (1991), also plays with mockumentary discourse in a more idiosyncratic way. In partly scripted, partly improvised episodes, Lurie goes on a series of fishing trips with celebrity friends Jim Jarmusch, Tom Waits, Matt Dillon, Willem Dafoe and Dennis Hopper. The use of

Hi-8 footage means that the series' aesthetic is that of a small-budget information series, and it generally has a similarly measured pacing and narrative style to match the slow pace of the fishing action itself. Matching this laid-back aesthetic, Lurie's band, the Lounge Lizards, is used as low-key musical accompaniment. Veteran non-fiction narrator Robb Webb provides laconic linking narration between scenes, and comments which offer ironic counterpoint to the footage on screen (in a quiet moment he insists that 'the action is fast and furious', and when Dillon stubbornly and awkwardly refuses to engage Lurie in conversation while fishing Webb says 'I think this is John's best show'). His commentary seems designed to especially parody the signature style of Jacques Cousteau nature documentaries, offering lyrical and extravagant claims for the philosophy of fishing and the meaning of the journeys of Lurie and his guests. The action in each episode veers between lazy sequences of the fishermen quietly fishing in remote locations as they engage in meandering conversations, and absurd adventures (Lurie and Defoe appear to die of starvation while fishing on a frozen lake in Maine; the host and Hopper are hypnotised by the giant squid they chase in Thailand). Similarly the series utilises mockumentary form but is never constrained by it, with Lurie integrating slow motion, sound effects and shots that would not be plausible from a documentary crew (such as 'point of view' shots from a shark that Jarmusch battles, and the giant squid that Webb's voice-over later admits may be fictional).

Another series in close proximity to mockumentary is *Double Take* (2003),[3] a British television mini-series by photographer Alison Jackson. The series has no overarching narrative, but consists of short vignettes, with visual references that range across key parts of the continuum of surveillance techniques which have become naturalised within contemporary society: CCTV footage integrated into wider regimes of law enforcement and security surveillance, the miniature camera footage that has become a staple tool within investigative television reporting or the paparazzi footage that is a staple of entertainment broadcasting. The video footage is deliberately grainy, sometimes blurred (or quickly coming into focus), shot from a roving hand-held camera intent on capturing footage from behind obstacles and through windows. The targets of such layers of surveillance are a series of look-alikes role-playing public figures who will be immediately familiar to the British public, such as footballer David Beckham, singers Elton John and Mick Jagger, Prime Minister Tony Blair and his wife, and various members of the British royal family. Using cues such as hairstyle, costume and dialogue (supposedly overheard private conversations that were added in post-production), the intention is partly to parody the public personas of such familiar figures by suggesting that they engage in contrasting behaviour when in private.

In a DVD commentary, Jackson explains that her technique involves combining the iconic with the intimate and personal. The British royal family, for example, are revealed in the kind of everyday activities that play against their public profile, such as the Queen getting her legs waxed, playing games with her maid, giving driving lessons to her grandson Prince William, or struggling to operate a mobile phone. The overall effect is to provide a charge of authenticity, forcing viewers to do a 'double take' to make sure that the characters are not really who they appear to be, together with the shock and pleasure inherent in unexpected voyeurism (public figures are viewed in their underwear, or in otherwise unwittingly revealing movements). Although at one level a simple exercise in titillation, in fact the series works best at those times when it encourages a layered sense of appreciation for both the skill and quality of the impression and the ways those impressions play with viewers' expectations of the public persona of its targets.

Jackson's wider objective is to satirise the banality of surveillance footage within the cultures of consumption in which television audiences are themselves implicated. Viewers are encouraged to reflect upon their own ambivalence toward such tabloid forms of visual culture. Certainly Jackson, in the face of criticism of such television work and the photographic art she has created using the same practice,[4] justifies the programme ultimately as an effort to interrogate the wider public belief in the integrity of any photographic image, which persists despite the increasing visual literacy of audiences.[5]

There are other programmes which use mockumentary discourse in more limited ways. *Jimmy McDonald's Canada* (2005) is essentially a clip series consisting of 1960s footage from the archives of Canadian television network CBC, but presented as the long-lost black and white episodes of a supposedly popular current affairs programme from that period hosted by Jimmy MacDonald (Richard Waugh). The series positioned its archival footage within a new narrative frame by having MacDonald introduce each clip (often while smoking) and add a heavily conservative commentary upon the now severely dated social and cultural discourses of the 1960s television stories. An additional segment, also in black and white, featured Marg Margison (Teresa Pavlinek), dressed in conservative 1960s style, offering traditional advice to women. The result was an ambivalent perspective on an earlier era of television, combining a parody of that era's television discourse with nostalgia for the actual events that are contained in the clips.

Any number of series have also touched on mockumentary elements through stunt-based comedy which relied on the unwitting participation of everyday people, derived from the formula of ambush comedy established by the long-running *Candid Camera* (1948–50) tradition. Garry McDonald played a spoof interviewer with his own series called *The Norman Gunston Show* (1975–79), which played for three seasons in Australia from May 1975 and was later broadcast in Britain. With balding hair slicked over his forehead and his face dotted with pieces of toilet paper after having cut himself shaving, Gunston surprised celebrities and other public figure with rude and hostile questions and served as a forerunner of similar fake reporters and talk show hosts of the 1990s from performers such as Steve Coogan (*The Knowing Me, Knowing You With Alan Partridge Show* (1994)), Caroline Aherne (*The Mrs. Merton Show* (1994–98)) and Paul Kaye (as ambush reporter Dennis Pennis in *Anyone for Pennis?* (1997)) (Lewisohn, 2003: 337).

In a similar vein, Sacha Baron Cohen featured in segments on the British Channel 4 programme *The 11 O'Clock Show* (1998–2000) as Ali G, a middle-class white obsessed with American hip-hop gangster style who surprised unwitting interviewees (generally figures of authority or expertise) by asking deeply ignorant and uninformed questions designed to elicit uncomfortable admissions. Cohen employed this fake interviewer technique in key segments of his British series *Da Ali G Show* (2000), both in studio interviews using his Ali G persona and in filmed reports as 'Borat Sagdiyev'. The Sagdiyev character was played as a Kazakh filmmaker attempting to document aspects of British culture, a premise which Cohen later developed into the successful mockumentary *Borat: Cultural Learnings of America for Make Benefit Glorious Nation of Kazakhstan* with a narrative based on more elaborate ambush situations. The Borat segments in *Da Ali G Show* are a combination of stunt and satiric mockumentary, as he adopts an air of unsophisticated cultural naïveté in encounters with unsuspecting spokespeople for traditional activities such as playing cricket or fox hunting, or for English etiquette. Faced with Borat's seeming lack of comprehension, his victims find themselves helpfully deconstructing English traditions in ways that reveal the deeply ingrained assumptions of their class origins or similar cultural contradictions.

Mockumentary segments from *The Daily Show*

The uses of actual footage placed within a new narrative frame and of ambush interviewing are often strong elements of fake news programmes, such as the sophisticated and highly popular American satirical news programme *The Daily Show with Jon Stewart* (1996–) from the Comedy Central network. The *Daily Show* itself follows a rich tradition of current affairs parodies, including the 'Weekend Update' segment from *Saturday Night Live* discussed in the previous chapter, British and American versions of *That Was The Week That Was* (1962–63), a Canadian series called *This Hour Has 22 Minutes* (1992–), and a number of mockumentary series (discussed in the following chapter). Running four days a week in the United States, *The Daily Show* itself is a perfect illustration of the naturalisation of mockumentary discourse within television satire.

Jon Stewart took over as host of *The Daily Show* in 1999 and serves as writer and co-executive producer. His initial cast of regulars included Stephen Colbert, Rob Corrdry, Samantha Bee, Ed Helms, Lewis Black and Bob Wiltfong (Colapinto, 2004). Stewart has taken the programme into the realms of political satire, combining a critique of the lack of real political debate and analysis within contemporary television news media with a sophisticated understanding of the American political process itself. A key strategy employed by the programme is the deconstruction of the aesthetics and discourses of television news coverage of current events, with Stewart and his colleagues using a variety of means to reveal the superficial, entertainment-centred agenda which shapes such coverage.

Stewart's address on the programme is to a politically educated audience, even if the forms of humour that he employs are often very broad. Baym argues that *The Daily Show* should be

10. The sophisticated pastiche of television news presentation from the popular American news satire *The Daily Show with Jon Stewart* (1996–).

'understood not as "fake news" but as an alternative journalism, one that uses satire to interrogate power, parody to critique contemporary news, and dialogue to enact a model of deliberative democracy' (Baym, 2005: 261). Considerably more sophisticated than the humour of *SNL*'s 'Weekend Update' segments and that of the comedians of late-night talk shows, *The Daily Show* employs a number of techniques that draw explicitly from mockumentary discourse for their satirical effect (Figure 10). Warner refers to *The Daily Show*'s agenda as 'political culture jammers', as the programme's team of comedians adopts the style of political branding and turns it back on itself.

A typical episode consists of a number of segments, including an initial monologue from Stewart in which he highlights one or more televised current events, skilfully edited clips or performances from the other comedic actors playing reporters on the programme and a studio interview. Stewart's opening address features 'the strategic use of video' to highlight the gaps and contradictions within both political and televisual news discourse (Warner, 2007: 27). Warner notes that a key aspect of this technique is its indirectness, with Stewart typically refraining from a direct critique of news coverage, instead both guiding a commentary and leaving the audience space to make up their own minds. Dempsey argues that Stewart's ease in being able to put together a montage of journalists or political pundits all using the exact same phrase suggests a degree of implicit collaboration on their part, or sheer laziness in not being able to develop independent thought outside of authoritative discourses (Dempsey, 2007).

Stewart's address often then segue's into a fake 'live' report or commentary from one of his fellow comedians. The apparent live reports feature a correspondent, labelled as the 'resident expert' depending upon the nature of the item, standing in front of an obvious blue screen projection. The 'correspondent' offers commentary that highlights the absurdities of political discourse by treating them as a given and extending them to their logical conclusion, while Stewart plays with a straight face, expressing surprise at recent political developments and asking rational, common-sense questions as prompts. As Gettings notes, the audience is always aware of the ontological status of information that is conveyed throughout these segments, as they are clearly flagged to the audience, usually through consistent types of performance and the use of comedic graphics (Gettings, 2007: 19–23).

Another regular segment consists of edited reports from one of the programme's roving comedic reporters, and these most clearly resemble sustained exercises in mockumentary. Resembling the format of Cohen's encounters as 'Borat', these are more visually sophisticated in that they are made to more closely mimic edited news items. The correspondents play with mostly straight faces, asking actual spokespersons to explain themselves in ways that unwittingly reveal the absurdity of their own rhetoric (Gettings, 2007: 22). The *Daily Show* reporters at other times also represent themselves as deliberately combative, shallow and manipulative in constructing news items that will play as great television, revealing the tendencies of actual television news reporters by offering a broad caricature of their interviewing techniques and constructed on-screen personas (McKain, 2005: 419). Finally, in the studio interviews Stewart adopts a Socratic interview style (Warner, 2007: 29; Barad, 2007), claiming ignorance of guests' expertise and asking for responses which force them to explain themselves. One of the deliberate ironies of this segment is that Stewart, playing a fake news anchor, can often ask pointed and perceptive questions that the interviewee would rarely confront in an actual encounter with American television news media (Baym, 2005: 273).

The programme's exercises in deconstructing the nature and quality of television news discourse are centred especially within an American context, and there have been debates within the local news media over the significance of the programme in relation to political knowledge, with widely circulated reports that younger and college-aged viewers were more likely to gain their knowledge of political candidates from the programme than from other sources. While some commentators decried the implication that viewers would rely on comedy programmes for information, others noted that viewers needed to be more educated and informed than viewers of real news; that they needed to understand the references to actual events in order to appreciate the nature of the programme's mixture of parody and satire. Interestingly, the rise of *The Daily Show* has prompted television networks to include news satires in their own programming (John, 2004: 14) – an extension of the familiar tradition of fake April Fool's Day news reports but without the underlying sense of critique that is such a distinctive feature of Stewart's series.

A spin-off programme from *The Daily Show* is *The Colbert Report* (2005–), featuring former 'correspondent' Stephen Colbert as a caricature especially of the openly conservative anchors that tend to feature on the Fox News network (such as Bill O'Reilly). Dempsey's description of this programme is perceptive:

> Satirizing the excesses of personality-driven cable news show hosts with the most gratuitous examples of rhetoric, Colbert *embodies* the kind of bad reasoning that Stewart merely exposes. Colbert's character embraces the irrational fully, and makes explicit the biased agendas of those he satirizes. (Dempsey, 200: 131, original emphasis)

Colbert's debut programme (17 October 2005) famously introduced the word 'truthiness' to public discourse, which he defined as referring to things which are believed to be true, irrespective of whether the facts are able to support such a conclusion – a subtle commentary on the nature of the neo-conservative discourse of the George W. Bush administration. Overall, however, *The Colbert*

Report moves further away from mockumentary discourse than *The Daily Show*. It focuses more on politically nuanced skit comedy, featuring guests and interviewees who are cued more for cameo roles than serving as the objects of satirical inquiry.

All of the examples discussed above illustrate something of the range of the partial application of mockumentary discourse within television series. None of these series engages in mockumentary in a sustained manner, but they use it for specific segments or as one element within a wider use of strategies for creating narratives, perspective and commentary by drawing upon familiar non-fiction codes and conventions. The examples which follow, in contrast, are efforts at sustained mockumentary discourse, but using short-form episodic structures.

Short form mockumentary series

Marion and Geoff, Look Around You (2002–5) and *Posh Nosh* (2003) are all series which experiment with the possibilities of sustained mockumentary over an entire series. They draw from quite different agendas and reference distinct non-fiction television forms. They are all British series, demonstrating the manner in which the British broadcasting system has allowed for some experimentation with formats through the provision of space for 'incidentals', short segments that could operate within the space between programmes of varied length that screened without advertising (in contrast to the more regimented American scheduling constraints).

Posh Nosh was a mock cooking show which drew upon instructional cooking programmes, a long-established staple of television schedules, and the more recent popularity of celebrity chefs. The smugly upper-class husband-and-wife team of Minty and Simon Marchmont (Richard E. Grant and Arabella Weir) hosted the show's 10-minute episodes. Billing their programme as offering 'extraordinary food for ordinary people', Simon and Minty constructed meals of 'only the finest ingredients' and served exquisitely crafted servings within the 'correct' plate and table settings. Presenting recipes from the fully equipped kitchen of their Victorian country house, the hosts revealed themselves through their chosen recipes, language and gestures, including their idiosyncratic descriptors for cooking procedures ('pillage the fish', 'vulgarise the nuts', 'interrogate the mussels', 'strip-search the broccoli' and so on). Most of their ideal ingredients are outrageously expensive, including those made from endangered animals and from Third World countries as the end products of exploitation. Simon captured their culinary creations through carefully posed photographs and the Marchmonts publicised their elite restaurant, a cook book (Simon: 'Also available in paperback, if you're not serious') and other merchandise. At the end of each programme there was a mock advertisement for a top-of-the-range food item (sample product: 'Costa Rican coffee-flavoured chocolate coffee beans'), accompanied by choral music and a velvet-toned voice-over by Joanna Lumley extolling its virtues.

Distanced from an awareness of the more basic and functional place of food in most people's lives, the couple are also in deep denial about their own dysfunctional relationship. Although no overall narrative is constructed through the series, each episode adds some information about its central characters. Simon is transparently gay and snidely hostile toward Minty and her more modest class background, who pretends not to notice but sublimates her unhappiness through cooking and eating. Their oblique references to unhappy past events and their true feelings are revealed through asides made to each other in between strict instructions given to their viewers. Both Minty and Simon drink frequently throughout each programme; Simon has a tendency to save his most eloquent pronouncements for identifying and assessing the flavours of his wine. The limited space for action, and necessary focus on actually presenting a complete (though fake) recipe[6] meant that the series tended to operate on one-liners rather than accumulating the narrative complexity that characterises the more effective examples of television mockumentary.

The two series of *Look Around You* respectively parodied 1970s television learning modules and 1980s popular science programmes, offering a nostalgic parody of now dated television formats and satirising the underlying scientific discourse on which they drew upon. (The first series of 10-minute programmes screened on BBC2 in December 2002. A second series was extended to 30-minute episodes, screening January–February 2005.) Each episode focused on a particular subject – such as 'maths', 'germs', 'ghosts', 'the brain', 'computers' or 'music' – which was then presented through a series of everyday, but absurd, textbook experiments.

The first series referenced (British) Open University and Television for Schools and Colleges programming, where students could watch programmes at home while consulting their textbooks. Each episode began with a shot of an expectant adult student ready with textbook open, followed by the presentation of nonsensical facts accompanied by a command for viewers to 'write that down' in their copybooks. Its presentation relied on voice-over, with demonstrations set in a bright white or blue studio, and various props such as beakers and microscopes intended to simplistically replicate the authority of a science laboratory. The second series parodied popular science programmes from the 1980s and was fronted by four in-studio presenters (including co-writers and co-producers Peter Serafinowicz and Robert Popper). Everything about this series was carefully referenced to that decade, including the fashion and hair of presenters and their deliberately measured and authoritative presentation style. The in-studio presenters for this second series gradually emerged as a stable set of characters, revealed through enthusiastically offering themselves as guinea pigs for increasingly bizarre experiments. The original series was constructed as if it had a 1970s school-aged audience, and the same cheerful tone was employed to address a more general audience in the second series. There were frequent pauses for effect (as if the presenters expected viewers to nod in agreement while watching at home), with comforting smiles and a friendly conversational tone of voice.[7] The production style likewise combined a slow, measured editing pace with a reliance on a standard set of long, medium and close-up shots, all eye-level, brightly lit, carefully framed frontal shots. These were overlaid with simplistic two-dimensional graphics and cheesy synthesiser theme music.

Neither series attempted anything ambitious in narrative terms. The first series of 10-minute programmes essentially reworked the same single joke premise, contrasting a sober approach of presentation with absurd scientific information (sample fact: 'germs originated in Germany'). With the second series, the producers introduced a linking device for each episode, an 'Invention of the Week' segment featuring an award given to a budding inventor (including eccentrics who provided prototypes of a noise-reduction spray, a food orchestra and a memory helmet). These segments built toward the series final where the winning invention appeared to be judged, in a chaotic 'live' broadcast, by British royal Prince Charles (seamlessly integrated through the use of actual archival footage from the 1970s). Outside of a parody of dated television formats, the series offered an extended satire of the simplistic, popularised version of scientific discourse which is typically presented through television. The stereotypical representation of a scientist used here wore a white coat and glasses, was male, and had poor social skills but an enthusiasm for the 'latest' technology and a technological determinist vision of the future.

Neither *Posh Nosh* nor *Look Around You* moved beyond anything more than a limited use of mockumentary form. Here the appropriation of non-fiction forms was used simply to create a series of immediately obvious parodic references. The storytelling possibilities of mockumentary are barely explored by either series. A final example of short-form mockumentary series which is much more inspiring as a demonstration of this potential is *Marion and Geoff*, a series produced and directed by Hugo Blick and co-written with Rob Brydon that is one of the exemplars of mockumentary from any medium.

Marion and Geoff presents highlights from the video diary of Keith Barret (played in a superb comedic performance by Brydon, based on a character he developed for radio). Rather than simply being used as a gimmick, the video diary format (see chapter 4) is employed here to open new possibilities for comedic narrative. The aesthetic of the series is consistent with the video diary format but is effectively extended by being played out over an entire series, increasing the potential to accumulate a complex narrative. In the first season of 10-minute programmes (screened by BBC2 in September–November 2000) Keith keeps the camcorder on the dashboard of his cab and regularly switches it on to record the latest events in his life (Figure 11). In fact, all we know of other people in Keith's life is gleaned from his own perspective of events and the occasional clue from locations that can be seen through the driver's side window onto the street.

Producer Blick has suggested that 'intense distillation' is integral to the 10-minute form (Rochlin, 2004: E9), and this is a useful description of the narrative density that the series accumulates. Through various tales told by Keith, we identify with his character and the details of his life. His personal life is in ruins after his wife Marion leaves him for her business partner Geoff, who is gradually taking over the role of father to Keith's two young boys (his 'little

11. Taxi driver Keith Barret (Rob Brydon) adjusts his dashboard mounted camcorder in the first series of *Marion & Geoff* (2003).

smashers'). All his attempts to reconnect with his family, or any form of human relationship, seem destined to end in disaster, despite the earnestness and innocence of his intentions. Even a brief flash of hope at the end of series 1 is somewhat bittersweet. He crashes on the way to see his new-found girlfriend and the last shot of this series is of Keith in the passenger seat of his girlfriend's car, with her kids in the back seat. As she tells him to turn off the camera (our only glimpse of another human being through Keith's lens), he turns it towards himself and we briefly see his body swathed in bandages. He has finally become 'whole' again, and tellingly no longer needs the camera as his companion and confidante.

The second season (broadcast January–March 2003) extends the premise to half-hour episodes and is set 2 years later, with Keith once again alone and now serving as chauffeur to a family which is itself disintegrating. In this series Keith becomes more engaged with the world, which only serves to highlight his inability to comprehend the mendacity and selfishness of those around him. He develops dysfunctional relationships with members of his employer's family. And he becomes an unwitting catalyst for the unravelling marriage of Marion and Geoff, while his own fortunes appear to be more and more out of his control.

The drama, comedy and tragedy within these monologues derive from Keith's relentless, almost delusional, optimism in the face of a series of crushing disappointments. In fact, it is the everyday nature of Keith's disappointments that encourages us to identify with him and to wish that he can overcome obstacles in his path. The series becomes increasingly bleak, however, as the remnants of his former life slowly erode, and the series becomes more of a black comedy. It is a measure of the quality of the writing that the simple narrative form used here is able to sustain any number of wider themes resonating with contemporary capitalist society: the sadness and emptiness of individual lives in large cities; the tragedy of those left behind in the rush for wealth and upwardly mobile ambitions; and the desperation of those outside of the apparently happy norm of the nuclear family. The series could also be seen as drawing upon post-feminist discourses on the instability of contemporary masculinity (Keith is very much the sensitive new-age man, the house husband when in his marriage, while ex-wife Marion is an upwardly mobile alpha female).

A key aspect of the comedic tension the series generates derives from the sense of ambiguity over Keith's confessional relationship with his camera. The 'raw footage' captured by Keith has the appearance of having been edited to emphasise dramatic moments in his personal narratives, with quick fades in the middle of scenes to skip irrelevant detail and some brief montage sequences set to music. However, Keith never gives any explicit indication that he is engaged in creating a television series, nor explains what his own motivation or agenda might be for participating in such a production (at times it is as if his diaries have been unknowingly passed on to a television executive who has shaped the footage into series form). He has strict rules about when he may use his camera, politely turning it off whenever he has passengers or receives a phone call out of respect for the others' privacy. In part, Keith suggests the wider tendency of 'everyday' people to place their trust in television to provide a forum for their personal failings, and this consequently replicates the video diary's initial objective of establishing a dialogue with a wider audience. However, at times Keith does not seem to have enough self-awareness to realise how he appears to his audience (an early episode features him playing innocently with his father's sniper's rifle while looking at his wife's lover through the scope, a shot rich with suppressed violence and Freudian significance).

In fact the series would not work as effectively if we detected a more complicit agenda from Keith. Central to his persona is a degree of naïveté, and crucially this is where the series differs from now conventional reality television programmes. Instead of the expectations of celebrity status, or at least an awareness of how he is represented by the camera, his commentary and narrative are simply offered to the wide-open public space, with no expectation of an audience, let alone a reply. The fictional Keith retains an authenticity and clear sense of autobiography which has tended to become subsumed into the more commercialist production agendas which typically frame the use of the video diary technique within mainstream television. Brydon's character indirectly suggests a more innocent period of camcorder history, a time before the acknowledgement of performance was such an integral part of our expectations as viewers. We are unused to users of camcorders displaying such openness and lack of awareness of how they might be perceived. Keith's fictional monologues consequently retain an apparent pathos and authenticity ironically absent from most constructions of television reality, even those within the less commercialist agenda of the pioneering British video dairy series *Video Nation*.

On another level, however, Keith's entire appearance is a performance of sorts, as he is at pains to not acknowledge to the camera the quiet desperation of his life which lurks just beneath the surface. We expect him to explode, to break down in tears (he does, very briefly in one episode), but we are denied the complete dropping of his beatific façade. It is this tension in the variety of contradictory expectations which the series establishes that explains much of its effectiveness. Keith is immediately familiar in his performance yet refreshingly 'virgin' as a camcorder participant.

A very different set of relationships between Keith and his on-screen representation is constructed in a 1-hour special entitled *A Small Summer Party* (2001) that was produced between the two series of *Marion and Geoff*. This dramatises a key moment which Keith relates in the first series (in episode 6 of season 1), when he is finally forced to acknowledge the relationship between his wife and Geoff after finding them together in his marriage bed. This one-off special also uses a mockumentary approach, but abandons the dashboard video diary for a more complex home movie format offering virtually a real-time account of the traumatic incident. Set at a barbeque organised by Keith to celebrate Marion and Geoff's business relationship, the programme seamlessly cuts between four apparently continuous records of the afternoon: one from an unnamed friend whom Keith has invited to record the event; another from a camcorder operated by his two boys playing in and around the house in astronaut suits; a third camera arriving by car with family guests; and the fourth camcorder brought into the house by neighbours trying to capture evidence of Keith's family's disruption of the neighbourhood.

All of the filming uses natural lighting, and the movements and sound effects associated with each camera suggest something of the 'personality' of its apparent operator(s). For example, we hear the sound of the boys' breathing on the soundtrack (amplified by their astronaut suits) whenever the screen cuts to their child's-eye level, very shaky hand-held footage, which consists of much lurking on internal stairs to spy on their parents and guests. We gain knowledge of events only peripherally, with each camera accidentally overhearing conversations or capturing the reactions of participants in events rather than glimpsing the events themselves, and Marion and Geoff's faces are only seen in-frame very briefly, towards the end of the programme.[8] Despite the perpetual motion of the cameras, the overall effect is to capture the emptiness of the occasion itself, and the absence of any familial warmth in Keith's home.

The special is consistent with Keith's version of this most traumatic of events in his life, but is less engaging than the regular series because his character is not central to the action. We are given a much more dispersed set of perspectives through the multiple camcorder approach, while never gaining the emotional resonance of any character's direct confession to camera. Instead of an autobiographical account of the incident, these perspectives position Keith more as the unwilling object of surveillance, as the various cameras relentlessly capture every detail of his humiliation. Keith is continually trapped in different corners of his suburban cage, and there is a claustrophobic atmosphere which contrasts with the freedom of personal expression he enjoys behind the wheel of a car in the regular *Marion and Geoff* series. He literally has no place to hide as every emotion and expression of the traumatic event is captured for posterity.

As with the regular series, there is no direct clue to suggest how such a 'documentary' might have come about; this aspect of the mockumentary is deliberately fudged. Brydon has since brought his Keith Barret character more directly into a public forum as the host of *The Keith Barret Show* (2004–5), which follows a more conventional British tradition of fake talk shows (although with a considerably gentler touch than its predecessors). Together with the two series of *Marion and Geoff* (10-minute and conventional half-hour format) and the 1-hour special, these programmes collectively suggest the richness of narrative rewards that can come from the careful crafting of a mockumentary series, and also the difficulty of maintaining a narrative arc using the premise. The following chapters explore these same aspects of mockumentary practice in relation to examples of sustained, longer-form mockumentary series.

Notes

1 Unfortunately, the case studies in this book are exclusively from English-language broadcasting. This is not because mockumentary discourse itself is limited, but derives from a difficulty in gaining access to other examples, and more particularly from this author's lack of capability with other languages.

2 *Walking with Dinosaurs* (1999), *Walking with Beasts* (2001), *Walking with Cavemen* (2003) and *Walking with Monsters* (2005).

3 A fifty-minute pilot screened on BBC2 in December 2001, with the series following in March–April 2003.

4 See www.alisonjackson.com.

5 Jackson in an interview included on the DVD for the series.

6 An accompanying website maintains and extends the fiction, in this case offering recipes and further details on the food philosophy of Simon and Minty. See www.bbc.co.uk/comedy/poshnosh/.

7 Both series are supported by online sites which replicate their educational tone of address, graphic style and absurdist content. See www.bbc.co.uk/comedy/lookaroundyou/.

8 Neither character ever appears in the two series of *Marion and Geoff*. Here Geoff is played by veteran vérité comedian Steve Coogan.

8

Surveillance and discipline: fake news and mock-reality TV

Some mockumentary series target the 'sober' discourse of television institutional forms, either those of apparently authoritative television news and current affairs programmes or the variety of associated documentary hybrids which pay lip service to public service ideals of informing and educating their audiences. There is much to mock here, given the increasingly commercialist agenda of television production, fighting to attract and retain viewers within a market of proliferating channels and other forms of media, particularly entertainment media. Even within institutions with strong public service traditions, such as the BBC in Britain, such patterns are obvious and disquieting for critics. Mockumentary plays with these tensions within television non-fiction discourses, appropriating televisual forms of non-fiction and fact-fiction representations of the world to tease out the agendas and compromises in their construction. The three sections in this chapter discuss contrasting mockumentary responses to constructions of authority: fake news programmes; satires of archetypal hybrid format *Cops*; and two series which re-imagine legal enforcement and discipline hybrids from the criminal's point of view.

And now for the news ... : *The Day Today,* *Brass Eye* and news satire

The range of discourses operating through the televisual fact-fiction continuum offers rich potential for satirical appropriation. A key target of one group of mockumentary series is television news. As Ericson et al suggest, it is possible to view news discourse as a perpetual search for social, political and cultural deviance, particularly in forms that can be characterised as disruptive to an assumed equilibrium within society (Ericson et al, 1987; 1991). The visual aspects of this news discourse are a preoccupation within television news production. Increasingly, forms of surveillance are becoming central to such a frame, with television news at the forefront of appropriating wider cultures of surveillance into everyday news bulletins. The most recent evidence of this is an active encourage-ment of the wider audience to contribute material through amateur camcorders, and newer versions of amateur surveillance through devices such as phonecams. The result is an emerging form of televi-sion news intersecting with the surveillance-centred agendas which have always been core to documentary hybrids.

There is any number of fake news television programmes glob-ally, many often directly inspired by the fake news segments from influential 1960s and 1970s satirical series such as *Monty Python's Flying Circus* and *Saturday Night Live* (discussed in chapter 6). All seek to deconstruct television news discourses that are familiar to their local viewers, offering a mixture of parody and satire of spe-cific current events and the manner in which these are presented to audiences within the increasingly commercialised forms of tele-vision news. Not all of this might be strictly considered mockumen-tary, as most tend to simply explore elements of the various agendas that characterise *The Daily Show*: parody of news media, satire of television discourses, commentary on contemporary social and political issues. Once again, we see within fake news programmes a spectrum of creative choices made by producers, derived from distinct production agendas and the specific television forms which are referenced. Collectively, fake news programmes suggest the complexity of news discourse itself, even as its broad patterns are easily identified and targeted through parodic appropriation.

Among the more sophisticated news satires has been the British series *The Day Today*. The genesis of the series lay in satirist Christopher Morris bringing together writer/producer Armando Iannucci, Steve Coogan and Patrick Marber to produce a news media parody for the *On The Hour* Radio 4 programme, before migrating the format over to television. In *The Day Today*, Morris played a somewhat smug, aggressive, slick-haired anchor-person, Coogan regularly appeared as hapless sports presenter Alan Partridge and Marber as inept political reporter Peter O'Hanrahanrahan. Other regular characters included weatherman Sylvester Stewart (David Schneider), American reporter Barbara

Wintergreen (Rebecca Front), and business correspondent Collaterlie Sisters (Doon Mackichan). Each of the cast also appeared as a host of more occasional characters, especially either reporters on location or their interviewees.

The Day Today, unlike the American *Daily Show*, was uninterested in contemporary political issues, but focused more particularly on a cutting satire of television news discourse itself. The show faithfully recreated the look and sound of television non-fiction presentation, but then teased elements of this presentation in particular directions in order to highlight the nature of their construction to viewers. The title sequence for the programme was a masterpiece in graphic satire (Ellis, 2000: 96), extrapolating the fluid and densely layered style of television news graphics into more extreme directions. They were created by Russell Hilliard and Richard Norley, creators of the ITN news graphics, who welcomed the opportunity to spoof their style (Lewisohn, 2003: 534). Superimposed over a base layer of news footage, a series of rotating globes would emerge out of cross-hairs to shoot at the viewer, beginning with a recognisable blue-green earth and moving through globes signifying different news segments. The 'economic' globe had coinage morphed over its surface, the 'sports globe' was a blue soccer ball (football) with white continents superimposed, followed by a sphere with a grid-like mosaic of news items on its surface. This collapsed into a series of intersecting blue and red discs that overlapped each other in rapid sequence before being 'stamped' by the title of programme, which comes flying in from off-screen. Ironically, the satirical impact of this sequence has lessened since the initial broadcast of the series, as news presentation has become increasingly layered as part of the overall commitment to network branding based on sophisticated motion graphics within televisual space (the deliberately spectacular opening title sequence of *The Daily Show* is one attempt to respond to such trends).

A similar approach was used for the visual design of each *Day Today* episode, with an excessive use of graphics, particularly to mark cuts between scenes or stories (for example, the frame would suddenly shrink to a sphere and speed off right-screen, with accompanying sound effects). Fittingly, the segment where graphics totally took over was the weather segment – traditionally the scene of the most elaborate experiments with graphic technology as weather presenters are sutured into layered presentations of weather maps, photorealistic landscapes and weather footage. In *The Day Today*, weather presenter Schneider was clearly just another layer in a graphic sequence featuring a confusing mass of iconic weather information moving rapidly across representations of the United Kingdom, at times morphing completely into an iconic shape himself. Following the wider television news branding trend, each episode also incorporated regular promotional slogans for the series in between story segments, revealing both its entertainment-centred agenda and the absurdity of slogans being attached to news programmes (some samples: 'ultra-news', 'game warden to the events rhino', 'bag piping fact into news')

Morris and his co-presenters appeared in expensive formal dress, with heavy makeup and carefully coiffed hairstyles, sitting behind enormous and imposing desks in a dark, cavernous studio space with large screens on the wall behind. There was no studio or canned laughter, with the 'news' presented straight-faced to camera. Morris's presentation style as lead anchor was distinctive, particularly in the manner in which he used his voice. As with conventional news delivery, he cued viewers' expected responses by either dramatically emphasising key words within a sentence or switching tone when changing from 'hard' news to 'soft' news. What pushed his narration into satire was partly how aggressively he put emphasis on words (and not always the obvious words) and the suddenness of his shifts in tone – highlighting the elements of performance that are integral to news presentation.

The on-screen relationships between the various presenters suggested a clear hierarchical division between Morris and the other presenters in the news team, who were all suggested as dysfunctional in some sense. Coogan's sports commentary was based more on excitement over dramatic footage than any understanding of the nuances of the sporting code itself (Figure 12). Likewise, Mackichan's economic news consisted of an overwhelming variety of incomprehensible statistical information, often presented graphically, and articulated by her in an almost robotic tone of voice. Instead of the familiar semi-scripted repartee and apparently easy familiarity between news presenters, Morris would address his colleagues in unexpected ways, engaging Coogan in long, inane conversations that would leave him repeatedly failing to begin his sports news, flirting with Front's traffic reporter, distastefully passing on to Mackichan (sometimes with overheard snide comments) and

12. Steve Coogan as the clueless sports reporter Alan Partridge, in a 'live'
segment from the seminal British mockumentary series *The Day Today* (1994).

virtually interrogating Marber's incompetent on-location reporter
during a live feed, forcing him to acknowledge that he did not have
any actual facts to support his statements.

Many stories made frequent use of Morris's voice-over narration, with rhetorical flourishes which matched their absurd content.
Each story might use any number of elements, including real archival footage, presented within a completely new narrative frame.
This was particularly the case with each episode's opening preview,
which included actual footage of public figures familiar to British
audiences, such as politicians, with Morris providing an absurd story
in voice-over. In their narration these rapid montages were a combination of the absurdity of *Monty Python*'s non-fiction parodies
and the photograph and gag story technique of 'Weekend Update'
segments from *Saturday Night Live*. As noted above, these were not
designed to comment on topical events, but reflected the overall
agenda to target television discourse itself. The content of stories
was always ludicrous (black-market dentistry, horses loose in the
London Underground, the IRA using 'bomb dogs' to target inner-

city Britain) but the focus was more on the manner in which reports were constructed, with correspondents mixing information with speculation, and stories centred on replaying spectacular footage presented in as manipulative a manner as possible (such as flash zooms into details within a frame, and the use of dramatic music). Narratives were constructed out of disparate pieces of footage, each taken out of context and used simply for rhetorical effect or to provide a meaningless visual flourish. The filmed segments could sometimes just offer a visual riff on a topic, such as Morris presenting a story on the suspected brain disease of politicians that simply provided a new narrative for the actual stock footage of politicians walking in and out of offices and buildings that provides familiar visuals for political news stories.

Other sequences of the programme targeted familiar segments of television news. Rebecca Front appeared as American reporter 'Barbara Wintergreen' from the fictional 'CBN' network, with a large, static hairstyle and a broad accent. Her stories were carefully crafted to highlight distinctive aspects of American news feeds incorporated into British news programming. Wintergreen presented endless variations on one story, the execution of serial killer Chapman Baxter (Marber), focusing on the trivial, banal or bizarre aspects of Baxter's (repeated) execution. These CBN stories were visually distinct from the rest of the series, with a washed-out video aesthetic and a constantly moving camera and rapid cutting between shots within a single scene, often including blurred footage. The series also directed its attention towards the still novel trends of hybrid formats, such as the dramatic reconstructions of crime in *Crimewatch UK* (1984–) and of emergency rescues in *999* (1990), or the packaging of spectacular incidents caught on amateur camcorders that constituted *You've Been Framed* (1990–). In each case the series' commentary was dismissive of such trends, effectively presenting the argument that these represented a 'dumbing down' on the part of their audiences as much as of the television networks. Over the course of the series other television genres were targeted, including MTV-style music programmes, youth education programmes and docusoaps.

A regular vox-pop segment titled 'Speak Your Brains' took the series into the territory of more stunt-based comedy, with a disguised Morris asking members of the British public narrowly framed and leading questions about obscure topics. Here the message was to suggest not just the highly selective and manipulative manner in which such notions of 'public opinion' were constructed, but also the lack of any attempt by interviewees to counter or question the premise of the questions. In the fifth episode of *The Day Today*, Morris invented a story on the clamping of homeless people on city streets, and elicited a shocked response from singer Kim Wilde. This segment proved to be a forerunner of the style Morris adopted for his follow-up series, which took the rhetorical approach of *The Day Today* into more aggressive, stunt-based satire.

Christopher Morris's deconstruction of television non-fiction discourse was taken to its next logical development with *Brass Eye*, comprised of a 1997 series and a notorious special episode in 2001. The original series consisted of episodes centred on a single theme ('Animals', 'Drugs', 'Science', 'Sex', 'Crime' and 'Decline'), allowing Morris to adopt a pseudo-current affairs approach, including developing a more coherent overall frame for each episode. As in *The Day Today*, key elements of televisual presentation were recreated, although with a higher degree of visual density, especially incorporating sequences with rapid-paced free-association visual puns that drew more generally upon audiences' familiarity with television aesthetics. Instead of having an ensemble cast for support, Morris played multiple characters himself, appearing as the in-studio presenter and in various reporter roles. The same satiric techniques from Morris' earlier series were used here to construct a seemingly rational frame for barely plausible (fictional) issues that each episode could 'campaign' against. The agenda of this series, in other words, was to target the agenda-setting power of media and the dangers this power could have within a competitive media environment. Here *Brass Eye* acted upon specific assumptions about the agenda of television news. It attacked the tendency for news media (particularly but not exclusively television news media) to focus, intensify or even generate public hysteria over social and political issues. These media-heightened panics could then be represented as flashpoints for the national psyche and used both as a means of generating ratings for the networks and reinforcing efforts to position them at the centre of socio-political debates.

Morris often invented an interest group campaigning on a fake issue, then approached a number of prominent celebrities and politicians for their endorsement of a seemingly worthy cause. His success exposed (depending upon your cynicism) the gullibility of public figures, their deference to those with apparently legitimate television credentials, their laziness in checking facts for themselves or their willingness to exploit any such opportunities to raise their public profile. Morris, dressed in a token disguise, was able to get these figures to repeat to camera often absurd public service announcements (PSAs). In the 1997 series, the 'Drugs' episode was particularly effective as a hoax for its participants, enticing a member of parliament (David Arness) to sound the alarm in the British House of Commons over the emergence of the completely fictional drug supposedly nicknamed 'cake'.

The 2001 *Brass Eye* special extended this approach to the subject of 'Paedophilia'. The programme itself is a densely layered construction, including sophisticated graphics, fake 'live' broadcasts, historical narratives using archival footage, dramatic 'reconstructions', vox-pop and fake focus groups using real people, faked undercover reporting and various stunts, including an apparent studio invasion by a militant paedophile organisation. One sequence manoeuvres Michael Hames, former head of the Obscene Publications Branch into ruminating on the relative obscenity of grotesque (fictional) works of art. The usual celebrity PSAs focused this time on anxieties over online games, with Morris getting even reporters and broadcasters to warn viewers to be vigilant against (fictional) technologies that allowed paedophiles to get the keyboards of remote internet users to release date-rape gases, or to turn children's computer screens into remote cameras or somehow transform them into physically interactive screens controlled by a sexual predator's gloves.

The clear target of the special was widespread public anxiety over the online sexual predation of children. From Morris's perspective this was media-generated hysteria which tended to overwhelm more rational public debate. One narrative running through the programme was a series of live reports on an increasingly angry protest outside a prison over the possible release into the community of a known paedophile, despite the fact that he was near death and in a coma. The hypocrisy of television coverage is made explicit by Morris as presenter: in introducing a lurid reconstruction of the man's crimes, he explains, 'We believe his story is too upsetting to transmit. We only do so tonight with that proviso.' The presence of television news crews at the prison protest is seen to increase the hysteria and possibilities for violence – quite literally, as the crew throw a dummy into the crowd and encourage its members to demonstrate how they would stomp on the convict. Overall, the programme is a sustained exercise in dark satire, but ironically its ultimate message was overwhelmed by political criticism of the broadcast. The programme infuriated those who had unwittingly participated in its satire and prompted over two thousand complaints to broadcaster Channel 4 over Morris's comedic treatment of what many viewers considered a serious social issue.

Mockumentary news satires which have followed in the wake of *The Day Today* rarely achieve anything like its satirical bite. Most target emerging trends in television news presentation. *CNNNN: Chaser Non-Stop News Network* was an Australian series which explored local current events and issues through a close pastiche of the American news network CNN (Cable News Network). CNN gained a global profile when it became among the first news networks to broadcast 24 hours a day and quickly emerged as one of a small number of iconic news networks. *CNNNN* was created by an ensemble cast of performers, including Craig Reucassel, Chris Taylor, Julian Morrow, Dominic Knight, Charles Firth and Chas Licciardello (most of whom have since gone on to more wide-ranging stunt-based comedy with *The Chasers' War on Everything* (2006–)). The series copied the aesthetic of CNN, with a news anchor desk located in a busy news office, variations on a blue-dominated set design and the use of simplistic and dramatic graphic language to dominate the screen, including its distinctive scrolling 'newsbar' offering real-time headlines. *CNNNN*'s take on the newsbar was to substitute headlines in the same vein as the satirical newspaper *The Onion*, offering absurdist stories within news genres featuring recognisable Australian and world figures.[1] The implicit argument of the series was that such networks were based more on entertainment than on actual news gathering and focused heavily on self-promotion. Fake promotions for other *CNNNN* programmes extended the premise (the most distinctive of these was for a 'CNX News Slam', which offered viewers 'just the big hits – less explanation, more detonation').

The series also parodied CNN efforts to develop celebrity status for news anchors, constructing elaborate soft-focus promotions for fake anchors Taylor and Reucassel. The famous CNN network identification spots featuring the voice of James Earl Jones solemnly intoning 'This is CNN' here became a series of slogans such as 'House of Newstainment', 'We Report, You Believe', 'Because Opinion Matters More Than Fact', 'You're Either With Us or Against Us', 'Resistance is Futile', 'One Network Under God' and 'Building Empires One War at a Time'. As these suggest, the underlying argument of *CNNNN* was that networks such as CNN not only were dominated by an entertainment agenda but also mindlessly repeated discourses supportive of President George W. Bush's 'War on Terror'. One recurring stunt segment provided more focused disquiet over the formation of American foreign policy by collating vox-pop interviews staged by the comedians with real American citizens who revealed their ignorance of even basic facts about global events and issues.

While each episode was based around a specific fictional event, the series' key theme was really the absence of actual, coherent and detailed information being provided by news organisations, with anchors continually interrupting each other with 'live' reports or interrupting interviews with experts to provide fractured forms of the 'latest, breaking news' rather than taking time to put anything into a wider context. One central technique was to compress the narrative of real events into absurd lengths. As an incomplete piece of information was apparently discovered, it was immediately accepted as fact by the anchors, transformed into a graphic headline and its implications explored with an in-studio expert – all within the space of a few seconds. The emphasis was on endless speculation, including the repeated suggestion that any event 'might be linked to Al Queda'. Despite a core narrative for each episode, there was not always any effort to retain a sense of coherence, with constant interruptions for fake advertisements. Other segments targeted specific Australian current affairs programmes such as *A Current Affair* (1971–), recreated on *CNNNN* as 'A Chaser Affair', and other forms of popular reality programming.

Another Australian mockumentary series, *Real Stories* (2006), took its cue more exclusively from current affairs programming. Devised by comedians Hamish Blake, Andy Lee, Tim Bartley and Ryan Shelton, the series derived from a mockumentary short film which mimicked a current affairs item to present a story about a couple who unwittingly purchased a show home and were consequently forced to accommodate regular visits from real estate agents. *Real Stories* repeated the format in half-hour episodes, each presenting four segments that effectively functioned as mockumentary shorts which appropriated a tabloid current affairs approach. The series used the format to play with assumptions associated with a series of Australian stereotypes, producing stories that did not need to rely on developing more extended narratives (stories included coverage of a man 'grounded for life', a celebrity sex-tape director, a town observing 525,599 minutes of silence in honour of all fallen Australian soldiers and comedy writers available for personal hire). Actual news presenter Jennifer Adam fronted the programme, introducing each item and exhibiting an obviously scripted fake warm sincerity to viewers (in the final episode, she promises that she loves each and every viewer from the bottom of her heart).

A very different approach is used for *Broken News* (2005–), a British series which virtually abandons any effort at narrative. Episodes are constructed to mimic what might appear on screen if a viewer were restlessly grazing over a series of news channels, sometimes returning to an earlier channel but never long enough to view a complete report. The result is extremely fragmented in narrative terms, but also effective in suggesting the banality and conformity of television news presentation. Most of the stories focus on trivial information, are centred on spectacular footage or are updates of previous stories without any new information, particularly placing a premium on 'liveness' over explanation. Reporters at times simply interview each other for reactions to events or offer speculations on events that are assumed to be about to happen. News presenters across diverse programmes (and nations) are shown to share the same language patterns, right down to their accents – in contrast to segments featuring people with everyday voices, who here are often incomprehensible because of their regional dialects. The series is somewhat frustrating to watch, despite the relative sophistication in replicating the layered graphics of news presentation, as it never progresses beyond its simplistic premise and rarely makes use of the satiric possibilities of its jump cuts between incongruous materials.

Klutz cops: *Operation Good Guys* and *Reno 911!*

A second group of mockumentary series falls within the same broad frame of playing with television constructions of authoritative and institutional discourses. Instead of referencing the conventions of news presentation, these series target the archetypal reality programme *Cops* and its brethren of hybrids centred on police enforcement. As detailed in chapter 4, *Cops* has been a consistent feature of global television programming since the late 1980s, retaining the key elements of its signature narrative and aesthetic style, even as other hybrid formats have appropriated, exhausted and abandoned the same elements. The familiarity and relative exhaustion of such hybrid patterns make them prime material for parody and satire. Those mockumentary series which directly reference such reality formats, either through a sustained appropriation of their signature styles or by exploring the possibilities of material which such programmes exclude, provide deliberately contrasting perspectives of law enforcement and crime to that of *Cops* itself.

The two series discussed here use the mockumentary approach to generate constructions of police officers that can best be labelled as 'klutz cops'.[2] British series *Operation Good Guys* (1997–2000) and the American *Reno 911!* (2003–) both operate to subvert any suggestions of competency, impartiality and authority in their representations of law enforcement institutions. Cameras instead document police incompetence and suggest that these officers are perhaps more dangerous to the wider public than the criminals whom they ineptly pursue. As such, whether through deliberate intention or not, these series work to subvert the specific discourses of police enforcement generated by *Cops* and similar reality formats, and consequently directly engage with the wider social discourses which support and nurture broader surveillance cultures.

Each of these programmes offers quite different comedic forms and contrasting commentaries on the variety of issues raised by reality formats. In part this is because they come from the very different production environments of Britain and the United States, and draw from the distinct traditions of reality programming within these contexts. Both draw from reality formats based on law enforcement, but each also incorporates elements of docusoap format, as the series follow characters not just over a number of episodes (a clear departure from the pattern of *Cops* and its ilk, which followed a specific police unit only for a single episode or segment of an episode) but also over a number of seasons. In part, the difference between these series also reflects the fact that they come from different periods in the development of mockumentary television, with *Operation Good Guys* treading an innovative and somewhat experimental path, while the later *Reno 911!* was able to draw from a more established field of precedents.

Operation Good Guys was created by Ray Burdis and Dominic Anciano, originally intending it to be a police drama before being encouraged by Hugo Blick to convert their idea to comedic form. Blick, later a key driving force behind the mockumentary *Marion and Geoff*, then served as producer, co-writer and fellow performer. As with many of the mockumentary series discussed in this volume, the series' production style centred on the improvisational talents of an ensemble cast, with scenes scripted only as a general narrative frame (suggesting in broad terms what needed to happen), while specific actions and dialogue were left to the players.[3] *Good Guys*, however, at the time of its production operated in unknown territory, helping to establish the possibilities of this production template and also effectively demonstrating some of the difficulties of maintaining creative consistency within such an approach (a difficulty that affects many of the series discussed in this and the next chapter).

The initial premise of the first series was that Det. Insp. Beach (David Gillespie) had taken it upon himself to invite a documentary crew to cover the formation of what he insisted was a 'crack undercover squad' tasked with bringing down local crime lord Smiler McCarthy (played, in a non-speaking role, by Blick). Co-creator Burdis played Beach's second-in-command, Det. Sgt. Ash, a sycophantic, effeminate sidekick but also apparently Beach's only friend. The homoerotic overtures to their friendship, which neither seemed to acknowledge, became more pronounced over the first series (which ended with Beach revealing his cross-dressing tendencies to his stunned squad members). Anciano was Sgt. Dominic de Sade, head of the squad's three-person Armed Response Team (ART), a closet sadomasochist who paraded around with his team in black uniforms, seemingly in constant training mode. Other key characters were the short-tempered undercover officer Bones, who frequently clashed with laid-back wannabe musician Strings (constantly playing Bowie-derived songs, even on undercover stakeout), undercover operative Gary Barwick (Gary Beadle), and vice officer Kim Finch (Kim Taylforth). Barwick's contributions to the squad were constantly handicapped by his disintegrating marriage and he ultimately developed a relationship with Finch, who performed all operations dressed as a prostitute. The final squad members were the gormless and inept Mark Kemp (Mark Burdis), the police Commissioner's nephew and often the cause of the squad's failure to successfully complete any actual undercover police operations, and accountant Roy Leyton (Roy Smiles), the only civilian in the squad.

The opening title sequence to the first season maintained the pretence that this was a reality series, listing the cast only by their characters' names. These initial episodes closely followed the format of the first wave of British police reality television programmes of the 1990s, with hand-held cameras in a strictly observational approach, avoiding music, captions or a voice-over. The key conventions used were interviews with members of the squad, intercut with layered vérité footage, and mock surveillance footage helping to document those operations from wider angles (generally in long shot, complete with prominent time codes and filenames). The vérité footage oscillated between closely framed, intimate hand-held footage of the squad in all their preparations for operations, with squad members aware of the crew's presence, and more surreptitious filming inside the squad's headquarters, as cameras filmed through glass walls, open doorways, around corners and down stairwells to capture conversations which squad members did not realise were being recorded.

The visual footage and interviews often complemented each other to provide several perspectives on an event, or were deliberately played against each other to reveal the gaps between the actions of their key characters and how they explained themselves in interviews. The most glaring examples of the latter were always centred on Beach himself, who (in a forerunner of Ricky Gervais in *The Office*) is continually caught out as the smooth, rehearsed patter he provides in his interviews contrasts with his open desperation as the façade of competence and authority crumbles in the presence of the cameras. Beach's explanation of each failed operation is pure management speak as he quotes from heroes such as J. Edgar Hoover (an in-joke, as Beach is later revealed to be a cross-dresser himself) and Elliott Ness. In early episodes he keeps asking the crew if they got what they needed, getting abrupt affirmative grunts from the crew. When things go wrong, Beach or other squad members immediately turn to the crew and ask if the camera can be turned off, or put up a hand to cover the lens. In the first episode, the hyper-aggressive Bones actually attacks the camera and chases

it down an alley, screaming for it to be turned off. When Bones
clashes with Strings in a briefing, Beach is suddenly in extreme
close-up, trying to block the lens and pleading with the documentary crew to not use the tape, as what they have witnessed is not
typical behaviour. Next we see Ash coaching the squad on how to
act, saying 'this time, no fighting' (the fictional documentary crew
obviously don't use the tamer, performed meeting scene, as we
immediately fade to the next scene).

The narrative arc of the first series follows the gradual diminish-
ment of the squad as they deplete their finances. They lose money
in attempted drug stings (Kemp hands over two thousand pounds
to a drug dealer who promises to be 'right back'), incur personal
and property costs as a result of harassing innocent suspects, and
especially suffer from the actions of accountant Leyton as he gradually siphons off their funds (in another sign of the squad's incompetence, as the series progresses Leyton buys a new car and
expensive clothes, appears in the squad's offices with two beautiful
girlfriends on his arms, all without anyone asking questions).
Throughout the series, the squad bond during adversity, and the
crew seem to become accepted as de facto members of the squad,
with the officers providing increasingly honest and unintentionally
revealing interviews, and at one stage (episode 4) Mark the cameraman comes out from behind his lens to party with Finch and her
flatmates, who flirt with the rest of the crew.

As funds dwindle, office equipment is sold off, the squad are
reduced to having a single payphone in the main office, and de Sade
and his ART team have to make do with less and less equipment.
In a brilliant sequence from the second episode, de Sade, his two
team members and the documentary crew stand next to a Mini
Cooper, trying to figure out how they will all get inside (they do,
with the sound man's microphone squeezed into frame near the roof
and the camera almost resting on the shoulder of one of the ART
men). In desperation, Beach organises a fund-raising event complete with variety entertainment, a staged rescue operation featuring the ART and fairground games (we see members of the
documentary crew playing). The large banner hanging over the
fund-raiser reads: 'Open Day: Meet Your Local Undercover Police'.
The final episode has the squad sitting on the floor of their now
completely bare offices as Beach reads them Leyton's postcard from
Spain revealing the scale of his embezzlement and mocking them.

The overall effect of *Operation Good Guys*, as suggested above, is a subversion of the usual representations of law enforcement constructed through reality programming. Instead of a highly professional, resourceful, intelligent, well-led and managed unit, the undercover squad reveal themselves to be more dangerous to innocent bystanders than are the criminals. The programme lasted for three seasons, although only the first season both used a mockumentary format exclusively and was able to maintain a satiric consistency across episodes. The second and third series retain the hand-held filming/interview approach, but largely abandon other aspects of the first series. There is little use of around-the-corner or hidden filming, or surveillance footage, and the producers introduced both a docusoap voice-over narrator and (most needlessly) a conventional sitcom laugh track. The content of these later series also became more inconsistent, with more frequent guest stars (a feature of the first series, but used with comparatively more subtlety) and increasingly absurd situations. The running joke of the second series was that the BBC had decided the team were not telegenic enough and that they were demoted by police headquarters because of public (televised) exposure of their incompetence. They are forced into extended training before Beach begs the BBC to allow the squad more air-time. In following episodes the squad organise and perform a television variety show, find themselves marooned on a deserted island (a parody of the BBC's *Castaway* (2000)) and serve as security detail for royalty.

Reno 911!, one of the longer-running television mockumentary series, also took its cue from the early wave of reality programmes that focused on law enforcement, in this case drawing from the American context, and in particular the signature style and approach of *Cops* (the title refers to a William Shatner-hosted reality programme *Rescue 911!* (1989–96) which focused on dramatic reconstructions of rescues). The premise of the series is that a reality programme is documenting the duties of officers from the (fictitious) Reno Sheriff's Department. Using actors who are veterans of sketch comedy and, as with *Good Guys*, a reliance on improvisation within loosely scripted episode frames, *Reno* closely matches the sense of spontaneity and immediacy which *Cops* generates around the encounters between police officers and petty criminals. There is no laugh track and many of the familiar conventions of *Cops* are closely appropriated. There is an opening disclaimer (in this case: 'Due to the graphic nature of this program, viewer discretion is advised'), establishing shots of the police buildings, captions to identify locations and police officers, the blurring of suspects' faces and the dominance of hand-held footage interspersed with surveillance footage (such as from cameras mounted on the dashboards of police vehicles). Other elements of the programme's packaging draw from the *Cops* template, but are also familiar from other hybrid formats, such as the use of a musical motif, quick montages of location shots between scenes and fake previews for the following week's episode.

Reno 911! has remained consistent in its aesthetic and narrative structure over its multiple seasons, although it has tended to become more inconsistent and erratic in its actual content (as with the feature film, titled *Reno 911!: Miami* (2007), based on the series). *Cops* itself uses a highly segmented narrative structure: there are no regular characters as such, with individual police officers appearing perhaps only briefly in interview situations (such as preparing for an operation or on patrol), and no consistent locations. With *Reno 911!* the producers have chosen to also follow a highly segmented narrative approach, while using the same stable set of characters and central location (the police headquarters) which are familiar elements of sitcom conventions. The result is something of a hybrid mix of sketch show and sitcom. Each episode (at least in the early seasons) generally followed a predictable pattern, using one or sometimes two key narratives that were broken up by regular segments that simply placed characters in a one-joke setpiece. These set-pieces often focused on the officers' encounters with civilians and suspects, with frequent use of running gags during each season, such as officers' safety presentations to local school children, testing bullet-proof vests on the firing range, public service announcements, practising live television statements from the Reno Sheriff's Department (the officers never realise that they are already live on air) and fake ads for security devices. Both the narrative and set-piece segments could draw upon the improvisational skills of the cast, within the overall structure for each episode. The narrative of each episode, as with many other mockumentary series, was built during post-production through a process of sorting through the best takes from each scene or set-piece (Ostrow, 2003).

The core of the series is the interchanges between the ensemble cast, each adhering to the broad template for their character, which generally stays within the ethnic and gender stereotypes typical of American sitcoms (until later seasons, where the characters start to reveal more absurd dysfunctional characteristics). The characters play across gender and sexual orientation (straight, gay, virgin, promiscuous), ethnicity (white American, African-American, Mexican-American) and politics (from liberal to closet fascist), but in deliberately provocative stereotypes. For example, Lt. Jim Dangle (Thomas Lennon) is a repressed homosexual who insists on wearing very short shorts, Deputy Trudy Wiegel (Kerri Kenney) is timid, naïve and depressive, Deputy Clementine Johnson (Wendi McLendon-Covey) is a flirtatious former topless showgirl and the two African-American characters Deputy S. Jones (Cedric Yarbrough) and Deputy R. Williams (Niecy Nash) (Figure 13) play variations on the stereotypes of 'laid-back' and 'sassy'. All of the core cast play multiple characters, both police officers and brief roles as stereotypical criminal suspects, dressed and using language

13. Niecy Nash, one of the ensemble cast who play incompetent members of the fictitious Reno Sheriff's Department in Comedy Central's *Cops* parody, *Reno 911!* (2003–).

that immediately marks them as 'drug addict', 'prostitute', 'car-
jacker', 'mugger' or some other social deviant (the blurring of suspects' faces helps to disguise the cast members, but part of the joke
is that we, the viewers, are also meant to be able to recognise them).

The core police characters are more or less matched in their
essential immaturity, as the relationships within their police department overall tend to resemble the petty jealousies, misunderstandings, lack of self-awareness, casual indifference, laziness and sexual
and ethnic tensions of a high school more than of a professional
institution such as the police. The police officers often play practical
jokes on each other, constantly complain about each other to the
cameras, but generally work together to protect themselves when
they need to (with the exception of the end of season two, when
the entire Department is investigated by internal affairs and they
all demonstrate spectacular examples of disloyalty). Their responses
to civilians, including possible criminal suspects, are also anything
but professional, ranging from sarcasm, fear and suspicion, the use
of unreasonable force and violence, to flirting and even dating while
on duty. One running joke concerns the repeated failure of a pros-
titution sting (largely seen through surveillance cameras) because
the officers are having too much fun. At some points the officers
even become victims themselves, generally through their own
incompetence, as they crash police vehicles or have them stolen,
are robbed of their night-stick or gun or are attacked with their
own mace.

Any time their behaviour gets out of hand and results in damage
or loss (as with *Operation Good Guys*), their immediate thought is
to cover up their incompetence, mostly by agreeing amongst themselves on a cover story and asking the camera crew to give them
the tape of what just occurred. At other times they are happy to
perform for the camera and to treat the (unseen) crew as confidantes or include them in their practical jokes. In episode 3, season
2 the cameraperson cannot scale a fence that Jones and Garcia
jump over in pursuit of a suspect, and all we can hear are the sounds
of a furious fight, including gunfire. But when the camera finally
manages to peer over the fence, the officers are revealed to have
staged the aural performance to cover the fact that they have lost
their suspect. Caught, Jones and Garcia simply run away. Occasionally
the presence of the camera spurs them to inappropriate behaviour.
In episode 10, season 1, Deputy Travis Junior (Robert Ben Garant)

gets thrown through a window while a number of officers subdue a suspect. Everyone agrees that it is the 'coolest thing that has happened since the cameras have been around', and all are bitterly disappointed when neither of the two camera people thinks they got the shot. Undeterred, the officers immediately restage the incident, including the role played by the suspect, after getting the thumbs up from one of the camera operators (we see his hand come into frame).

During season 2, the public profile of the Sheriff's Department officers (the result of the screening of the first season) prompts comments from possible suspects. One perpetrator (episode 3) recognises Dangle from the (fake) programme, who is forced to explain that their conversation may not be broadcast because he has no control over the editing of the series. In episode 5, Jones and Garcia encounter a woman in a domestic dispute who is thrilled to be filmed, but when they tell her that the incident is probably not dramatic enough to get on air she flashes her breasts and starts screaming. In episode 14, season 2, the same officers are at the centre of a Rodney King-style incident as they assault a suspect in a milkshake costume who then gets run over by a truck as he is trying to escape from them. The incident is captured on amateur videotape, from an angle that misleadingly suggests Jones and Garcia may have thrown him under the truck. The tape becomes a media sensation, prompting an internal investigation that leads to the firing and eventual arrest of all of the officers.

Over the course of the following series, the material becomes increasingly absurd, suggesting that the series premise is becoming exhausted. Characters are put into more outrageous plots and there are more frequent references to other forms of television programmes. These later seasons move away from the mock-*Cops* premise of the programme and occasionally abandon mockumentary mode altogether. Season 3 in fact largely takes on more of a docusoap structure after the officers are released from jail and scatter to endure meaningless jobs and dispiriting experiences before being reinstated after accidentally capturing a serial killer with a grudge against them. Despite the decline in quality over the season, the overall impact of the series, simply through sheer repetition of parodying television stereotypes and the exhaustive exploration of narrative possibilities over a number of seasons, is a comprehensive deconstruction of the language and aesthetic of televised police enforcement, with a secondary commentary on the wider investment in surveillance in American society. The series has accumulated a richness of detail through drawing upon a variety of social discourses, although this is not always apparent when viewing any single episode, where absurd plot twists and broad and often deliberately offensive humour dominate. In other words, any satirical effect from *Reno 911!* is accumulative, and more likely to be apparent to regular viewers of the series.

Convicts, outlaws and docusoap: *Paths to Freedom* and *Trailer Park Boys*

These final two examples are from Ireland and Canada, and while each also uses a broad focus on issues of law and order, they draw more on docusoap formats for their narrative structures and aesthetics. Both series put criminals at the centre of their narratives, taking a sympathetic perspective of former convicts and playing with the kinds of surveillance and discipline discourses typically embedded in television hybrids.

Paths to Freedom was a six-part mockumentary series, devised and directed by Ian Fitzgibbon for the Irish RTÉ channel, covering the first year in the lives of two convicts released back into society after serving their sentences. The title sequence for the series (repeated for each episode) showed the final processing and release of Jeremy Fitzgerald (Brendan Coyle) and Raymond 'Rats' Doyle (Michael McElhatton) from Mountjoy Prison, with each first introduced in a freeze-frame with his name and conviction listed on screen. The conventional (male) voice-over narrator outlines the purpose of the 'documentary' series: to examine the effectiveness of the Irish penal system by following two prisoners who have agreed to be filmed: 'For a year we followed them. Their trials and tribulations, their attempts to reclaim their lives as they took their first tentative steps on their paths to freedom.' The unseen narrator plays a key role in the series, providing a quick introduction to each scene and allowing for rapid cutting back and forth between the parallel narratives of Jeremy and Rats (the only person to call him 'Raymond' is the narrator). The shift from one narrative to another is always done through a distinctive visual transition accompanied by a 'whoosh' sound effect: the existing screen scales down to half the screen, on a black background, the second narrative quickly appears on the right hand side and then we zoom into this frame until it fills the screen. Outside of these effects, the approach is pure docusoap, with generally a single hand-held camera used within most scenes.

The two men play contrasting characters, providing the means for the producers of the series to play with a variety of Irish social discourses. Jeremy is a consultant gynaecologist, convicted of a drink-driving office that resulted in the paralysis of a recent immigrant to Ireland. He is upper class, quietly smug about his social status and furious at his conviction, which he considers deeply unjust. In an outburst in episode 3 he reveals that his agenda for participating in the 'documentary' is to clear his name ('to show that the law is an ass') and to publicise his book (titled 'Women Inside Out: the do's and don'ts of giving birth'). He is married to Helen (Deirdre O'Kane), whom we first see waiting by their expensive car in dark glasses, ignoring the camera crew as she waits to pick up her husband from prison. They live in a comfortable home in Dublin suburbia. When his wife tells the crew that Jeremy is excited about his book, he interrupts to say: 'Helen, children and dogs get excited. I'm pleased.'

Rats, in contrast, is from inner-city Dublin, unemployed and a frequent offender. Convicted of petty robbery, he is more naïve than Jeremy, and it always seems that he has agreed to be in the documentary because he didn't think to say 'no'. On his release he looks nonplussed that his wife Sharon (Neilí Conroy) is not there to greet him, tries to go back inside the prison to make a phone call, then has to walk home. Arriving at his small flat in a rundown apartment building, he discovers it completely empty, and his wife, children and most of his furniture gone.

Each episode of the series follows the contrasting trajectories of Jeremy and Rats as they try to put their lives back together. We come to know them from their surroundings, their partners and friends and their reactions to the disappointments and obstacles they encounter. The quality of the series lies partly in its attention to detail. Jeremy's closest friend, Barney (Darragh Kelly), is deferential to Jeremy's ego, a frequent partner for a round of golf at their private club, and shares his sense of injustice at Jeremy's conviction. Both express xenophobic views and suspicion about the 'real' state of injuries suffered by Jeremy's victim. Jeremy's assumptions of superiority and entitlement begin to disintegrate as he fails to secure a book contract and loses his licence to practice medicine, effectively making him unemployed as well. Everyone who reads his manuscript remarks on his obvious misogyny, and other distasteful aspects of his personality start to reveal themselves as he begins a downward spiral into depression and increasingly erratic behaviour. He sets up camp on his back lawn and retreats into fantasies centred on karate, Lord of the Dance and almost obsessive surveillance of his drink-driving victim (he tracks the man and his wife, dressed in commando gear and armed with a camcorder – almost resembling a hybrid filmmaker himself).

Our sympathies are increasingly with Rats, as he has no resources, and a wife who has left him for another man. He is forced into menial jobs such as security guard for a liquor store, fast-food worker and, eventually, helping his mother in her cleaning job. Throughout, he is constantly frustrated with his lack of opportunities, but also immediately philosophical and optimistic about his prospects for the future. Rats' best friend is Tomo (Peter McDonald), who is socially inept, has long greasy hair and horn-rimmed glasses and constantly wears a black baseball hat. When he is first interviewed by the crew he expresses jealousy that Rats had free meals and was able to take courses in prison. His interview is clumsy; he talks directly to the sound man, asking if he can hear him, pulls the boom microphone into frame and shouts into it. Together, Rats and Tomo form a double-act resembling two naïve children loose in the world, improvising plans based on their limited social experiences (a hilarious running joke through episode 3 is Rats and Tomo's inability to comprehend what they feel is the impenetrable Belfast accent when they travel from Dublin to track down Rats' wife Sharon).

There are also marked differences in the relationship between the two leads and the documentary crew who follow them. In the first episode Jeremy cautions the crew about letting their equipment scratch the interior décor of his car, and his friends expect the crew not to be an annoyance in their lives. As Jeremy's life disintegrates he resents the presence of the crew, becoming aggressive and abusing the soundman for being French. His wife, Helen, is initially aloof, then increasingly sarcastic as they continue to film, but gradually begins to treat the crew as confidantes. Beginning to drink more heavily, she starts openly flirting with the crew, then becomes abusive when they resist her advances. Rats, however, immediately treats the crew as his equals and frequently asks them for a ride in their van (he has only a bike) or for some money to buy cigarettes. All of his friends comment on the presence of the camera and introduce themselves to the crew members. After Rats forms a rock band with Tomo, he decides that his only real resource is the camera crew, and boycotts all filming until they agree to produce a music video for him (they film in his mother's flat, in bizarre costumes partly created through raiding her closet).

Paths to Freedom offers complete narrative closure. Once an initial premise has been established in episode 1, together with the traits of its two main characters, things proceed to their logical conclusions. The quality of the series derives from the performances of Coyle, McElhatton and the rest of the cast, the crafting of the details of their social environment (revealed through everything from dialogue to set design and costuming), together with the manner in which each episode inexorably moves towards the series' comic-tragic finale.

Trailer Park Boys, a Canadian production that, as of this publication date, is the longest-running mockumentary series, offers quite contrasting lessons in mockumentary storytelling. *Trailer Park Boys* began with a short mockumentary film which then became the basis for a low-budget movie by director Mike Clattenburg that premiered at Atlantic Film Festival in 1998. Its success in turn attracted producer Barrie Dunn and, together with lead actors John Paul Tremblay and Robb Wells, they developed the mockumentary television series (a later 2006 movie dropped the mockumentary premise). The core of the series is the focus on the everyday escapades of Julian (Tremblay) and Ricky (Wells), two convicts who continually try, but fail, to reform their lives by moving away from lifestyles centred on varieties of criminal behaviour (Figure 14). Julian plays the more level-headed and intelligent of the two, with ambitions to escape to a more conventional life, while Ricky is short-tempered, rarely considers the consequences of his actions and is more comfortable with what he knows best, including marijuana growing and poorly planned robberies. Each season tends to begin with both released from a Nova Scotia correctional facility, while season finales typically find them both arrested and back in familiar cells (they are comfortable there, it is their second home).

Outside of prison they live in Sunnyvale Trailer Park, where they are effective leaders of its community of lower-class

14. Central characters Julian (John Paul Tremblay) and Ricky (Robb Wells)
from the Canadian *Trailer Park Boys* (2001–), the longest running
mockumentary television series.

semi-permanent residents, including their best friend Bubbles (Mike
Smith), occasional romantic partners Sarah (Sarah Dunsworth) and
Lucy (Lucy Decoutere) and a host of secondary players, such as
Ricky's wheelchair-bound father (series producer Dunn). The boys
constantly battle for control of the park with trailer park supervisor
and former police officer Jim Lahey (John Dunsworth) and his
sidekick Randy (Patrick Roach). Much of the action over each
season revolves around the various get-rich schemes of Julian and
Ricky that draw in other park residents, while Lahey and Randy
attempt to get them arrested and sent back to jail.

At its heart *Trailer Park Boys* is a conventional sitcom, in the
sense that it is set within a single location, each episode ends with
a clear sense of closure, and the characters have remained extremely
consistent and associated with specific character traits across a
number of seasons. Their behaviour, dress and language are all
predictable – such as Julian's costume of black T-shirt and jeans and
the rum-and-coke drink he carries in most scenes. The stability of

the basic situation and core cast of *Trailer Park Boys* partly derives from the facts that all of its original cast and crew knew each other before the series and the series has been the primary vehicle for their careers. Mike Smith, who plays Bubbles, was the sound man for initial episodes, was then written into the show and was later added as co-writer with Clattenburg, Wells and Tremblay. Some of the props used in the programme actually belong to cast or crew members. The co-creators have retained control over its production and sought to maintain it as an alternative to conventional television programming.

The opening title sequence, with a theme song provided by a friend of director Clattenburg's, consists of a montage of sepia-coloured, idyllic exterior shots of scenes within trailer parks, with tidy backyards, children playing on its streets and heard on the soundtrack, together with birdsong. The sense is of a safe, secure world and almost a conservative presentation of family values, a message complemented with the sense of disruption of the park community whenever it is visited by local law enforcement. In a DVD commentary for the season 1 finale, Clattenburg argues that the premise for the series is '*Cops* told from the criminal's point of view', but it could more accurately be described as a Canadian mockusoap (see Chapter 9).

In early episodes of the first season Julian answers queries from other characters about the presence of the cameras with the vague response that a 'friend' is doing a documentary on his life. Certainly the production has maintained a low-budget look, with a reliance on digital cameras, and editing conducted on a Macintosh computer using the nonlinear editing programme Final Cut Pro. All filming is shot on location (in a number of real trailer parks), with flat, naturalistic lighting and sound. The footage is mostly hand-held (with some noteworthy exceptions, as discussed below), filmed with cameras that appear to merely follow action spontaneously within a scene, and there are small touches such as unexpected zooms which remind viewers of the mockumentary premise. There are a number of unusual shots that do not always gel with the series' fly-on-the-wall premise, such as mounted cameras on the roofs and doors of cars (which do not appear in shots from other cameras that are supposedly simultaneously filming), but director Clattenburg is otherwise able to consistently maintain a mockumentary format.

Over its course, however, the series has not always been able to maintain a consistency in the plausibility and quality of its narrative. To some extent this is inevitable, given the unexpected longevity of the series and the consequent exhaustion of narrative possibilities involving the core cast and largely single location (this is a natural difficulty all long-running series eventually exhibit). Partly this is also an inherent weakness in the production's reliance on improvisation, with each episode building just from a rough narrative frame and structured through post-production. However, there are also features of the mockumentary premise which have been left unexplored, or rarely touched upon, over the several years of the programme.

The first series hints at the alternative possibilities which the producers could have pursued. Julian's efforts to reform himself are partly prompted by the presence of the cameras, while Ricky initially struggles to present himself in a good light. Generally, however, the trailer park residents are invariably honest and straightforward toward the presence of the cameras and no one makes any real attempt to hide criminal activity from the crew (this is in fact an integral part of their appeal as characters). Not surprisingly, at the end of the first series, Julian and Ricky go back to jail, convicted partly by the various forms of evidence that have been recorded by the documentary crew. In subsequent series, however, no one modifies their behaviour around the camera crew and there is never again any suggestion that their footage is used against Julian and Ricky. Further than this, there is never any real feedback from the apparent broadcast of the series itself. All of the characters at various points reveal information that could dramatically change relationships between the trailer park residents, but this never seems to come back to haunt them. An occasional comment comes back to Ricky that he does not come across well on television, but nothing within the trailer park changes because of their television appearance. The producers have obviously decided to just fudge this issue in favour of maintaining the series' longevity, and the result is as if the series' characters never see themselves on screen and never ultimately have to deal with the consequences of the crew's presence.

Outside of these omissions, the relationship between the core characters and the fictional documentary crew develops several layers over the course of the programme. In a similar manner to

Reno 911! the cumulative effect is a useful commentary on the complex ethical issues inherent in the encounter between a documentary crew and their subjects. For the bulk of the series the crew are anonymous, with their characterisation indirectly constructed through their shot selection and apparent editing choices for the broadcast cut of the series. In general, they are completely integrated into the trailer park community and there appears to be mutual respect between crew and community. Julian and, especially, Ricky frequently abuse the camera operators for not leaving them alone – but considering that verbal abuse is part of the natural language of the park, this is almost a sign of affection towards the crew (it is also clearly a means to remind viewers of the mockumentary premise by calling attention to the presence of a fictional camera crew). There are occasional suggestions that the residents are irritated by the presence of the cameras, but usually these are countered by scenes where Julian or Ricky use the crew to document the activities of Lahey so that he can be blackmailed, or to aid their criminal activity (such as when they are apprehended by police officers in the second episode of the first season, and convince the officers that they are actually part of a documentary crew in the process of evaluating their performance). At other times the crew engage in hidden filming, against the explicit requests of residents, suggesting that they either have another agenda or are capable of lying as persuasively as do their subjects.

The close relationship between the crew and the trailer park boys allows for some satirical comments on the nature of televised crime. In an attempted drug deal (episode 4, series 1), the dealer opens fire on Julian and Ricky because he sees the crew and thinks that they must be the police. Later Ricky gets the sound man to help steal a piece of farm equipment; the sound man promptly gets shot by a farmer. There is brief chaos as Julian helps to drag the sound man into their truck, while Ricky helps with the sound equipment. They drop the injured man off at the local hospital and get a call from him later to thank them and beg 'don't let them fire me, this is the best job I've ever had'. In episode 5 of the first season, the crew tag along with the boys as they rob a convenience store. We cut to the surveillance footage of the event as they all burst into the store, leading to the superbly ironic image of Julian and Bubbles in careful disguise while their attending camera crew are not (suggesting that the crew consider themselves to be simply documenting the crime and therefore can not be accomplices).

Over the multiple seasons of the programme there are in fact frequent references to the wider fields of surveillance that capture the illegal activities of the trailer park boys. There are many scenes which follow a similar structure to the police operations in *Operation Good Guys*, with cutting between hand-held cameras and shots from surveillance footage (where the characters' voices are also captured). The finale to season 2 features Julian, Ricky and Bubbles on the run from the police, in a pickup truck towing a caravan full of marijuana, and we cut back and forth between shots inside the truck and police helicopter footage with police radio chatter on the soundtrack. At other times there is more playful use of alternative means of capturing footage, such as from Hi-8 footage when residents J-Roc (Jonathan Torrens) and Tyrone (Tyrone Parsons) try to make a pornographic film, or the home movie footage incorporated into Ricky's aborted wedding at the end of season 1. The result is a layered series of representations in which different kinds of videographic and cinematographic non-fiction capture the everyday lives of the trailer park boys. Despite the comparative simplicity of the narrative structure and core characters of the *Trailer Park Boys*, then, the series as a whole has accumulated a detailed exploration of the nature and complexity of key aspects of the televisual fact-fiction continuum.

Notes

1 The Onion website has since created the 'Onion News Network', providing short online clips that closely resemble the form and agendas of the news satires discussed here.
2 The idea of 'klutz cops' draws deliberately from the notion of 'klutz films' suggested by Jon Dovey (2000) in identifying the emergence of documentaries from filmmakers partly intent on deconstructing the authoritative perspective traditionally conferred by the genre. Examples of such filmmakers include Ross McElwee, Nick Broomfield, Michael Moore and Morgan Spurlock.
3 Burdis, in an interview included in the DVD of the series.

9

Mockusoaps: people and places

Many of the more interesting mockumentary series are clearly intended to be hybrids of docusoaps and sitcoms. They draw directly from audience's familiarity with docusoap, a key reason why these series, which we can term 'mockusoaps', have been most prominent within British televisual space, as this has also been a significant site of docusoap production. As with docusoaps, the mockusoap involves a focus on the everyday, on the voice and activities of the common people. Drawing on the well-established aesthetic traditions of observational documentaries, in particular the hand-held immediacy of cinéma vérité, mockusoaps pretend to document the everyday dramas of a collective of characters within specific locations. Mockusoaps involve character studies, typically derived from everyday discourses of gender, ethnicity and class within their national context of production. Operating within the broader agenda of comedy vérité, mockusoaps serve as an innovative take on sitcom conventions, using the encounter with a documentary crew as the basis of how they represent characters and their interrelationships. Some use comparatively subtle forms of humour for sitcom, eschewing a laugh track and resonating with a localised audience through accumulating observations. There is a different kind of relationship established with viewers here, relying on characters that resonate more with assumptions of everyday national traits and characteristics, generating a shock of recognition, a charge of the real that provides a distinct satirical edge to their comedy. In many cases this involves relying on a 'comedy of the cringe', as many critics have identified it, involving audiences' recognition of the authenticity of less admirable kinds of human behaviour.

The effectiveness of mockusoap, then, derives especially from a combination of aesthetic approach and a type of performance which is atypical of the long history of sitcom. Some of the series discussed in the previous chapter have elements of mockusoap tendencies. Both *Paths to Freedom* and *Trailer Park Boys* (discussed at the end of the previous chapter), for example, could be argued as more mockusoap than parodic pastiche of surveillance-based documentary hybrids. The series below, while generally operating more purely within the mockusoap vein, also reference particular nationally inflected documentary, hybrid and comedic traditions that would be familiar to their immediate localised audiences. The discussion here covers a number of distinctive examples within the spectrum of mockusoaps, drawing from the large corpus of British mockusoaps, but also including examples from Australia, New Zealand and the United States. Rather than deal with these series in a strictly chronological order, this chapter looks first at initial British efforts at mockusoap involving more episodic form, and then at examples which can be grouped together for their common thematic terrain, before ending with a comparative analysis of the British and American versions of what is perhaps the definitive mockusoap, *The Office*.

Episodic series: a collection of one-offs

There is an overlap here with the short-form and experimental mockumentary series discussed in chapter 7, not least because some involve the same stable of producers and performers. The three British series below, however, exhibit a greater confidence in the use of mockumentary formats than those earlier series, developing a consistency of perspective and approach across an entire series that suggests a stable construction of a documentary crew as implicit characters themselves. Each of the episodes of these three series, however, is relatively self-contained. Each is an anthology of mockusoaps: episodes focus on distinct characters and serve as enclosed mini-narratives and (except in a limited way in the last of these examples) do not look to revisit a large cast of characters or interweaving storylines within an overall narrative arc. They each offer useful demonstrations of some of the possibilities and challenges in operating within mockumentary mode. They are clearly referenced to different tendencies within British docusoaps, taking these as templates for experimenting with their possibilities as a basis for comedic form.

People Like Us

People Like Us was constructed as a satire of the kind of small-scale BBC documentary series with the worthy intention of presenting everyday British people to viewers. Each episode consisted of an encounter between inept reporter Roy Mallard (Chris Langham, the director of *Posh Nosh*) and someone with an everyday occupation, such as managing director of a small company, real estate agent, photographer, local police officer, solicitor, head teacher, bank manager, vicar, airline pilot or even just 'mother'. The series was distinct in its focus on developing the character of the documentary filmmaker himself. Most of the series discussed below are content to leave the production team relatively anonymous, simply suggesting an agenda and perspective through camera movement and selective editing. Over two series of six half-hour episodes each, Mallard attempted to discover what each person he interviewed actually did on a typical day. Tightly scripted, the series was designed to appear as naturalistic as possible, through performance and features such as natural lighting and sound (with each of these series, there was no laugh track).

The series originated as a BBC Radio 4 programme. It confused some listeners, who regularly complained about the poor reporting of Mallard, but developed a following over 3 years (from 1995 to 1997) before making the transition to television. The BBC shot two versions of the series pilot, one with Mallard visible on screen, the other where he was not (Rochlin, 2003). It was the 'unseen' characterisation which was chosen, providing a distinctive approach to character development and meaning that viewers were forced, as with the radio series, to largely imagine how Mallard appeared, cued by the nature of his interview questions and, especially, the reactions he generated from the people he interviewed. (There were some very brief images of Mallard, captured by the camera reflected in windows, or simply with his arm appearing in frame – but he is too shy to remain on camera.)

The humour of the series was comparatively subtle, and based especially on a continual disruption of viewers' expectations of the competence of BBC reporters. Each episode was highly structured, replicating the pattern of a series in the transition between television documentary series and early British docusoap. A banal opening credit sequence, using a collage of everyday images and accompanied by an insipid theme tune, was followed by what seemed initially to be a conventional expositional introductory sequence. As scenes of the locality of each interviewee rolled on the screen – standard shots of the main street of a small town, local people walking, exterior shots of buildings, before resting on an exterior shot of the location of the occupation of the week – Mallard's formulaic voice-over blandly introduced the community and the week's interviewees. Repeating meaningless statistics, tired narrational clichés and absurd non sequiturs in deadpan fashion, Mallard appeared to be role-playing what he conceived to be an authoritative voice-over. As with *Monty Python*, part of the satire here lay in the careful play with language that revealed both the craft and the banality of BBC conventions (the first episode states that 'this could be anywhere in Europe, but it's not', episode 4 informs viewers that they are in 'an area of Cheshire that's often called the Surrey of the North, except by people who live in places like Sussex for whom Surrey of the North is Surrey'). Mallard's voice-over is a constant presence through each episode, replicating conventional docusoap formula by focusing on the everyday routines of interviewees, but in this case calling attention to itself through its lack of real insight, rather than serving to neatly link sequences into a compelling narrative.

Each episode begins with Mallard arriving at a location and clumsily introducing himself to his interviewees. His social awkwardness immediately both irritates and underwhelms them (they invariably appear surprised later in the day if he reveals that he is married). From there the encounter slowly but inevitably heads downhill, not through a series of catastrophes but through a dripfeed of Mallard's inane, inappropriate or confusing questions, or simply the mere presence of the camera crew disrupting and distracting his interviewees' everyday business. He fails to gain an intimacy with his subjects and often becomes caught up in tensions within the small institutions or businesses he is visiting.

Part of the difficulty for Mallard, however, is that, invariably, nothing of any real interest actually happens during the day on which he has chosen to visit. The participants of each 'documentary' episode are distracted, harassed or generally depressed with their lives, and appear to so completely underestimate Mallard that they are completely natural in front of the camera, rarely considering how they might be representing themselves. In a sense, they are complete innocents as documentary subjects (on being told to 'just pretend we're not here', a minor character agrees and promptly enters his house and closes the door on the camera).

People Like Us ultimately works as a satire of documentary because of the gaps between voice-over, observational footage and interview style. Mallard, or his producers, have been unable to rescue his encounters into compelling episodes, through either a lack of talent or, more likely, a strict adherence to a production practice that simply churns through a formulaic approach to a subject and spits out the required 22 minutes of programming content (in the last episode of the second series Mallard reveals to an interviewee that he has been at the BBC for 17 years; he is as stuck in a dead-end job as they are).

Human Remains

Human Remains (2000) offers a different approach to mockusoap, although within the same episodic structure as *People Like Us*. This was a series of six half-hour episodes, produced by veterans of comedy vérité (Steve Coogan's Baby Cow Productions). A black comedy, the focus here is on using specific forms of comedic performance to offer a commentary on British social eccentricities. In this it reflects a key aspect of docusoap, particularly early British examples, which tended to look for distinctive personalities, social marginals or otherwise dysfunctional characters. Instead of looking for people representative of British society, such people were deliberately 'cast' as leads within docusoaps because of the ease with which their everyday dramas could be translated into compelling television narratives.

Human Remains draws from this pattern for inspiration in constructing a number of character studies of dysfunctional British couples. Each played by Rob Brydon (*Marion and Geoff*) and Julia Davis, the couples are brutally honest and open about the state of their relationships and personal foibles and, as with most of the characters in *People Like Us*, appear to be unaware of how the confessions of their private lives might appear on the small screen. The couples include an upper-class marriage of convenience; two swingers who run a bed and breakfast for a living while caring for a comatose relative; a repressed Christian couple; a prospective marriage between a bully and his compliant fiancé; and an aging small-time singing act that disintegrates over the woman's belated coming out.

Brydon and Davis developed each of their characters through improvisational rehearsal, creating performances that relied on subtle gestures that would be amplified by the intimacy of the television screen, or the building of layers of narrative detail through back stories that could be suggested partly through tone of voice, through pauses, or simply from what is not said. Their acting within each episode is an example of sustained improvisation, but honed and structured through post-production to create tightly structured character studies. Brydon and Davis' performances are enhanced by a deliberately restrained use of docusoap technique. There is no voice-over to introduce or summarise their stories, and the interviewer is only rarely heard. Instead, each couple is left to tell their own story through direct address to the camera.

The gaps between their respective representations of themselves and their partners and the truths about their everyday reality are made obvious through the juxtapositions between interview and observational sequences. Individual or joint interview segments overlap with footage that adds telling details to their narratives, generating unexpected layers of pathos or observations on their unhappiness. Each couple is interviewed and observed within their specific social environment, with footage capturing a sense of how they interact with each other and cutaways of the clutter of their living spaces used to provide colour to their stories. There are clear pointers to key British discourses around class, gender and ethnicity, but Brydon and Davis' skill means that these tend not to lapse into stereotype. The result is a series of episodes that appear to give an open, but still unintentionally intimate, glimpse into the private lives of each of the featured couples, with details that provide a convincing sense of history to their dysfunctional relationships.

That Peter Kay Thing

This approach of characters telling their own stories, using actors who appear in different personas across different episodes, is also followed by the mockusoap *That Peter Kay Thing* (2000). The combination of docusoap techniques and performance style used here has produced an effect quite distinctive from both of the series discussed above. *That Peter Kay Thing*, a seven-part series (including a pilot) of half-hour episodes, was developed from a one-off programme made for Channel 4's *Comedy Lab* (1998–) series (a showcase for new comedic talent and potential programme development). Each episode features comedian Peter Kay playing a number of both male and female characters within the same location, together with a cast of secondary characters who offer more straight-faced performances that he plays off. The pilot episode ('The Services') is set in a motorway service station in Bolton, with the following episodes set in similarly small, tightly focused locations around the same city. The situations include a club (an episode later extended and remade as the vérité sitcom *Phoenix Nights* (2001–2)), a bingo hall, an ice cream van, a performance arena, an aging local paper 'boy' receiving a community award and the story of a failed pop star. As can be gathered just from this listing, there is a slightly uneven tone and focus across the series, and while episodes are loosely connected through the reappearance of some characters, they otherwise function as stand-alone pieces.

Each episode is richly detailed, both in terms of Kay's multiple performances and in the manner in which the series is structured to mimic docusoap conventions. Actual docusoap narrator Andrew Sachs provides voice-over narration, introducing each character, linking scenes together and providing the expected summaries and previews before each advertising break and at the end of each episode. Unlike *People Like Us*, this narration could have been lifted straight out of a real docusoap. It provides a rational, deadpan structure within and against which Kay's more improvised comedic performances can operate. The series as a whole is overwhelmingly structured through dialogue, oscillating especially between Sach's and Kay's voices. Through each of his characters Kay effectively provides a series of monologues to camera, either seated in 'interviews' or more typically maintaining a commentary while moving through locations and interacting with other characters.

The dialogue-heavy scenes convey a sense that each character could easily be presented as part of a stand-up routine, with Kay dressing in different costumes and providing layers of detail through anecdotes and observations about people and events in his/her life. The docusoap format allows such content to be presented within spatial performances, in the sense that each character can be defined in relation to the physical and social spaces of each episode's location. But we never forget that this is Kay, and one layer of the series is undoubtedly meant to be an appreciation of his virtuoso skill as a comedian. This showcasing of comedic skill is also a feature of

Human Remains, but Brydon and Davis' performances are designed to be more naturalistic.

Another layer of *The Peter Kay Thing* is a commentary on aspects of the production of docusoap formats. There are lots of reflexive moments throughout the series, scenes where characters demonstrate that they are well aware of the presence of the camera, of the manner in which it might be framing and capturing their behaviour, and especially the impact that an appearance on television could have on their lives. Many characters are performing for the camera, or continually commenting on its presence, either warning others to behave correctly while it is on or complaining about its presence (at a department meeting in the pilot episode, one girl asks her manager if she gets time and a half because the Channel 4 crew is there). At other moments the camera operator appears to stumble, or to bump into obstacles while trying to follow one of Kay's characters.

A more subtle critique of docusoap's agenda occurs at the end of each episode, where there is a preview of the next (non-existent) instalment of the series – each episode, in other words, pretends to be an episode from a different series, focusing just on the characters it has introduced. Here Sach's voice-over offers a condensed narrative of incidents to come in the lives of each of the characters, a teaser that uses rapidly edited footage to emphasise emotional drama and trauma. This is a more typical pattern for docusoaps: the unfolding of a reality-based narrative, often with interweaving and not always connected storylines, over a number of episodes of a series.

The following examples of mockusoaps more closely reference this narrative structure, together with the familiar pattern of focusing on everyday people preparing for an event in which they have invested hopes and dreams, providing producers with a narrative arc that naturally builds dramatic tension over a number of episodes.

Small-town ambitions

The examples discussed in this section are from the periphery of global television production: Australia and Canada. Each of these series incorporates a wealth of intertextual references to local social and political discourses, and each enjoyed particular success with its local audiences. These, again, suggest the variety of the performance styles which have been employed within television mockumentary, as well as, in these cases, differing commitments to exploring mockumentary's inherent reflexivity toward the fact-fiction continuum.

The Games

The Games was an Australian series from the ABC channel. Co-written by John Clarke and Ross Stevenson, the series used mockumentary form to satirise the bureaucratic and political machinations required to stage the Sydney 2000 Olympic Games. Clarke and co-star Bryan Dawe have a long history on Australian television, largely based on satirising national and local politicians, using comparatively subtle means. For over 10 years the pair have performed 'interviews' in segments on Channel Nine's *A Current Affair* between a straight-faced reporter (Dawe) putting innocently common-sense questions to a familiar political figure (in other words, much the same technique that Jon Stewart adopts in *The Daily Show*). Clarke appears as the politician, but without any effort at impersonation through playing with his costume and voice. The humour in their encounter lies instead in a revealing of the absurdities of political discourse, through repeating public statements made by the politicians and explaining the 'logic' behind their policy declarations.

Clarke himself has made a career out of a signature style of comedic performance that centres on the playful use of language (inspired by *The Goons* and *Monty Python*), delivered in a laconic, partly improvised manner and often presented through encounters between his characters and a bemused straight man. It is a style which particularly lends itself to mockumentary, and there are key points in Clarke's career where he developed expertise in using the conventions of non-fiction television to perfect his humour. A New Zealander, Clarke achieved fame in his own country in the early 1970s with a character named Fred Dagg that drew on stereotypes inherent in local farming culture (the dominant local industry). In short segments on the (at that time) only national television channel, Dagg would be interviewed in a rural setting by actual reporters, explaining his philosophy of life and approach to sheep farming, while dressed in an iconic black singlet, baggy hat, walk shorts and gumboots. In 1975 Dagg announced that he was running in the local parliamentary elections, and throughout the campaign he riffed on the policies of actual politicians in mock television interviews. *The Games* played to Australian audiences familiar not only with Clarke's television characters, but also with other strands of popular local satire using comedy vérité forms (such as *Frontline* and the later *Kath and Kim*, covered in previous chapters).

The premise of *The Games* was that a documentary crew are allowed behind-the-scenes access to offices of the Administration and Logistics section of the Sydney Olympics organising body, as part of a public relations exercise. As they look for evidence of corruption and incompetence, Clarke and his administrative team juggle the presence of the cameras with the demands of interest groups, the International Olympic Committee (IOC), national politicians keen to associate themselves with a successful games and local news media. The focus of the series is really on discourses of management and administration, within an Australian context. The series is brilliantly effective in revealing the conflicts of interest and blatant politicking which lie behind the internationalist sporting rhetoric associated with the modern Olympics, in particular suggesting that the events themselves are never able to become the arena for pure sporting endeavours which they are promoted to be.

In keeping with Clarke and Dawe's signature style, most scenes in *The Games* revolve around characters arguing over the semantics of various policies, and especially attempting to make a problem disappear by relabelling it. Each episode begins with an improbable premise (for example, the administrators discover that the 100-metre track built for the Olympic Stadium is, inexplicably, only 94 metres long) and documents their immediate bureaucratic response of attempting either to blindly rationalise it or to seek someone else to blame. Episodes have the appearance of having been captured using two cameras (series director Bruce Permezel operated one of these). There are regular individual 'interviews' with the core character members, usually in sequences which cut between two interviews offering completely contrasting perspectives on the 'truth' of what is happening, and captions are used to introduce day/time and identify settings and characters. The presence of the crew is frequently acknowledged by their fictional subjects – they are greeted in the morning by characters and quickly become participants in the office activities.

The series incorporates some subtle commentary on the tensions inherent in any collaboration between documentary filmmaker and his/her subject, with continual references to the contest between the Olympics' needing to have a 'clean' public profile and the crew's need to get dramatic footage. The second series extended this commentary. It began with an innovative episode constructed as a current affairs story on the possible incompetence and corruption in Clarke's administration team, followed by a 'live' ambush interview with Clarke at his home. He unsuccessfully attempts to push the crew out the door, tries to shield his face from the horde of photographers on his doorstep and is captured making a panicked and threatening phone call to the ABC about the crew.

The other twelve episodes of this second series move back into the docusoap format of the first season. Unlike most second seasons of mockumentary series, this is distinctive in that it incorporates reaction to the public broadcast of the first season into its narrative. Forced to accept the presence of an ABC documentary crew again, this time because they are too broke to refuse their financial offer, the Olympics administrative team are caught on camera deciding how to best perform for the crew. At a team meeting with all of the wider staff in their administration, Clarke, Dawe and colleague Gina (Gina Riley) are forced to answer criticisms that the television series made them all a laughing stock and showed the key characters making fools of themselves. Other episodes in this second season include openly reflexive moments as the team occasionally help the crew to set up their camera and lights, and some moments that more playfully comment on the series' construction. The final episode, screened just before the real Sydney Olympics opened, suggests that Clarke and his fellow actors have been invited to play a part in the actual opening ceremony. John's response is bemused, stating that 'we're on a programme that a lot of people think is sending the Olympics up'.

We Can Be Heroes: Finding the Australian of the Year and Summer Heights High

Two other Australian mockumentary series are also structured around a focus on apparent docusoap subjects building towards a dramatic event. Both created by Chris Lilley, they use overlapping but still distinct mockumentary styles to showcase his virtuoso comedic performances. *We Can Be Heroes: Finding the Australian*

of the Year and its part-sequel *Summer Heights High* are similar to
That Peter Kay Thing in that their core characters are all played by
the same comedic actor, in performances that are edited down from
a body of improvisational work. Both of these series, however, are
more carefully crafted than Kay's, with each using an overall narrative structure which expertly replicates the appeal and complexity of docusoap narrative, creating layered forms of engagement for
audiences which allow a strong identification with his characters
over the course of a series.

We Can Be Heroes is constructed as a documentary series covering five people who are finalists for the Australian of the Year award
(an actual award given each year on Australia Day). The series
opens with a conventional voice-over by a female narrator (Jennifer
Byrne, a voice familiar from actual docusoaps), authoritatively
explaining the significance of the award, and the production's selection of five nominees as a focus for the series. Her introduction is
accompanied by carefully composed shots of everyday 'typical'
Australians, as the camera tracks in or swings down from a boom
to a mid-shot of each person in fixed pose. There is a polish to this
opening credit sequence which closely references prime-time docusoap productions, and which provides a conventional authoritative
frame for the series as a whole. Directed by Matt Seville, the series
has a consistent production style which includes a number of familiar docusoap elements, including captions to identify key characters,
exterior setting shots outside homes and buildings before cutting
to internal scenes, montages of vérité footage set to music or used
as counterpoint to interview material, and an upbeat leitmotif used
in transitions between characters. Graphic sequences appear at the
beginning of each episode, tracking across a map of Australia before
zooming into the location of each of the nominees as they are
introduced. There are no reflexive moments in this series, and no
effort to include members of the production crew as characters –
they are all as anonymous as a real docusoap crew. Without immediate cues such as a laugh track, viewers are effectively presented with
a convincing pastiche of a high-budget docusoap and are being
asked to identify the series as a mockumentary on content alone.

The series' fictional status, however, becomes obvious quite
early, as we recognise the same performer (Lilley) playing each of
the nominees apparently selected for this television production:
a selfish and arrogant ex-police officer (Phil Olivetti), an Asian

Ja'mie King
Sydney, New South Wales

15. Teenage narcissist Ja'mie King, one of the five characters Chris Lilley plays in the Australian mockumentary series *We Can Be Heroes: Finding the Australian of the Year* (2005).

physics postgraduate with acting dreams (Ricky Wong), an uncouth 17-year-old farmhand with a deaf twin (Daniel Sims), and a 47-year-old mother of two who excels at the sport of 'rolling' (Pat Mullins). The character who makes the most impression is a 17-year-old girl from a privileged background (Ja'mie King, pronounced 'Jar-may') (Figure 15) who automatically considers her own feelings before those of her friends and family. All of these characters are closely referenced to national stereotypes, tapping into a variety of Australian assumptions about gender, class and ethnicity that are showcased in order to be used as key targets of the series' satire.

There is a complexity to these characters that supports the series' broader satiric intent yet still allows viewers to develop sympathies with each of their stories. This is a quality that partly derives with the subtleties of Lilley's carefully crafted performances. He is able to build a depth to each character through drip-feeding details of their behaviour and attitudes through dialogue, little body gestures and fleeting facial expressions that all seem to 'reveal' the truth about themselves to the camera (as with Rob Brydon and Julia Davis in *Human Remains*, but here sustained over a six-part series). Teenager Ja'mie, for example, takes great pleasure in showing pictures of the eighty-five children, all from the same village, whom she sponsors through 'Global Vision'. She cannot actually pronounce any of their real names, so just refers to them as 'Usher', 'Denzel', or 'Eddie' depending on which African-American celebrity they remind her of. She raises money for 'her' children by going on a sponsored famine every week, which she notes also helps to keep her trim. As Lilley plays her, she constantly plays with her hair, self-consciously poses her body to best advantage in front of the camera and endlessly complains about the injustices committed against her by other people. It is a richly textured performance, providing a shock of recognition (especially for Australian audiences) even as we can appreciate Lilley's acting skill.

These performances are effective also because they operate within a carefully detailed social milieu. The camera frequently picks out personal artefacts and other details of their homes and working environments, used as cutaways to add colour to one of Lilley's in-character interviews. The most crucial factor supporting Lilley's performances, however, is perhaps the quality of actors in supporting roles. The close friends, relatives and working colleagues of each of the core characters (all Lilley) highlight and ground the parts of his performances that are nearer caricature. The effectiveness of the many instances of 'cringe comedy' at work in this series lies in their silent, pained or resigned responses to the behaviour of some of Lilley's characters. The exception is the character of Pat Mullins, whose good nature, sacrifices for her family and friends and warm relationship with her husband of 25 years are reinforced by his quiet support for all her activities. The real pathos of the series lies with her narrative, as she confronts a remission of her cancer and dies in the final episode.

This easy movement between comedy and drama adds depth to the series' narrative arc, allowing many of the characters, whom we have often seen treat their family and friends badly, to ultimately find redemption after each fails to be chosen as their state's finalist for the Australian of the Year award. The balance across the five characters' stories offers a complexity of possibilities for identification for audiences, and we move our sympathies back and forth to different characters as aspects of their lives are revealed to us. Lilley learned from the best aspects of *We Can Be Heroes* and applied these to its partial sequel, *Summer Heights High*. Set in a public high school, Ja'mie King returns as a single-semester exchange student, slumming for the cultural experience, with Lilley also playing Jonah Takalua, a break-dancing Tongan boy with behavioural problems and Greg Gregson (self-named 'Mr G.'), the school's drama teacher – played by Lilley almost as a diva-in-training. Each character's narrative allows for shifts in audience sympathies, as Mr G.'s egotism lurches out of control while he directs a musical based on a drug overdose by a popular student, while Jonah's disruptive behaviour is balanced with details about his family life and his genuine distress at being unfairly expelled from the school.

The reduction of *We Can Be Heroes*' five characters to just three here means a tighter focus and a more detailed exploration of their storylines. The series also dispenses with a voice-over narrator, allowing more space for these characters to tell their own stories and for secondary players to provide shades and colour to their relationships in mock interviews. Directed by Stuart McDonald, *Summer Heights High* also has a much denser camera style than the first series. There are frequent cuts between multiple camera positions within the same scene and regular montages of rapid camerawork, with pans, zooms and tracking of characters across the schoolyard and through corridors. These are combined with quick cuts between interview segments to give a much busier feel to this second series, despite the smaller set of main characters. There is also an unusual visual flourish in the use of an iris to open and close segments on each character.

Both of these series are relatively self-contained, in that they were designed with finite narrative arcs. Consequently, neither needs to build in an acknowledgement of the possible impact that the screening of the series might have on the lives of the main characters. There is no suggestion in *Summer Heights High*, for example, that students recognise Ja'mie from any previous exposure in a television series, or that the revelations of her behaviour captured by cameras for *We Can Be Heroes* affected her social status. Instead, each of these two series operates inside a kind of perfect bubble, where the camera catches the 'reality' of the key personalities (through many subtle 'flickers of authenticity'). The audience are encouraged to view and judge the characters they see on screen, and there is never any sense that their participation in a television production might in itself have implications for their lives.

The Tournament

A similar ethos operates within *The Tournament* (2005–6), a Canadian mockumentary series produced for the CBC network which more explicitly demonstrates its linkages to conventional sitcom. The first season of *The Tournament* covered the story of the quest of a junior ice hockey team called the Warriors to qualify for a prestigious novice tournament in Châteauguay, Quebec. The series' tagline was 'The game, the dream, the parents from hell', which flagged its real subject: a satire of parents who might obsessively visit their own sporting dreams and frustrations on their children. A text caution in the first episode suggests the overall tone: 'Due to scenes of appallingly petty adult behaviour, this show may not be suitable for children.' All of its characters are roughly sketched, and its actors rarely move beyond the norms of sitcom characterisation, with characters essentially remaining static throughout each of the two seasons, never learning from their mistakes. The humour is generally broad and obvious, using a host of Canadian national stereotypes, but the series is nonetheless engaging for its ability to resonate with more universal themes of parental responsibility and the need to grow out of youthful dreams and fantasies.

The central storyline focuses on the McConnell family: father Barry (Alain Goulem), hockey widow Janice (Paula Boudreau) and their 10-year-old son Robbie (Martin Huisman). Barry's own hockey career was cut short by injury, so he drives his talented but unambitious son to complete his frustrated dreams of glory. His obsession threatens chaos within each episode, as it undermines his marriage, leads to conflicts with other hockey fathers and even threatens to destroy any team spirit within his son's team. The narrative of the series is conventional, with each episode combining a main storyline interwoven with a secondary storyline, both of which intersect at the end with partial closure but unresolved underlying conflicts that invariably flare up in the next episode. Many episodes build toward a climactic hockey game, with later episodes featuring games that become more and more significant for Barry's hopes for his son's professional hockey career.

The mockumentary form allows the series to play with a number of layers of narrative information, chiefly the differences between what characters tell each other, what they will reveal directly to camera in interviews and what they are caught doing by a camera that often films from around the corner of buildings or through windows without their knowledge (all standard parts of a mocku- mentary narrative style). During hockey games, the editing pace intensifies, with lots of cutting back and forth from action on the ice to the emotional dramas on the sidelines (one of the recurring jokes is that Barry's obsession so distracts him that he rarely enjoys or even sees his son's success). Some of the key directors for the series had experience with Canadian mockumentary (Bruce McDonald directed *Hard Core Logo* (1996), an excellent punk descendant of *This is Spinal Tap*, and Trent Carlson directed *The Delicate Art of Parking* (2003)). Their craft shows in the consistency of the series' aesthetic. There are frequent reminders to the audi- ence that they are meant to be watching a documentary, with rough- focus pulls, or a shaking camera as the operator struggles to get into position to 'catch' the action. There are also more explicitly reflex- ive moments as characters object to something being filmed and turn on the camera crew.

The second season of *The Tournament* simply continues the same approach, but the situations become more and more absurd, with conflicts and alliances between hockey parents and a number of implausible subplots involving French Canadian coaches, Janice's pregnancy, and bizarre romantic entanglements. These all build towards a series climax which intercuts between a birth, a wedding and a junior hockey game involving an American team that somehow becomes a nationally televised 'live' event featuring cameos by actual sports announcers.

Searching for stardom

A second group of mockumentary series also uses a broad narrative arc where docusoap participants are apparently followed in their preparations for personal milestones. The four series discussed here also share a number of specific thematic concerns, with their core characters looking to develop careers within a media industry, a focus that meshes with the potential of mockumentary form to comment directly upon the nature of media practice. Each of these series features characters who are aware of how they might be represented by a documentary camera, who often have their own career-centred agenda for participating in a documentary pro- duction and who consequently have complex relationships with members of the television crews that are covering them. Two of the series discussed here, *Wayne Anderson: Singer of Songs* and *The Comeback* (2005) serve as contrasting applications of mockumentary discourse and very different avenues for the future development of television mockusoap.

Wayne Anderson: Singer of Songs

Wayne Anderson: Singer of Songs is a New Zealand mockumentary series that suggests one pole in a possible continuum of mockusoap approaches, one based on a performance style that is quite distinct from most of the series discussed here. In *Wayne Anderson* the distinctions between mockumentary and docusoap are deliberately played with, in a similar manner to Sacha Baron Cohen's *Borat* or the seminal dramatic vérité series *Tanner '88*, where a performance is often positioned within a space where not all participants understand what is real and what is faked. The result offers particular challenges and pleasures to audiences, particularly those who appreciate its satiric detail. In *Wayne Anderson*, Wayne Anderson plays himself as a forty-something lounge singer who is confused and frustrated by his failure to achieve fame. Cameras and a narrator follow the singer and his not-quite-convincing agent (he abandons his main career as a video store clerk to focus on managing his only client) as they attempt to organise a national tour through New Zealand small towns, culminating in a hoped-for triumphal return to the city of Auckland as a headline act. The series was put into a late timeslot on a local channel and only developed an audience through word of mouth, chiefly from people who needed others to see the programme so that they could help to decide whether it was real or not.

The appearance of the programme is that of a low-key, low-budget docusoap, following the template of early British docusoap of focusing on people who have ambitions larger than their talents. There is a brief credit sequence which incorporates underwhelming shots of the Auckland suburb of Manurewa, where Anderson lives in a small house overflowing with vinyl records and memorabilia of singers such as Tom Jones, Elvis Presley and Engelbert Humperdinck. Each episode focuses on a small milestone that Anderson is trying to achieve, such as a performance in a lounge bar or an appearance on local television. Hand-held cameras follow his preparations, he is interviewed on his aspirations, and on his responses to the inevitable anticlimax as things do not gel as he hoped. The low-key style includes enough space in each episode to allow quiet moments where Anderson is framed against the banality of his environment, an understated comment on the prospects of fulfilling his ambitions.[1]

The narrator, and Anderson's and all other performances are completely straight-faced. He is invariably optimistic, but fusses over relatively unimportant details of his preparations and appears to be genuinely unaware of how pathetic he might appear to viewers. Much of the impact of the series may escape non-New Zealanders, as there are continual references to locations and situations that resonate with local knowledge. For example, Manurewa itself is a lower-class, economically depressed suburb, and the idea of someone assuming that he can launch a national career from such a situation immediately carries a sense of almost doomed ambition. The series accumulates small but telling details, all plausible in themselves but building toward a sense of inevitable failure – including Anderson's favourite food (takeaway chicken), his choice of costume (flared collars and white trousers), his selection of material and his agent's poor choice of tour vehicle (a Daihatsu hatchback, which naturally breaks down in the middle of nowhere). In local towns he encounters bar owners, publicists, even local mayors, who are often real people playing along with the premise of the series.

The Wayne Anderson promotional campaign has consistently maintained the fiction. An official website offers a suitably cheesy series of images and a profile of the man and his music,[2] and Anderson provided in-character interviews to bemused local reporters to promote a second series, *Wayne Anderson: Glory Days* (2008):

> I see people with half my talent succeeding in the music industry, which makes me think they must know somebody in the business. My main problem is that the music I'm into stopped being fashionable about the time I started my career. If I'd been born 30 years earlier, I'd be a star by now. I'd be rich. (Quoted in Smithies, 2008: 14)

In some interviews, conducted in the house in Manurewa that was used for the series, he expressed frustration that people would consider the first documentary series a comedy: 'Well, I was a little confused. I had envisaged it to be more of a serious music thing. There's a bit of that in it, but there's more comedy in it than what I envisaged. I'm a bit eccentric. Which is good, because you laugh at yourself' (quoted in Witchell, 2008: 34). The second series follows Anderson as he tries to start his own radio station, 'Radio Classy', and initiate a tour of Japan.

The Festival and Pilot Season

There are other examples of mockumentary series focused on small-town ambitions of fame and fortune which have provided more explicit satirical perspectives on media practices. Both *Pilot Season* (2004) and *The Festival* (2005) partly operate as in-jokes, incorporating a number of cameos from the industry that each series targets (American television and independent film).[3] As with *Wayne Anderson*, the premise is simple: their subjects are small-town wannabes desperately pushing their noses up against the window of fame and success and encountering failures that are all the more excruciating because they appear to be documented by a documentary camera crew.

The Festival is a six-part Independent Film Channel series cover-ing the desperate efforts of first-time filmmaker Rufus Marquez (Nicolas Wright) to screen his film at the 'Mountain United Film Festival (M.U.F.F.)'. The festival itself stands in for any number of the plethora of film events which serve as sites for intense competi-tion between budding directors, producers and actors desperate to enter the film industry, and where a 'buzz' surrounding a film can secure a distribution deal and kick-start a promising acting or directing career. Marquez as a character is a mixture of traits fitting the stereotype of an ambitious, art-school trained auteur. He has a naïve and idealistic perspective of the industry, a fragile ego (not least because he has an ex-girlfriend who has achieved more success than he has as a director) and a conviction that he is already an auteur. His film is pretentiously titled 'The Unreasonable Truth of Butterflies', it is the only thing he has ever created and he is terri-fied of releasing it into the world. He is something of an easy mark for the unsavoury distributors who frequent the festival and battle for the rights to his unseen film. Part of the drama of the series, played out over a number of episodes, is tension over whether the film can sustain the anticipation that has unaccountably built up for its premiere. As the repeated efforts to actually screen the film fail (over a series of episodes), Marquez's mental health gradually disintegrates and he manages to antagonise everyone with his paranoia and immaturity.

Marquez has a tense relationship with the documentary film crew who are capturing these exchanges, especially with first-time director Cookie Armstrong (Miranda Handford), who initially has a purist's insistence on only capturing the 'truth' (she refuses to give Marquez a ride in the crew's van, leaving him in the snow) and struggles to manage her own film with a minimal budget, resentful cameraman and manipulative producer. She becomes more of a character as the series progresses, frequently entering the frame and questioning participants on their motives and thoughts at inappropriate times. The core message of the series is that all of the participants in the festival inevitably make personal and professional compromises in order to succeed (the series offers a bitterly negative perspective on the industry).

A similarly dark perspective on the Hollywood film and television industry underlies *Pilot Season* (2004), a mockumentary series derived from a mockumentary film from writer/director/actor Sam Seder called *Who's the Caboose?* (1997). The film is one of the number of film industry mockumentary in-jokes about actors attempting to find success in Hollywood, and while the series uses a similar premise it is smarter and more satirical. Using largely the same actors, and picking up 8 years later to find out what has happened to key characters, the six-part series focuses on the so-called 'pilot season' in American television production, where there is intense competition and outright desperation to become part of the next 'big' television series. The first step is the successful launch of a pilot for a series, and *Pilot Season* uses the natural drama of a countdown to the end of the pilot season to frame the intense relationships between its co-stars. In terms of aesthetics, the series closely references docusoap form, with a voice-over narrator providing links between interlinked storylines, and montage sequences accompanied by music or used in counterpoint to extracts from interviews with key characters.

In essence, the series is a sitcom about people who are desperate to be in a sitcom, but the mockumentary form allows for some layers to the performances by Seder and a cast of seasoned improvisational actors, such as Sarah Silverman as Susan (Sam's ex-girlfriend), Andy Dick, David Cross (who has also been in *Arrested*

Development), H. John Benjamin, David Waterman and Isla Fisher. All are consumed with their own ambitions, and desperate to at least appear successful (to each other and for the camera) even if they are not, but the documentary camera continually catches them in situations that reveal the yawning gap between their hoped-for and actual circumstances. And as is typical of sitcom conventions, characters completely fail to learn from their mistakes. As Seder's career gradually disintegrates, his distress is compounded its being recorded by the camera crew, even as he must witness others enjoying accidental and undeserved success.

The sharpness of the series' satire in fact partly rests on continual references to recent Hollywood folklore, and many of the incidents in the series would probably resonate mostly strongly with those in the industry. There are appearances by a number of television executives, and a key storyline focuses on the competition to sign up Ross Brockley, who essentially appears as himself, replicating his own story as a hot young actor who has appeared only in commercials. The focus on people who are seemingly willing to sacrifice their privacy and dignity, to compromise the most treasured parts of their lives and relationships, for the opportunity of fame and fortune makes for rich mockusoap material. The mockumentary series which to date has most successfully exploited this premise, however, is *The Comeback*.

The Comeback

The Comeback is a high point in reflexive mockusoap, a series which takes the reflexive potential of mockumentary and integrates it into a layered set of representations and commentary on the nature of media-defined celebrity and identity. The lead character is Valerie Cherish (Lisa Kudrow) an actor who has previously enjoyed popular success as a sitcom actress and who refuses to accept that the industry and her previous audiences might now find her too old for television roles. The series uses a show-within-a-show premise, as Cherish allows her life to be documented by a television crew which she then leverages to gain a small part in a new sitcom that is in development by the same network. In the process, the series satirises both conventional sitcom and the hybrid format of reality sitcom.

The key innovation of the series, one that no other mockumentary seems to have attempted, is to present itself as a rough cut of the footage captured by the crew. This allows the series, shot using two digital cameras simultaneously (Careless, 2005), to plausibly incorporate a variety of scenes that could be expected to be edited out of a broadcast-worthy production. The result is that the series partly operates as the 'making of' a reality sitcom. From the very first scenes we see Cherish attempting to negotiate with the crew's director (Jane played by Laura Silverman) over what they will film and rehearsing the performances she wants to give to them. In other words, we see Cherish in the process of attempting to create and maintain a particular public persona. The difficulty for her, and the key to the series' satire, is that the crew obviously have a totally different agenda to her; while she imagines that she and the crew are collaborating in a series that aims to mesh with her constructed public persona as a caring, selfless, generous and talented actor, they are gathering footage that can easily destroy her reputation and the remnants of her career.

The complexities and compromises here are played out in Cherish's relationship with the director, Jane. Cherish imagines an emphathetic and collaborative relationship with her director, believing that Jane respects her creative input. She frequently looks to the camera, motions, and asks for a 'time-out' whenever the camera appears to capture something she finds embarrassing. At key points, when it becomes obvious that she has lost control and is implicitly pleading for footage not to be included, or for a modicum of respect and privacy, she tells Jane that she just needs to 'know that I'm being heard', then reads more into Jane's 'yes' than she should. But Cherish is also the author of her own downfall, continually agreeing to allow access to intimate areas of her life (she allows a surveillance camera to be set up in her bedroom, and agrees to maintain a video diary that keeps recording more than she wishes as she mishandles the 'off' button) (Figure 16).

The impact of the series partly lies in the manner in which it manages to generate sympathy for Cherish even as it continually shows how easily she compromises relationships and other people's lives and careers in the pursuit of her own ambitions. Partly this is a product of the quality of performance by Kudrow , who convincingly moves between a variety of forms of performance, from Cherish's almost-talented comedic performances on her sitcom, to her frustrated passive-aggressive relationship with the sitcom's producers, to the 'performance' she gives to other people in the

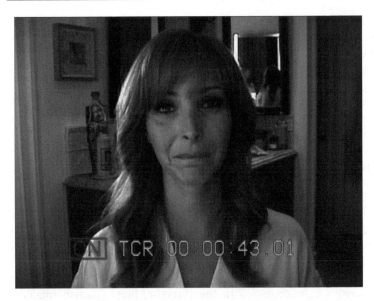

16. Valerie Cherish (Lisa Kudrow) tries to put a brave face after yet another personal disaster, in a video diary sequence from the highly reflexive mockusoap *The Comeback* (2005).

industry and to the reality cameras and, finally, to the desperately fragile woman she reveals when her façade drops. Cherish is a fundamentally unstable character. Her insecurities over a lack of control of her own career consistently lead her into embarrassing situations, then she takes herself to the brink of complete humiliation in order to rescue her dignity. Kudrow adds sympathy to Cherish by giving her a lonely childhood and adolescence, and through her continually having to face the everyday humiliations of a woman within an industry that values female youth over talent and experience (on the sitcom, Cherish is forced into the role of a batty upstairs aunt, rather than the hoped-for lead role). Her response to her situation is to pretend that everything is as she expected, and that she continues to be (as she imagines she was) a much-loved and respected star.

Through documenting Cherish backstage as she works on the sitcom, *The Comeback* also provides space to satirise the making of situation comedies, and television more broadly. The sitcom itself, titled 'Room and Bored', is in constant danger of creative collapse, as writer/producers Tom Peterman (Robert Bagnell) and Paulie G. (Lance Barber) especially struggle to retain control and inspiration in the face of interference from network executives. While Peterman works to accommodate to the network's demands, Paulie G. takes out his bitterness over such compromises on Cherish. All of the sitcom's production crew are also irritated by the presence of Cherish's reality crew (a subtle commentary on the anger of television writers with the emergence of television forms which appear to allow their easy replacement).

Reality programmes are also more directly targeted in *The Comeback*. Jane and the reality crew are seen constantly interacting with their subjects and negotiating access in ways that subvert any pretence of 'fly on the wall' filmmaking. One early scene has a production meeting at Cherish's sitcom loudly interrupted as the crew all attempt to clumsily squeeze into the room to capture the unfolding 'reality'. In a later episode an airline worker at the airport declines to serve Cherish, refuses to appear on camera and switches with her co-worker after declaring that she thinks reality 'is over'. Cherish's 12-year-old stepdaughter, in contrast, is completely at ease with the cameras, bringing her friends over to show them off. At the network's showcase for the upcoming season, Cherish's sitcom and reality sitcom are part of a programming line-up that includes 'Take That', featuring newlyweds encouraged to physically beat each other, and 'Search for America's Next Great Porn Star'. Cherish herself continually devalues reality programmes, taking the entire series of *The Comeback* to realise that, while she is a bit player in the sitcom, she is the star of her own reality series.

The series as a whole is ultimately about the types of desperation that it assumes are at the core of personalities that are attracted to television hybrids. After a disastrous first screening of her reality show, where all of Jane's footage has been edited in the most misleading and exploitative manner possible, Cherish finally turns on the reality crew. Her fury at Jane's breach of trust only abates when she realises that the savage caricature of her that has been viewed by the American public has made her a star, and she willingly submits to the adulation and promise of a revived career. It is an unusual moment in sitcom history, as a series that appears to be leading towards Cherish's ultimate redemption and the triumphant reclamation of her dignity decides instead to complete the circle of its satire on the dehumanising and exploitative ethos of popular reality programming. *The Comeback*, then, strays far from the conventions of the sitcom genre, which perhaps explains its relative obscurity and its failure to reach a popular audience (it was cancelled after the one season). The series ultimately suggests both the satiric potential of mockumentary form and the challenges for producers in constructing innovative television comedy that still plays to the broader generic expectations of the medium's audience. The final two examples of series discussed in this volume offer telling demonstrations of how mockusoap producers have successfully handled such challenges.

The British and American versions of *The Office*

The original British version of *The Office* and its American equivalent, which began broadcasting in 2005, are high points in the development of mockusoaps. Each has enjoyed such popular and critical success that these two series have effectively defined for most audiences what television mockumentary should be (in other words, they have achieved the kind of status that *This is Spinal Tap* achieved for cinematic mockumentary). Both have proved hugely influential, not only resonating with their respective national audiences but also appealing to global audiences, prompting a number of descendants (there are to date German, French, Canadian and Chilean versions of *The Office*) and inspiring numerous viewer-created homages and parodies which have flourished online. Interestingly, neither series was immediately popular. The British *Office* initially generated audiences largely from word of mouth and did not achieve real success until a DVD of the series was released, while the American version suffered at first from comparison to the original series before developing its own distinctive voice and an independent following. Both series have since won a number of awards for excellence in comedy and comedic television.

The discussion here is not intended to be comprehensive in analysing these texts (there are already excellent critiques of each series: Mills, 2004; Brabazon, 2005; Walters, 2005; Wisnewski, 2008), but to position each series more clearly within the trajectories of mockusoap development outlined in the previous chapters in this volume. Despite beginning with the same basic premise and largely employing the same mockumentary textual strategies (especially

an aesthetics referenced to docusoap formats), there are key distinctions between each series. These are differences which serve as
a useful illustration and summary of key patterns in the development of television mockumentary series in particular.

Critics and commentators have offered a variety of terms to
describe the distinctive nature of the British series. Mills uses the
term comedy vérité (see chapter 6) to suggest a 'faux-improvisa-
tional style', where the type of performance exhibited by the series
is what marks it out from more conventional sitcoms. Neither Mills
nor Walters ever refers to the series as a mockumentary, despite
Walters' extremely detailed analysis, while Gilbert labels *The Office*
an 'anti-sitcom sitcom' to suggest a focus on its distinct comedic
style (Gilbert, 2003: B10). Many commentators position the series
within a broader British tradition often labelled the 'comedy of
cringe', including particular comparison with the comic style of
John Cleese as Basil Fawlty in *Fawlty Towers* (1975–79) (Press,
2003; Brabazon, 2005). Critics of the American *Office*, in turn,
quickly grouped this series with a number of innovative sitcoms,
including *Curb Your Enthusiasm* and *Arrested Development* (discussed in chapters 6 and 7 according to Mills's label of comedy
vérité). All of these commentaries recognise the sophisticated
nature of the comedy of each series: the manner in which familiar
fact-fiction conventions associated with the docusoap are incorporated into largely conventional sitcom narrative, creating space for
styles of performance that are still distinctive and atypical for
sitcom as a genre.

The original British *Office* was created by Ricky Gervais and
Stephen Merchant, with Gervais noting in many interviews that he
drew inspiration from (American) mockumentaries such as *This is
Spinal Tap* and television series such as the vérité *Larry Sanders
Show*. Both were apparently also aware of the successful templates
provided by British mockumentaries such as *People Like Us* and
Operation Good Guys. Walters has provided a detailed account of
the gestation of the series (2005), outlining the co-creators' internship in radio comedy and their development of short-film treatment
of the premise of the series which they could pitch to the BBC.

Over six episodes the first season of *The Office* focused on a
small number of key characters in the local branch of paper
company Werner Hogg in the depressed industrial area of Slough,
Berkshire. Despite the continued threat of the branch's closure,

17. Manager David Brent (Ricky Gervais) cannot hide his smugness in an interview sequence from the original British version of mockusoap *The Office* (2001–3).

manager David Brent (Gervais) appears delighted at the presence of the cameras, constantly interrupting the work of his subordinates to perform jokes and otherwise play out the role of the beloved leader that he assumes he is (Figure 17). In his interview segments, he typically expounds upon his philosophy of management, his many talents and the positive impact he imagines he is having on his employees.

> You grow up, you work half a century, you get a golden handshake, you rest a couple of years and you're dead. And the only thing that makes that crazy ride worthwhile is, 'Did I enjoy it? What did I learn? What was the point?' That's where I come in. You've seen how I react to people. I make them feel good, make them think that anything's possible. If I make them laugh along the way, sue me ... and I don't do it so they'll turn around and go, 'Ooh, thank you David for the opportunity, thank you for the wisdom, thank you for the laughs.' I do it so one day someone'll go, 'There goes David Brent ... I must remember to thank him.' (David Brent, episode 6, season 1)

Set mostly within the confines of an open-plan workplace, the action of each episode revolves around the generally banal every-day activities of an office (even to the extent of occasional long and close-up shots of a bubbling water cooler, or the mechanical opera-tions of a photocopier, within an otherwise soundless environment). Relationships between the employees are invariably uncomfort-able, partly because of the presence of the cameras but partly also because they seem to have little in common with each other apart from the shared misery of their working lives.

The only positive relationship we see is the repressed flirtation and sexual tension between salesman Tim Canterbury (Martin Freeman) and receptionist Dawn Tinsley (Lucy Davis), a compli-cated friendship that moves more to centre stage during the six-part second season. Their perpetually frustrated potential romance (she is engaged) is suggested through comparatively muted form: sug-gestive body language, fleeting facial expressions when they are together and, especially, the lightness and wit of their shared sense of humour (McAleer, 2008: 61). Their potential romance provided the key dramatic tension throughout the two seasons of *The Office*, a 'will-they-or-won't-they' storyline that is a staple narrative device for sitcom. The second season never resolved this romantic tension, ending on the bleak note of Dawn's departure overseas with her fiancé. Two 2003 Christmas specials, however, effectively built towards a more conventionally satisfying narrative conclusion, bringing together Dawn and Tim who eventually openly acknowl-edge their feelings for each other.

The British *Office* is a tightly scripted and shot comedic gem, with Gervais and Merchant taking great pains to sustain the con-sistent premise that everything we are watching is the product of a documentary crew's encounters with the core cast members. Initially choosing the mockumentary approach at least in part simply because it suited a low budget (just as many budding filmmakers had before them), they soon realised that it also had advantages in terms of the speed at which they could work. With little actual directing experience, the pair experimented initially (in their pilot) with the use of a voice-over narrator, using John Nettles from the docusoap *Airline*, and briefly considered the possibility of making the documentary crew openly incompetent (Walters, 2005: 16).

The series otherwise closely references a docusoap aesthetic, using naturalistic lighting and sound and developing a layered set of representations of each of the characters and their interactions with each other within the confines of their apparent workplace. In classic mockusoap fashion, scenes are constructed from individual partly confessional interviews with characters, observational sequences where the characters are obviously highly conscious of the presence of the camera, and more surreptitious filming where the camera quietly lurks in semi-surveillance mode behind office equipment and outside doorways or windows to capture the employees at their most natural and with their guard down. Gervais, on the value of a strict mockumentary approach, notes:

> We were trying to find a way of disguising the plots so that they didn't undermine the realism, so that you wouldn't see the narrative mechanics at work. We wanted the illusion that you were merely watching scenes from an office but that they were actually building up into a picture of the world, becoming more than the sum of their parts. (Walters, 2005: 15)

The camera, in other words, alternates between roles as 'cool observer, intruder and intimate interviewer' (Anonymous, 2006: 20). The play between these layers of narrative information that this provides closely informs our understanding of the differences between characters' private thoughts and feelings and those they offer to other people. The result is both a complex perspective on the social dynamics and politics of a modern office environment and a commentary on the significance of issues of performance and authenticity within docusoaps as a 'reality' form.

The series plays to audiences' familiarity with docusoap, and not just in the sense of recognising the form, in accepting that the aesthetic can provide a charge of authenticity. Docusoaps also educate their audiences to some extent about the nature of everyday performance, and especially about the ways people behave when they are conscious of the presence of a camera (partly through Roscoe's 'flickers of authenticity', or the dropping of a façade). In a sense, as argued in chapter 4, the reflexivity of docusoap has provided the groundwork for *The Office*'s satire of media ambitions. As with George Constanza (Jason Alexander) from *Seinfeld*, another character based on cringe comedy, viewers often cringe in anticipation whenever Brent hovers into view, ready to interrupt his employees as they are being filmed and grab the camera's attention. The tension that his presence creates is because he assumes that he is able to control how he appears on camera. He has seen the ability of (British) docusoaps to propel their subjects into instant stardom, but has not closely watched how such programmes appear to capture character flaws. As with Valerie Cherish from *The Comeback*, he does not seem to realise how accurately the camera is able to capture his performances and to reveal his ambitions, and that his simple desire to be at the centre of everything will appear so nakedly to viewers. When his expectations, of laughter from subordinates or confirmation of the status he believes he has, are not validated there is an uncomfortable silence – heightened by the presence of the camera and often exquisitely prolonged through editing, by slightly delaying a cut to the next shot or scene (Meyer and Schneider, 2008: 138).

The timing, of both edits between shots and camera movements within shots, in the British *Office* is integral to its humour. Mills notes the distinctive nature of the manner in which interactions between characters are filmed, with the camera often panning to another character for a reaction, but crucially missing the initial few seconds. This creates a less conventionally structured sense of characters' interactions but increases the possibilities of creating humour from the pauses and gaps in people's conversations (Mills, 2004: 72). As with docusoap, people make no attempt to ignore the camera (the pretence of cinéma vérité itself), and there are many moments where Tim looks at the camera, to the audience, to rescue him from a Brent-inspired moment of embarrassment.

The Christmas specials have a slightly different construction, referencing more populist docusoap conventions such as the use of captions and a generally more interventionist approach toward the characters. It is at the crew's prompting that Dawn and her fiancé are enticed back to England and into the final encounter with Tim (the crew even pay for their tickets). This is a comparatively rare mockumentary series, in fact, which fully integrates the impact of the broadcast of an initial series on its characters. When we revisit the cast supposedly after 3 years we find that, as expected, Brent has attempted to trade his assumed celebrity status into a pop career, and the television crew are apparently encouraged by the ratings potential of a Tim–Dawn romance to prompt a reunion that neither appears capable of engineering themself. All the strands of the series are allowed to build towards their unexpectedly conventional conclusion. Even Brent is offered redemption at the end of these specials, finding the promise of a real relationship and the suggestion that he has outgrown his emotionally stunted sidekicks.

Gervais and Merchant's decisions to acknowledge this sense of broadcast and audience feedback, and to give a definite closure to *The Office*'s narrative arc, are two of the key differences between this series and its American version. There are other differences, most either derived from conventions within American sitcom traditions or imposed by the nature of American television production. Each series followed the broader pattern of differences between British and American production models, with the American *Office* being adapted by producer Greg Daniels (unlike the writer-led production of the British version). Daniels began by using the same aesthetic and narrative template for the American series, even to the extent of using the same actual script for its first episode while adapting details to the American context (for example, the paper company is now named Dunder Mifflin, and the local branch is based in Scranton, Ohio). From there, however, the two series have started to diverge.

As Kevin Reilly, president of NBC Entertainment is reported to have remarked: 'Americans need a little bit more hope than the British' (Friend, 2006). The overall sense of the American series is reflective of local sensibilities and expectations of characters, especially a toning down of the satirical bite of the original, and over the course of five series featuring an expanded roster of secondary characters that did not appear in the British *Office*. Instead of the black comedy of the original, the American version increasingly focuses on the office employees' commitment to each other as a surrogate family. The cast of the American *Office* are also divided among a variety of demographic groups, touching on a number of stereotypical character traits, and as a whole demonstrate performances that are generally lacking the subtlety and consistency of the British version. All of these features are in keeping with conventional American sitcom.

On the other hand, the complexity of a narrative that has accumulated over a number of seasons with no definite end point (as with the *Trailer Park Boys*) has meant that there are also strong elements of soap opera, in a sense taking the mockusoap full circle back to its origins. Within the more sprawling set of narrative possibilities that the American *Office* has featured are episodes that focus on the private lives of characters, stories set outside of the office, as well as a variety of mostly dysfunctional office romances. The sense of a detailed and ongoing fictional world extends to

18. Pam Beesly (Jenna Fischer) and Jim Halpert (John Krasinski) play out the tentative, perpetually frustrated romance at the centre of the early seasons of the American version of *The Office* (2005–).

NBC's production of webisodes featuring secondary characters, designed to maintain audience interest in the programme during the hiatus between seasons.

Some of the core character dynamics are retained from the British version, but again modified for the assumed sensibilities of local audiences. The central romance in the American *Office* is between Pam Beesly (Jenna Fischer) and Jim Halpert (John Krasinski), and initially followed the pattern of the frustrated romance of Tim and Dawn before bringing them together as a couple at the end of season 3 (Figure 18). Their flirtation is common knowledge, and declared and confessed to both camera and other characters in ways that would never have happened in the British version. Both Pam and Jim are also more ambitious and active in their relationships with other people than are their British counterparts (she calls off her own wedding; he moves to corporate headquarters in New York for a season). The manager of the branch is Michael Scott (Steve Carell, a veteran of *The Daily Show*), as self-absorbed as Brent but with different character flaws and a more detailed personal history (a troubled childhood and difficult relationship with his stepfather) that generally make him a more sympathetic figure (Terjesen, 2008: 28). He has talent as a salesperson, just not as a manager. He is fiercely loyal to his work 'family' but continually misjudges his relationships with them. He is more unstable than Brent, with less-focused ambitions, and typically oscillating between moments of clarity and agitated self-delusion (Rocknak, 2008; Evans and Murphy, 2008: 99).

The broader production environment of American television has also imposed some structures on the American *Office*. Unlike the condensed narratives of the six-part British version, Daniels and his team have played out their storylines over seasons of up to twenty-three episodes. While the British broadcasting system allows episode lengths of up to 29 minutes, between advertising, the more heavily advertising-saturated American schedule only allows 22-minute episodes. These institutional factors appear to have helped to foster a faster-paced style, virtually eliminating the quieter moments that are so distinctive of the British *Office* – the long shots of the 'dead time' during a work day, which aided that series' bleak sense of an everyday working office.

With working scripts that are less tightly written than the British version, and a detailed set design replicating a working office, the actors (especially Carell) have more freedom to improvise within scenes (this is especially evident in the DVD extras included on releases of the American series, with a wealth of alternate takes and scenes attached to each episode). Episodes are consequently constructed more in post-production, through the selection of alternate takes and a laborious editing process (from main editor David Rogers) that works to build toward a structure consistent with a documentary feel (Anonymous, 2006: 24).

Within a general similarity in aesthetics to the British *Office*, the American approach typically also entails a more dynamic encounter between character and camera. The series' director of photography, Randall Einhorn (who had a background as a documentary and hybrid cinematographer, working most notably on *Survivor*), has argued that the camera is quite deliberately constructed as a character in some episodes. Here he recalls a specific instance where Pam explicitly collaborates with the crew:

> Pam, in an on-camera interview, tells the camera, 'If you guys see anything, keep me posted.' Then the camera sees something and points it out to Pam by running up to her. She asks, 'What is it?' The

camera pans over, shows her something and pans back to her, and she says, 'Thanks, guys.' The camera is definitely there. (Quoted in Anonymous, 2006: 21)

In season 4, the crew discover the relationship between Jim and Pam by following her car, then confront the two with their footage to prompt a confession. The overall relationship between the camera crew and their subjects is more fluid and dynamic, with a greater sense of collaboration. This flows through the interview segments, which are considerably more confessional than in the British *Office*. This in itself could be a quality that reflects the broader confessional nature of American television, which provides such a distinctive aspect of the local talk shows and informs American television hybrids. Like *Trailer Park Boys*, however, it is also a key sign of an open-ended narrative structure, with no real effort at incorporating feedback from an audience. There is no suggestion that earlier seasons have actually been broadcast, that members of the office have seen what their colleagues have said about them, or what the camera has revealed about their relationships. The series remains in a perpetual limbo, exploiting the sense of intimate, unfettered access to these characters over a series of years as they live in a bubble outside of any media responses. In direct contrast to a similar documentary exercise like the *Seven Up* series, its participants never have to live with the struggle to reconcile the differences between their self-image and mediated images. *The Office* remains in perfect stasis, suspended between sitcom and docusoap, while its characters develop within narrow narrative confines.

The distinctions between just these two versions of the series demonstrate just how much the outcomes of any television production are dependent upon a combination of factors, some institutional and operating through the broader production design, while others are more closely derived from the decisions of key creative personnel collaborating within a weekly production practice. The products of such complex collaborative production practices can be distinctive, and in turn have a significant impact on the types of response and interpretation of audiences. It is no coincidence, for example, that each of the two series discussed here has generated fan communities that strongly favour one version of *The Office* over the other, as each provides distinctive combinations of aesthetics, performance style and narrative constructions within its broader appeal to national social and cultural discourses.

Notes

1 In documentary terms, the overall effect is similar to that of *American Movie: The Making of Northwestern*, which similarly confused audiences about its status as non-fiction.
2 See www.wayneanderson.tv/.
3 In this sense, they are the television equivalent of the many film mockumentaries which reference making of documentaries – see chapter 2.

Conclusion

Mockumentary is a complex discourse that intersects with the dynamic collection of generic and hybrid discourses and forms that is the fact-fiction continuum. Mockumentary involves referencing and appropriating texts that range across print, audio and audio-visual media and is at the centre of the increasingly incestuous relationships between analogue and digital media. Each medium has appropriated and refashioned mockumentary for its own purposes, with media producers engaging with the discourse's 'call to play' to produce layered texts that, in the best examples, appeal to audiences through a variety of modes of reading and interpretation.

Television as a medium is characterised by a collective density of textual forms, made available in streams of programming that should be seen as a textual space accessible by viewers increasingly capable of leveraging digital technologies to design their own viewing experiences. A 'text' in such an environment can be defined, in terms of the product of an individual production practice, as the collective of programmes that constitute a series or more generally as an instance of narrative embedded within broader televisual metanarratives that include advertising and other programming content. Television producers are thus able to exploit the intertextuality built into the broadcasting environment itself as a means to couch a particular programme within a broad terrain of televisual and cultural discourses.

Mockumentary thrives in such an environment, perhaps more naturally here than in any other medium (aside from digital media, although televisual patterns of intertextuality reappear here as well). And television in turn has been integral to the genealogy of mockumentary, although this is not always acknowledged by documentary and other media theorists more intent on searching for examples less complicit with commercialist institutions. The highly segmented, advertising-saturated televisual space is more typically dismissed as the scene of simplistic, apolitical, compromised and token efforts at textual experimentation than it is acknowledged as a site for genuine artistic expression (a similar attitude prevails against the overwhelming archives of audio-visual complexity that constitute online sites such as YouTube, which inevitably combine both the banal and the sublime). Where critics do acknowledge the quality of an individual television programme or series, this is typically accompanied by the complaint that such texts are unfortunately the exception. Commentators rarely judge the finest examples of cinematic expression together with the medium's most disappointing output, but in a television schedule similar comparisons can be difficult to avoid (perhaps the proliferation of DVD releases of television series will enhance the critical appreciation of the best examples of television forms).

Mockumentary discourse on television reveals much about the medium itself. It is a discourse regularly employed by advertisers who rarely explore its potential for intertextual aesthetic and narrative complexity. Dramatic mockumentary here has stuttered as a production approach, overwhelmed by broader patterns of dramatic vérité that dominate so much of contemporary television drama. While dramatic mockumentary has helped to reinvigorate cinematic science fiction and horror narratives, television producers have shown little interest in exploring this side of the discourse, outside of one-off programmes such as *Ghostwatch* or novelty episodes within dramatic series. Instead, it is parody and satire which dominates television mockumentary, the product often of small communities of practitioners who are adept at playing with combinations of a variety of generic conventions to create distinctive aesthetic and narrative forms.

The high points of television mockumentary are arguably mockumentary series, the culmination of a broader set of parodic and satiric traditions that have played a significant role throughout television's global history. The exemplars of this trajectory are series which deserve to be recognised as among the finest examples of television content: from the news satire of *The Day Today*, to the hapless encounters between a documentarian and his subjects of *People Like Us*, the detailed video diaries of *Marion and Geoff*, the play with bureaucratic discourse in *The Games*, the exploration of media ambition at the heart of *The Comeback*, the virtuoso performances of *Summer Heights High*, and *The Office*'s satiric exploration of the sociality of contemporary workspaces.

Each of these series is tapping into broader patterns favouring parodic and satiric discourse within contemporary televisual space. When a satirical news programme such as *The Daily Show* becomes a cultural touchstone, it is a sign of a broader recognition that television has the capacity of performing acts of critical literacy in relation to broader cultural and political life. Similarly, Gray talks of 'parody as a critical form of intertextuality' (Gray, 2006: 4), using the dominance of *The Simpsons* within the American cultural mainstream since the early 1990s as evidence of the broader complexity of modes of reading that have become central to engagement with popular media texts. It is perhaps no accident that mockumentary forms a key part of the satiric strategies used by *The Daily Show* itself, as the discourse has an inherent potential to draw together techniques of reflexivity that have become naturalised within televisual space.

The best examples of mockumentary generate layered forms of engagement for their audiences, providing narratives which can be enjoyed for their own sake (through the identification of characters and their storylines) and degrees of intertextual commentary on the fact-fiction forms which they appropriate. Mockumentary builds upon the reflexive tendencies within the broader field of television documentary culture, particularly those hybrid forms which incorporate complex messages about issues of performance and authenticity. Mockumentary can reveal the complex motivations and expectations of participants in such productions, the creative labour that is behind apparently spontaneous scenes of actuality and, more specifically, the negotiations and compromises that are at the heart of any mediation of reality. These are all tendencies within the television fact-fiction continuum that are familiar to television mockumentary audiences, just as they inform and inflect documentary cultures in other media.

There are a number of ways to interpret the broader implications of a climate dominated by the playful and subversive agendas of reflexive media. Banning insists that a media sphere characterised by a high degree of reflexivity within non-fiction forms is ultimately destructive of a wider belief in the forms of common knowledge that are essential to a working democracy. He argues that we are entering an environment dominated by 'radical scepticism', which he defines as 'an inability in deliberation to discern between fact and fiction, knowledge and opinion, and information and promotion' (Banning, 2005: 86). Although not referring to mockumentary, his arguments could be taken as a warning of the ultimate effect of important parts of the agendas of the discourse:

> Reflexive representations occur across literature, film, video, news, and philosophies of thought and they are not by nature deleterious to society. Reflexivity draws conscious attention to the constructed nature of representation and to what can be taken as real [...] Too often the potential of reflexive representations to raise critical awareness and rhetorical capacity for deliberation in public discourse is lost, however, because reflexive representations are occurring with such frequency and without critical awareness of their use or significance. (Banning, 2005: 91)

In these terms, the normalisation of mockumentary discourse, which mockumentary television series suggests, is a dangerously corrosive point in contemporary culture, a logical end point in which the inherent tendencies of parody and satire eventually overwhelm the discourse and forms which they reference (Harries, 2000: 127). In terms of documentary, then, we would reach a point where we could no longer easily distinguish between examples of documentary comedy, reflexive documentary, documentary hybrids and mockumentary itself.

The opposite contention would be that satiric discourse is a sign of the richness and vibrancy of culture, of a willingness to play with those discourses and forms that are previously seen to be sacred, not least those typically associated with dominant institutions (as has been the case for documentary for much of its history). In Harries' terms, the most important operation of parody (the less aggressive form of satire) is to target those aspects of a genre which are tired and in need of revision and renewal. Parodic texts, then, are central to an essential process of a 'weeding out' of clichéd conventions that allows for the continued healthy growth of the media sphere itself (Harries, 2000: 123).

The television mockumentary exemplars listed above do not offer conclusive evidence for any of these claims. The ultimate effects of such demonstrations of discursive play, once again, are a matter of debate and conjecture, as they involve the most poorly understood and least researched aspect of media practice: that of reception. Much of the work in this volume is focused on textual analysis that engages with the patterns of production practice and textual construction that characterise the exemplars of television mockumentary. It lays the groundwork for detailed ethnographic research into the modes of reading employed by differently situated viewers, modes shaped by interpretive contexts which are at least partly determined by access to the critical literacy skills outlined above. The broader assumption of these discussions is that mockumentary contributes to a climate in which the distinctions between media constructions of 'fact' and 'fiction' are both more difficult to determine and their identification at the textual level is increasingly the work required of audiences as a part of everyday media engagement. We can return here to Hutcheon's notion of the 'paradox of parody' (Hutcheon, 2000: 75), which refers to a tension between the reinforcement of forms through close referencing, and the ability of some parodic texts to transcend such acts of appropriation. Where a mockumentary text ultimately fits within this set of possibilities, and what its eventual role might be in the broader currents suggested above, ultimately depend on the interpretations of its audiences.

Filmography

Mockumentaries discussed in this text are included below. For a more comprehensive listing of film and television texts, excluding the hundreds of mockumentary short films, see www.waikato.ac.nz/film/mock-doc.shtml (which is maintained by the author).

Mockumentary

#1 Fan: A Darkomentary (2005) dir: Dee Austin Robertson, United States, short film, 20th Century Fox Home Entertainment, DVD, 12 min.

500 Bus Stops (1997) dir: Willy Smax, Britain, television mini-series, British Broadcasting Corporation (BBC), DVD, 23 min. episodes.

A Mighty Wind (2003) dir: Christopher Guest, United States, feature film, Warner Bros. Pictures, DVD, 87 min.

A Sense of History (1992) dir: Mike Leigh, Britain, short film, October Films, 22 min.

A Small Summer Party (2001) dir: Hugo Blick, Britain, television series, British Broadcasting Corporation (BBC), DVD, 50 min.

Alien Abduction: Incident in Lake County (1998) dir: Dean Alioto, United States, television programme, United Paramount Network (UPN), 50 min.

Alternative 3 (1977) dir: Christopher Miles, Britain, television programme, Shocking Videos, DVD, 52 min.

Bad News Tour (1983) dir: Sandy Johnson, Britain, television programme, Channel 4 Television Corporation, DVD, 30 min.

Best in Show (2000) dir: Christopher Guest, United States, feature film, Warner Bros. Pictures, DVD, 90 min.

Blair Witch Project, The (1999) dir: Daniel Myrick and Eduardo Sánchez, United States, feature film, Lions Gate Films, DVD, 89 min.

Bob Roberts (1992) dir: Tim Robbins, United States, feature film, Artisan Entertainment, DVD, 102 min.

Borat: Cultural Learnings of America for Make Benefit Glorious Nation of Kazakhstan (2006) dir: Larry Charles, United States, feature film, Twentieth Century-Fox Film Corporation, DVD, 82 min.

Brass Eye (1997–2001) dir: Michael Cumming, Britain, television series, Channel 4 Television Corporation, DVD, 25 min. episodes.

Broken News (2005–) dir: John Morton, Britain, television series, British Broadcasting Corporation (BBC), DVD, 25 min. episodes.

Buried Secret of M. Night Shyamalan, The (2004) dir: Nathaniel Kahn, United States, television programme, The Sci-Fi Channel, DVD, 124 min.

Burkittsville 7, The (2000) dir: Ben Rock, United States, short film, Alliance Atlantis Communications / Artisan Entertainment / Showtime Networks, DVD, 30 min.

C'est arrivé près de chez vous (*Man Bites Dog*) (1992) dir: Rémy Belvaux, André Bonzel, Benoît Poelvoorde, Belgium, feature film, The Criterion Collection, DVD, 95 min.

Cloverfield (2008) dir: Matt Reeves, United States, feature film, Paramount Home Entertainment, DVD, 85 min.

CNNNN: Chaser Non-Stop News Network (2002–3) dir: Bradley Howard, Australia television series, Australian Broadcasting Corporation (ABC), DVD, 23 min. episodes.

Comeback, The (2005) dir: various, United States, television series, Home Box Office Home Video (HBO), DVD, 23 min. episodes.

Curse of the Blair Witch (1999) dir: Daniel Myrick and Eduardo Sánchez, United States, television programme, Haxan Films / The Sci-Fi Channel, DVD, 44 min.

David Holzman's Diary (1967) dir: Jim McBride, United States, feature film, Direct Cinema Limited, DVD, 73 min.

Day Today, The (1994) dir: Andrew Gillman, Britain, television series, Framestore CFC, DVD, 23 min. episodes.

Death of a President (2006) dir: Gabriel Range, Britain, feature film, Newmarket Films, DVD, 90 min.

Delicate Art of Parking, The (2003) dir: Trent Carlson, Canada, feature film, Cinéma Libre / Horizon Entertainment DVD, 86 min.

Double Take (2003) dir: Alison Jackson, Britain, television miniseries, Channel 4 Television Corporation, DVD, 23 min. episodes.

Eddie Monsoon: A Life (1984) dir: Sandy Johnson, Britain, television programme, Channel 4 Television Corporation, DVD, 30 min.

Falls, The (1980) dir: Peter Greenaway, Britain, feature film, British Film Institute (BFI), DVD, 195 min.

Festival, The (2005) dir: Phil Price, Canada, television series, Independent Film Channel (IFC), DVD, 23 min. episodes.

Forgotten Silver (1995) dir: Costa Botes and Peter Jackson, New Zealand, television programme, Zeitgeist Films, DVD, 50 min.

Fuckland (2000) dir: José Luis Marquès, Argentina, feature film, Atomic Films S.A., Cinecolor / Symphony Pictures / Videocolor, 84 min.

Games, The (1998–2000) dir: Bruce Permezel, United States, television series, Australian Broadcasting Corporation (ABC), DVD, 23 min. episodes.

Ghostwatch (1992) dir: Lesley Manning, Britain, television programme, British Broadcasting Corporation (BBC), DVD, 90 min.

Hard Core Logo (1996) dir: Bruce McDonald, Canada, feature film, Miramax Films / Rolling Thunder, DVD, 92 min.

History of White People in America, The (1985–86) dir: Harry Shearer, United States, television series, MCA / Universal Home Video, VHS, 22 min. episodes.

Human Remains (2000) dir: Matt Lipsey, Britain, television series, British Broadcasting Corporation (BBC), DVD, 23 min. episodes.

Husbands and Wives (1992) dir: Woody Allen, United States, feature film, Columbia TriStar Home Video, DVD, 108 min.

Independent, The (2000) dir: Stephen Kessler, United States, feature film, Allumination Filmworks, DVD, 81 min.

Interview with the Assassin (2002) dir: Neil Burger, United States, feature film, ContentFilm International, DVD, 85 min.

Jimmy McDonald's Canada (2005) dir: Greig Dymond, Canada, television miniseries, Koch International, DVD, 23 min. episodes.

Larry David: Curb Your Enthusiasm (1999) dir: Robert B. Weide, United States, television programme, Home Box Office (HBO), DVD, 57 min.

Last Broadcast, The (1998) dir: Stefan Avalos and Lance Weiler, United States, feature film, Metrodome Distribution / Wavelength Releasing, DVD, 86 min.

Lisa Picard is Famous (2000) dir: Griffin Dunne, United States, feature film, First Look International, DVD, 90 min.

Look Around You (2002–5) dir: various, Britain, television series, British Broadcasting Corporation (BBC), DVD, 9 min. episodes (season 1), 30 min. episodes (season 2).

Making of ... And God Spoke, The (1993) dir: Arthur Borman, United States, feature film, Artisan Entertainment, DVD, 82 min.

Marion and Geoff (2000–3) dir: Hugo Blick, Britain, television series, British Broadcasting Corporation (BBC), DVD, 9 min. episodes (season 1), 30 min. episodes (season 2).

More Bad News (1988) dir: Adrian Edmondson, Britain, television programme, Channel 4 Television Corporation, DVD, 51 min.

No Lies (1974) dir: Mitchell Block, United States, short film, Direct Cinema Limited, 16 min.

Norbert Smith: A Life (1989) dir: Geoff Posner, Britain, television programme, Channel 4 Television Corporation, 50 min.

Normal Ormal: A Very Political Turtle (1998) dir: Metin Hüseyin, Britain, television programme, Tiger Aspect Productions, 50 min.

Nothing So Strange (2002) dir: Brian Flemming, United States, feature film, GMD Studios / Parallax Productions / Unsharp Mask, DVD, 78 min.

Office, The (2001–3) dir: Ricky Gervais and Stephen Merchant, Britain, television series, British Broadcasting Corporation (BBC), DVD, 29 min. episodes.

Office, The (2005–) dir: various, United States, television series, NBC Universal Television Distribution, DVD, 22 min. episodes.

Operation Good Guys (1997–2000) dir: Dominic Anciano, Hugo Blick and Ray Burdis, Britain, television series, British Broadcasting Corporation (BBC), DVD, 23 min. episodes.

Opération Lune (Dark Side of the Moon) (2002) dir: William Karel, France, television programme, Point du Jour, DVD, 52 min.

Paths to Freedom (2000) dir: Ian Fitzgibbon, Ireland, television miniseries, Radio Telefís Éireann (RTÉ) / British Broadcasting Corporation (BBC), DVD, 25 min. episodes.

People Like Us (1999–2001) dir: John Morton and Willy Smax, Britain, television series, British Broadcasting Corporation (BBC), DVD, 23 min. episodes.

Pilot Season (2004) dir: San Seder, United States, television mini-series, Trio Network, 23 min. episodes.

Posh Nosh (2003) dir: Chris Langham, Britain, television series, British Broadcasting Corporation (BBC), 10 min. episodes.

R2 D2–Beneath the Dome (2001) dir: Don Bies and Spencer Susser, United States, short film, 20th Century Fox Home Entertainment / Lucasfilm, DVD, 20 min.

R2PC: Road to Park City (2000) dir: Bret Stern, United States, feature film, Phaedra Cinema, DVD, 83 min.

Real Life (1979) dir: Albert Brooks, United States, feature film, Paramount Pictures, DVD, 98 min.

Real Stories (2006) dir: Tim Bartley, Australia, television series, Network Ten / Radio Karate / Roving Enterprises, DVD, 23 min. episodes.

Real Time: Siege at Lucas Street Market (2001) dir: Max Allan Collins, United States, feature film, Troma Team Video, DVD, 71 min.

Reno 911! (2003–) dir: Michael Patrick Jann and various, United States, television series, Paramount Home Video / Comedy Central, DVD, 23 min. episodes.

Reno 911!: Miami (2007) dir: Robert Ben Garant, United States, feature film, Twentieth Century-Fox Film Corporation, DVD, 84 min.

Return of Spinal Tap, The: (A Spinal Tap Reunion: The 25th Anniversary London Sell-Out) (1993) dir: Jim Di Bergi, United States, feature film, Import, DVD, 110 min.

Rutles, The: All You Need is Cash (1978) dir: Eric Idle and Gary Weis, Britain, television programme, Rhino Home Video, DVD, 71 min.

Series 7: The Contenders (2001) dir: Daniel Minahan, United States, feature film, USA Films, DVD, 91 min.

Shadow of the Blair Witch (2000) dir: Ben Rock, United States, Artisan Entertainment, The Sci-Fi Channel, television programme, DVD, 45 min.

Slaves of Hollywood (1999) dir: Terry Keefe and Michael Z. Wechsler, United States, feature film, Filmopolis Pictures, DVD, 73 min.

Smashey and Nicey: The End of an Era (1994) dir: Daniel Kleinman, Britain, television programme, Tiger Aspect Productions, 50 min.

Special Bulletin (1983) dir: Edward Zwick, United States, television programme, National Broadcasting Company (NBC) / Warner Home Video, VHS, 103 min.

Summer Heights High (2007) dir: Stuart McDonald, Australia, television series, Australian Broadcasting Corporation (ABC), DVD, 23 min. episodes.

Take the Money and Run (1969) dir: Woody Allen, United States, feature film, Anchor Bay Entertainment, DVD, 85 min.

That Peter Kay Thing (2000) dir: Andrew Gillman, Britain, television series, Channel 4 Television Corporation, DVD, 23 min. episodes.

They Shoot Movies, Don't They?: The Making of Mirage (2000) dir: Frank Gallagher, United States, feature film, Goldhil Entertainment, DVD, 87 min.

This is Spinal Tap (1984) dir: Rob Reiner, United States, feature film, The Criterion Collection, DVD, 82 min.

Tournament, The (2005–6) dir: Trent Carlson, Bruce McDonald and Peter Svatek, Canada, television series, Adjacent2 Entertainment, DVD, 23 min. episodes.

Trailer Park Boys (2001–) dir: Mike Clattenburg, Canada, television series, Showcase Television / Topsail Entertainment / Trailer Park Productions, DVD, 23 min. episodes.

Waiting for Guffman (1996) dir: Christopher Guest, United States, feature film, Sony Pictures Classics, DVD, 80 min.

Wayne Anderson: Glory Days (2008) dir: Glenn Elliott, New Zealand, television series, ButoBase, 23 min. episodes.

Wayne Anderson: Singer of Songs (2005) dir: Glenn Elliott, New Zealand, television series, ButoBase, DVD, 23 min. episodes.

We Can Be Heroes: Finding the Australian of the Year (2005) dir: Mathew Saville, Australia, television series, Australian Broadcasting Corporation (ABC), DVD, 23 min. episodes.

Welcome to Hollywood (1998) dir: Tony Markes and Adam Rifkin, United States, feature film, Home Box Office (HBO) / Phaedra Cinema, DVD, 89 min.

Who's the Caboose? (1997) dir: Sam Seder, United States, feature film, Pilot Season Productions, 94 min.

Wicksboro Incident, The (2003) dir: Richard Lowry, United States, feature film, Vanguard Cinema, DVD, 80 min.

Without Warning (1994) dir: Robert Iscove, United States, television programme, CBS Television / Warner Bros. Pictures, DVD, 100 min.

Zelig (1983) dir: Woody Allen, United States, feature film, MGM/UA Home Entertainment, DVD, 79 min.

Zero Day (2003) dir: Ben Coccio, United States, feature film, Home Vision Entertainment (HVE), DVD, 92 min.

Others

11 O'Clock Show, The (1998–2000) dir: various, Brtiain, television series, 30 min. episodes.

1900 House, The (1999) dir: various, Britain, television series, 45 min. episodes.

2001: A Space Odyssey (1968) dir: Stanley Kubrick, Britain, feature film, 141 min.

24 Hour Party People (2002) dir: Michael Winterbottom, Britain, feature film, 117 min.

999 (1990) dir: Brian Lighthill and Nick Metcalfe, Britain, television series, 30 min. episodes.

A Current Affair (1971–) dir: various, Australia, television series, 30 min. episodes.

A Show Called Fred (1956) dir: Richard Lester, Britain, television series, 30 min. episodes.

Airline (1998–) dir: various, Britain, television series, 22 min. episodes.

America's Funniest Home Videos (1990–) dir: various, United States, television series, 23 min. episodes.

America's Most Wanted (1988–) dir: various, United States, television series, 50 min. episodes.

American Movie: The Making of Northwestern (1999) dir: Chris Smith, United States, feature film, 107 min.

American Splendor (2003) dir: Shari Springer Berman and Robert Pulcini, United States, feature film, 101 min.

An American Family (1973) dir: Alan Raymond and Susan Raymond, United States, television series, 60 min. episodes.

An Inconvenient Truth (2006) dir: Davis Guggenheim, United States, feature film, 100 min.

And Now for Something Completely Different (1971) dir: Ian MacNaughton, Britain, feature film, 88 min.

Anyone for Pennis? (1997) dir: various, Britain, television series, 30 min. episodes.

Arrested Development (2003–6) dir: various, United States, television series, 23 min. episodes.

Artificial Intelligence: A.I. (2001) dir: Steven Spielberg, United States, feature film, 146 min.

At Last the 1948 Show (1967) dir: Ian Fordyce, Britain, television series, 30 min episodes.

Babylon 5 (1994) dir: various, United States, television series, 45 min. episodes.

Barry Lyndon (1975) dir: Stanley Kubrick, Britain, feature film, 184 min.

Behind the Music (1997–2004) dir: various, United States, television series, 48 min. episodes.

Big Brother (1999–2006) dir: Marc Pos, Netherlands, television series, 50 min. episodes.

Biography (1987–) dir: various, United States, television series, 48 min. episodes.

Bowling for Columbine (2002) dir: Michael Moore, United States, feature film, 120 min.

Candid Camera (1948–50) dir: Allen Funt, United States, television series, 22 min. episodes.

Cane Toads: An Unnatural History (1998) dir: Mark Lewis, Australia, television programme, 47 min.

Cannibal Holocaust (1980) dir: Ruggero Deodato, Italy, feature film, 95 min.

Capturing the Friedmans (2003) dir: Andrew Jarecki, United States, feature film, 107 min.

Castaway (2000) dir: various, Britain, television series, 60 min. episodes.

Cathy Come Home (1966) dir: Ken Loach, Britain, television programme, 75 min.

Chasers' War on Everything, The (2006–) dir: various, Australia, television series, 26 min. episodes.

Chelovek s kinoapparatom (*Man With a Movie Camera*) (1929) dir: Dziga Vertov, Soviet Union, feature film, 68 min.

Chronique d'un été (*Chronicle of a Summer*) (1960) dir: Jean Rouch, France, feature film, 85 min.

Citizen Kane (1941) dir: Orson Welles, feature film, United States, feature film, 119 min.

Civil War, The (1990) dir: Ken Burns, United States, television series, 42 min. episodes.

Colbert Report, The (2005–) dir: Jim Hoskinson, United States, television series, 22 min. episodes.

Comedy Lab (1998–) dir: Steven Lock / Jalaal Hartley, Britain, television series, 25 min. episodes.

Comic Strip Presents . . . , The (1982–2005) dir: various, Britain, television series, 30 min. episodes.

Complete and Utter History of Britain, The (1969) dir: Maurice Murphy, Britain, television series, 30 min. episodes.

Cops (1989–) dir: various, United States, television series, 23 min. episodes.

Coronation Street (1960–) dir: various, Britain, television series, 22 min. episodes.

Cosby Show, The (1984–92) dir: various, United States, television series, 22 min. episodes.

Crimewatch UK (1984–) dir: various, Britain, television series, 50 min. episodes.

Cruise, The (1998) dir: Christopher Terrill, Britain, television series, 55 min. episodes.

Culloden (1964) dir: Peter Watkins, Britain, television programme, 69 min.

Curb Your Enthusiasm (2000–) dir: various, United States, television series, 23 min. episodes.

Da Ali G Show (2000) dir: various, Britain, television series, 25 min. episodes.

Daily Show with Jon Stewart, The (1996–) dir: various, United States, television series, 23 min. episodes.

Day Britain Stopped, The (2003) dir: Gabriel Range, Britain, television programme, 90 min.

De Grote Donorshow (*The Big Donor Show*) (2007) dir: unknown, Netherlands, television programme, BNN TV, 80 min.

Do Not Adjust Your Set (1967–69) dir: Adrian Cooper, Britain, television series, 30 min. episodes.

Don't Look Back (1967) dir: D. A. Pennebaker, United States, feature film, 96 min.

Donnie Darko: The Director's Cut (2001) dir: Richard Kelly, United States, feature film, 133 min.

Drinking for England (1998) dir: Brian Hill, Britain, television programme, 50 min.

Driving School (1997) dir: Francesca Joseph, Britain, television series, 22 min. episodes.

Ellen (1994–98) dir: various, United States, television series, 22 min. episodes.

ER (1994–) dir: various, United States, television series, 42 min. episodes.

Extreme Makeover (2002–5) dir: Shanda Sawyer, United States, television series, 42 min. episodes.

Fahrenheit 9/11 (2004) dir: Michael Moore, United States, feature film, 122 min.

Family, The (1974) dir: Franc Roddam and Paul Watson, Britain, television series, 30 min. episodes.

Father Knows Best (1954–60) dir: William D. Russell / Peter Tewksbury, United States, television series, 24 min. episodes.

Fawlty Towers (1975–79) dir: John Howard Davies / Bob Spiers, Britain, television series, 30 min. episodes.

Feltham Sings (2002) dir: Brian Hill, Britain, television programme, 60 min.

Fishing with John (1991) dir: John Lurie, United States, television series, The Criterion Collection, DVD, 30 min. episodes

French and Saunders (1987–) dir: various, Britain, television series, 30 min. episodes.

Frontier House (2002) dir: Nicolas Brown and Maro Chermayeff, United States, television series, 42 min. episodes.

Frontline (1994–97) dir: various, Australia, television series, 23 min. episodes.

Frost Report, The (1966–67) dir: various, Britain, television series, British 30 min. episodes.

Game, The (1997) dir: David Fincher, United States, feature film, 128 min.

Germania anno zero (*Germany Year Zero*) (1948) dir: Roberto Rossellini, Italy, feature film, 78 min.

Gladiators, The (1969) dir: Peter Watkins, Sweden, feature film, 102 min.

Grey Gardens (1975) dir: Ellen Hovde, Albert Maysles, David Maysles and Muffie Meyer, United States, feature film, 100 min.

Hancock's Half Hour (1956–60) dir: Alan Tarrant / Duncan Wood, Britain, television series, 25 min. episodes.

Hill Street Blues (1981–87) dir: various, United States, television series, 42 min. episodes.

Homicide: Life on the Street (1993–99) dir: various, United States, television series, 60 min. episodes.

Hurdes, Las (*Land Without Bread*) (1933) dir: Luis Buñuel, Spain, short film, 30 min.

I Love Lucy (1951–57) dir: various, United States, television series, 25 min. episodes.

In This World (2002) dir: various, Britain, feature film, 88 min.

It's Garry Shandling's Show (1986–90) dir: Michael Winterbottom, United States, television series, 30 min. episodes.

Jerry Springer Show, The (1991–) dir: various, United States, television series, 42 min. episodes.

Joe Schmo Show, The (2003) dir: Danny Salles / Sean Travis, United States, television programme, 42 min. episodes.

Jurassic Park (1993) dir: Steven Spielberg, United States, feature film, 127 min.

Just Shoot Me (1997–2003) dir: various, United States, television series, 22 min. episodes.

K Street (2003) dir: Steven Soderburgh, United States, television series, 23 min. episodes.

Kath and Kim (2002–) dir: Ted Emery, Australia, television series, 24 min. episodes.

Keith Barret Show, The (2004–5) dir: Tony Dow, Britain, television series, 30 min. episodes

Kingdom Hospital (2004) dir: Craig R. Baxley, United States, television miniseries, 40 min. episodes.

La terra trema (1948) dir: Luchino Visconti, Italy, feature film, 160 min.

Ladri di biciclette (*Bicycle Thieves*) (1948) dir: Vittorio de Sica, Italy, feature film, 93 min.

Larry Sanders Show, The (1992–98), dir: various, United States, television series, Home Box Office (HBO) / Sony Pictures Television, DVD, 23 min. episodes.

Last Waltz, The (1978) dir: Martin Scorsese, United States, feature film, 117 min.

Leave It To Beaver (1957–63) dir: various, United States, television series, 24 min. episodes.

Man of Aran (1934) dir: Robert Flaherty, Britain, feature film, 76 min.

M.A.S.H. (1972–83) dir: various, United States, television series, 25 min. episodes.

Monty Python's Flying Circus (1969–74) dir: Ian MacNaughton / John Howard Davies, Britain, television series, 30 min. episodes.

Mrs. Merton Show, The (1994–98) dir: Dominic Brigstocke and Pati Marr, Britain, television series, 30 min. episodes.

My Name is Earl (2005–) dir: various, United States, television series, 22 min. episodes.

Nanook of the North (1922) dir: Robert J. Flaherty, United States / France, feature film, 79 min.

Natural History of the Chicken, The (2000) dir: Mark Lewis, Australia, television programme, 60 min.

Norman Gunston Show, The (1975–79) dir: John Eastway, Australia, television series, 30 min. episodes.

NYPD Blue (1993–2005) dir: various, United States, television series, 45 min. episodes.

Oprah Winfrey Show, The (1986–) dir: various, United States, television series, 42 min. episodes.

Osbournes, The (2002–5) dir: Sarah K. Pillsbury et al, United States, television series, 22 min. episodes.

Paisà (1946) dir: Roberto Rossellini, Italy, feature film, 125 min.

Panorama (1953–) dir: various, Britain, television series, 40 min. episodes.

Paradise Lost: The Child Murder of Robin Hood Hills (1996) dir: Joe Berlinger and Bruce Sinofsky, United States, feature film, 150 min.

Peuple migrateur, Le (*Winged Migration*) (2001) dir: Jacques Perrin, Jacques Cluzaud and Michel Debats, France / Italy / Germany / Spain / Switzerland, feature film, 98 min.

Phoenix Nights (2001–2) dir: Jonny Campbell and Peter Kay, Britain, television series, 25 min. episodes.

Police Five (1962–92) dir: various, Britain, television series, 30 min. episodes.

Police Tapes, The (1977) dir: Alan Raymond and Susan Raymond, United States, television film, 88 min.

Pornography: The Musical (2003) dir: Brian Hill, Britain, television programme, 55 min.

Practice, The (1997–2004) dir: various, United States, television series, 42 min. episodes.

Prehistoric Park (2006) dir: Sid Bennett / Karen Kelly / Matthew Thompson, Britain, television series, 50 min. episodes.

Primary (1960) dir: Robert Drew, United States, feature film, 60 min.

Punishment Park (1971) dir: Peter Watkins, United States, feature film, 88 min.

Queer Eye for the Straight Guy (2003–) dir: various, United States, television series, 42 min. episodes.

Real Life (1992–94) dir: various, Australia, television series, 23 min. episodes.

Real World, The (1992–) dir: various, United States, television series, 42 min. episodes.

Rescue 911! (1989–96) dir: various, United States, television series, 50 min. episodes.

Roger & Me (1989) dir: Michael Moore, United States, feature film, 91 min.

Roma, città aperta (*Rome, Open City*) (1945) dir: Roberto Rossellini, Italy, feature film, 100 min.

Roseanne (1988–97) dir: various, United States, television series, 22 min. episodes.

Royle Family, The (1998–2000) dir: Mark Mylod / Steve Bendelack / Caroline Aherne, Britain, television series, 28 min. episodes.

Saturday Night Live (*SNL*) (1975–) dir: various, United States, television series, 90 min. episodes.

Sciuscia (*Shoeshine*) (1946) dir: Vittorio de Sica, Italy, feature film, 93 min.

Scrubs (2001–) dir: various, United States, television series, 24 min. episodes.

SCTV (1976–81) dir: George Bloomfield / Milad Bessada / John Blanchard, Canada, television series, 25 min. episodes.

Seinfeld (1990–98) dir: various, United States, television series, 22 min. episodes.

Sex and the City (1998–2004) dir: various, United States, television series, 23 min. episodes.

Significant Others (2004) dir: Robert Roy Thomas, United States, television series, 23 min. episodes.

Simple Life, The (2003–7) dir: Claudia Frank, United States, television series, 22 min. episodes.

Simpsons, The (1989–) dir: various, United States, television programme, 23 min. episodes.

Sixth Sense, The (1999) dir: M. Night Shyamalan, United States, feature film, 107 min.

Smallpox 2002: Silent Weapon (2002) dir: Daniel Percival, Britain, television programme, 100 min.

South Bank Show, The (1978–) dir: various, Britain, television series, 50 min. episodes.

Space Cadets (2005) dir: Tony Gregory, Britain, television series, 48 min. episodes.

Spellbound (2002) dir: Jeffrey Blitz, United States, feature film, 97 min.

SportsCenter (1979–) dir: Jeff Winn, Greg Richards, Michael Feinberg and Kevin Kreppein, United States, television series, 42 min. episodes.

Star Wars Episode II: Attack of the Clones (2002) dir: George Lucas, United States, feature film, 142 min.

Super Size Me (2004) dir: Morgan Spurlock, United States, feature film, 100 min.

Survivor (2000–) dir: Mark Burnett, United States, television series, 42 min. episodes.

Sylvania Waters (1992) dir: Brian Hill, Australia / Britain, television series, 30 min. episodes.

Tanner '88 (1988) dir: Robert Altman, United States, television miniseries, 23 min. episodes.

Tanner on Tanner (2004) dir: Robert Altman, United States, television miniseries, 120 min.

Tarnation (2003) dir: Jonathan Caouette, United States, feature film, 88 min.

Ten (2002) dir: Abbas Kiarostami, France / Iran / United States, feature film, 94 min.

That Was The Week That Was (1962–63) dir: various, United States, television series, 50 min. episodes.

That Was The Week That Was (1964–65) dir: Marshall Jamison, Britain, television series, 30 min. episodes.

This Hour Has 22 Minutes (1992–) dir: various, Canada, television series, 22 min. episodes.

Touching the Void (2003) dir: Kevin Macdonald, United States, feature film, 106 min.

Truman Show, The (1998) dir: Peter Weir, United States, feature film, 103 min.

Umberto D. (1952) dir: Vittorio de Sica, Italy, feature film, 89 min.

Unbreakable (2000) dir: M. Night Shyamalan, United States, feature film, 106 min.

Unscripted (2005) dir: George Clooney and Grant Heslov, United States, television series, 23 min. episodes.

Up the Junction (1965) dir: Ken Loach and James Taggert, Britain, television programme, 75 min.

Vertical Features Remake (1978) dir: Peter Greenaway, Britain, short film, 45 min.

Video Nation (1993–) dir: various, Britain, television series, 15 min. approx episodes.

Video Nation Shorts (1998) dir: various, Britain, television series, 2 min. episodes.

Village, The (2004) dir: M. Night Shyamalan, United States, feature film, 108 min.

Walking with Beasts (2001) dir: Nigel Paterson, Britain, television series, 30 min. episodes.

Walking with Cavemen (2003) dir: Richard Dale / Pierre de Lespinois, Britain, television series, 30 min. episodes

Walking with Dinosaurs (1999) dir: Tim Haines / Jasper James, Britain, television series, 30 min. episodes.

Walking with Monsters (2005) dir: Tim Haines / Chloe Leland, Britain, television series, 30 min. episodes.

Wal-Mart: The High Cost of Low Price (2005) dir: Robert Greenwald, United States, feature film, 95 min.

War Game, The (1965) dir: Peter Watkins, Britain, television programme, 48 min.

War Room, The (1993) dir: Chris Hegedus and D. A. Pennebaker, United States, feature film, 96 min.

Wednesday Play, The (1964–70) dir: various, Britain, television series, 75 min. episodes.

West Wing, The (1999–2004) dir: various, United States, television series, 42 min. episodes.

Wife Swap (2003–) dir: Martin Fuller and Sam Maynard, Britain, television series, 45 min. episodes.

World in Action (1963–98) dir: Stephen Segaller, Mike Hodges, Michael Apted, John Goldschmidt and Ian McBride, Britain, television series, 30 min. episodes.

Xena: Warrior Princess (1995–2001) dir: various, New Zealand, television series, 45 min. episodes.

X-Files, The (1993–2002), dir: various, United States, television series, 45 min. episodes.

Young Ones, The (1982–84) dir: Paul Jackson / Geoff Posner, Britain, television series, 35 min. episodes.

You've Been Framed (1990–) dir: David Kester / Andrew Nicholson / Chris Power, Britain, television series, 30 min. episodes.

Bibliography

Andrejevic, M. (2004) *Reality TV: The Work of Being Watched*, Lanham, Rowman & Littlefield Publishers, Inc.

Andrew, G. (2005) *10*, London, British Film Institute.

Ang, I. (1989) 'Wanted: audiences. On the politics of empirical audience studies', in E. Seiter, H. Borchers, G. Kreutzner, and E. Warth (eds), *Remote Control: Television, Audiences, and Cultural Power*, London, Routledge, pp. 96–115.

Ang, I. (1991) *Desperately Seeking the Audience*, London, Routledge.

Ang, I. (1996) *Living Room Wars: Rethinking Media Audiences for a Postmodern World*, Routledge, London.

Anonymous (2006) 'Another day at the office', *Videography*, 31:2, pp. 20–4.

Arthur, P. (2004) '(In)Dispensable cinema: confessions of a "making-of" addict', *Film Comment*, 4:4, July/August, pp. 38–42.

Austin, T. and W. de Jong (eds) (2008) *Rethinking Documentary: New Perspectives, New Practices*, Maidenhead, McGraw-Hill.

Baker, M. (2006) *Documentary in the Digital Age*, Oxford, Focal Press.

Banash, D. (2004) '*The Blair Witch Project*: technology, repression, and the evisceration of the mimesis', in S. L. Higley and J. A. Weinstock (eds), *Nothing That Is*, pp. 111–23.

Banning, M. (2005) 'Truth floats: reflexivity in the shifting public and epistemological terrain', *Rhetoric Society Quarterly*, 35:3, pp. 75–99.

Barad, J. (2007) 'Stewart and Socrates: speaking truth to power', in J. Holt (ed.) The Daily Show *and Philosophy*, pp. 69–80.

Bayer, G. (2005) 'Artifice and artificiality in mockumentaries', in G. D. Rhodes and J. P. Springer (eds), *Docufictions*, pp. 164–78.

Baym, G. (2005) '*The Daily Show*: discursive integration and the reinvention of political journalism', *Political Communication*, 22:3, pp. 259–76.

Benford, S., C. Magerkurth et al. (2007) 'Pervasive Games: bridging the gaps between the virtual and the physical', in F. v. Borries, S. P. Walz and M. Böttger (eds) *Space Time Play*, pp. 248–50.

Björk, S. (2007) 'Changing urban perspectives: illuminating cracks and drawing illusionary lines', in F. v. Borries, S. P. Walz and M. Böttger (eds) *Space Time Play*, pp. 276–9.

Bogost, I. and C. Poremba (2008) 'Can games get real? A closer look at "documentary" digital games', in A. Jahn-Sudmann and R. Stockmann (eds) *Computer Games as a Sociocultural Phenomenon: Games Without Frontiers, Wars Without Tears*, Houndmills, Palgrave Macmillan, pp. 12–21.

Bolter, J. D. and R. Grusin (2000) *Remediation: Understanding New Media*, Cambridge, MA, MIT Press.

Borries, F. v., S. P. Walz and M. Böttger (eds) (2007) *Space Time Play: Computer Games, Architecture and Urbanism: The Next Level*, Basel, Birkhäuser.

Bourdon, J. (2000) 'Live television is still alive: on television as an unfulfilled promise', *Media Culture Society*, 22:5, pp. 531–56.

Bousé, D. (2000) *Wildlife Films*, Philadelphia, University of Pennsylvania Press.

Brabazon, T. (2005) '"What have you ever done on the telly?" *The Office* (post) reality television and (post) work', *International Journal of Cultural Studies* 8:1, pp. 101–17.

Brooker, W. and D. Jermyn (eds) (2003) *The Audience Studies Reader*, London, Routledge.

Brookey, R. and R. Westerfelhaus (2002) 'Hiding homoeroticism in plain view: the *Fight Club* DVD as digital closet', *Critical Studies in Mass Communication*, 19:1, March, pp. 21–43.

Bruzzi, S. (2000) *New Documentary: A Critical Introduction*, London, Routledge.

Butler, J. G. (2001) 'VR in the ER: *ER*'s use of e-media', *Screen*, 42:4, pp. 313–31.

Caldwell, J. (2002) 'Prime-time fiction theorizes the docu-real', in J. Friedman (ed.) *Reality Squared*, pp. 259–92.

Caldwell, J. T. (1995) *Televisuality: Style, Crisis, and Authority in American Television*, New Brunswick, NJ, Rutgers University Press.

Cantril, H. (1940) *The Invasion From Mars: A Study in the Psychology of Panic*, Princeton, NJ, Princeton University Press.

Careless, J. (2005) 'Perfecting the illusion of reality', *Videography*, 30:7, pp. 43–5.

Carpenter, H. (2000) *That Was Satire That Was: The Satire Boom of the 1960s* – Beyond the Fringe, The Establishment Club, Private Eye *and* That Was the Week That Was, London, Phoenix.

Castonguay, J. (2004) 'The political economy of the indie blockbuster: fandom, intermediality and *The Blair Witch Project*', in S. L. Higley and J. A. Weinstock (eds) *Nothing That Is*, pp. 65–85.

Caughie, J. (2000) *Television Drama: Realism, Modernism, and British Culture*, Oxford, Oxford University Press.

Colapinto, J. (2004) 'The most trusted name in news', *Rolling Stone*, 28 October, pp. 58–62.

Corner, J. (1996) 'British TV dramadocumentary: origins and developments', reprinted in Alan Rosenthal (ed.) *Why Docudrama?: Fact-Fiction on Film and TV*, Carbondale, Southern Illinois University Press.

Corner, J. (1999) *Critical Ideas in Television Studies*, Oxford, Oxford University Press.

Corner, J. (2000) 'What can we say about "documentary"?', *Media, Culture & Society*, 22:5, pp. 681–8.

Corner, J. (2001a) 'Documentary in a post-documentary culture? A note on forms and their functions', European Science Foundation 'Changing Media – Changing Europe' programme. Team One (Citizenship and Consumerism) Working Paper No. 1, www.lboro.ac.uk/research/changing.media/publications.htm, accessed January 2007.

Corner, J. (2001b) '"Documentary" in dispute', *International Journal of Cultural Studies*, 4:3, pp. 352–9.

Corner, J. (2002a) 'Performing the real: documentary diversions', *Television New Media*, 3:3, pp. 255–69.

Corner, J. (2002b) 'Sounds real: music and documentary', reprinted in A. Rosenthal and J. Corner (eds) (2005) *New Challenges for Documentary*, 2nd edition, Manchester, Manchester University Press, pp. 242–52.

Corner, J. (2003) 'Finding data, reading patterns, telling stories: issues in the historiography of television', *Media Culture Society*, 25:2, pp. 273–80.

Corner, J. (2006) '"A fiction (un)like any other"?', *Critical Studies in Television*, 1:1, pp. 89–96.

Cottle, S. (2004) 'Producing nature(s): on the changing production ecology of natural history TV', *Media Culture Society*, 26:1, pp. 81–101.

Couldry, N. (2002) 'Playing for celebrity: *Big Brother* as ritual event', *Television New Media*, 3:3, pp. 283–93.

Dahlgren, P. (1992) 'What's the meaning of this? Viewers' plural sense-making of TV news', in P. Scannell, P. Schlesinger, and C. Sparks (eds) (1992) *Culture and Power: A 'Media, Culture and Society' Reader*, London, SAGE Publications, pp. 201–17.

Darley, A. (2003) 'Simulating natural history: *Walking with Dinosaurs* as hyper-real edutainment', *Science as Culture*, 12:2, pp. 227–56.

Dayan, D. (2001) 'The peculiar public of television', *Media Culture Society*, 23:6, pp. 743–65.

de Siefe, E. (2007) *This is Spinal Tap*, London, Wallflower Press.

de Siefe, E. (n.d.) 'History of the mockumentary: the treachery of images', www.spinaltapfan.com/articles/seife/seife1.html, accessed November 2006.

Dempsey, L. P. (2007) '*The Daily Show*'s exposé of political rhetoric', in J. Holt (ed.) The Daily Show *and Philosophy*, pp. 121–32.

Dena, C. (2007) 'Creating alternate realities: a quick primer', in F. v. Borries, S. P. Walz and M. Böttger (eds) *Space Time Play*, pp. 238–41.

Dilucchio, P. (1999) 'Did *The Blair Witch Project* fake its online fan base?', *salon.com*, www.salon.com/tech/feature/1999/07/16/blair_marketing/index.html, accessed January 2006.

Doherty, T. (2003) 'The sincerest form of flattery: a brief history of the mockumentary', *Cineaste*, 28:4, pp. 22–4.

Dovey, J. (2000) *Freakshow: First Person Media and Factual Television*, London, Pluto Press.

Dovey, J. (2008) 'Simulating the public sphere' in T. Austin and W. de Jong (eds) *Rethinking Documentary*, pp. 245–56.

Dowd, M. (1988) 'Eighty-eightsomething', *The New Republic*, 1 August, pp. 37–40.

Doyle, A. (1998) '*Cops*: television policing as policing reality', in M. Fishman and G. Cavender (eds) *Entertaining Crime: Television Reality Programs*, New York, Aldine de Gruyter, pp. 95–116.

Edwards, J. (2005) 'Taking a whack at Wal-Mart', *Brandweek*, 46:38, p. 38.

El-Miskin, T. (1989) '*Special Bulletin*: transfictional disavowal', *Jump Cut: A Review of Contemporary Media*, 34, pp. 72–6.

Ellis, J. (1992) *Visible Fictions: Cinema: Television: Video*, London, Routledge.

Ellis, J. (2000) *Seeing Things: Television in the Age of Uncertainty*, London, I. B. Tauris Publishers.

Ericson, R. V., P. M. Baranek and J. B. L. Chan (1987) *Visualising Deviance: A Study of News Organisation*, Milton Keynes, Open University Press.

Ericson, R. V., P. M. Baranek and J. B. L. Chan (1991) *Representing Order: Crime, Law, and Justice in the News Media*, Milton Keynes, Open University Press.

Evans, J. and P. Murphy (2008) 'Authenticity or happiness? Michael Scott and the ethics of self-deception', in J. J. Wisnewski (ed.) The Office *and Philosophy*, pp. 93–104.

Farrell, G. (1999) 'TV Commercials offer too much of a good thing all over again', *New York Times*, 1 October, p. C5.

Fetveit, A. (1999) 'Reality TV in the digital era: a paradox in visual culture?', *Media Culture Society*, 21:6, pp. 787–804.

Fiske, J. (1989) 'Moments of television: neither the text nor the audience', in E. Seiter, H. Borchers, G. Kreutzner, and E. Warth (eds), *Remote Control: Television, Audiences, and Cultural Power*, London, Routledge, pp. 56–78.

Fiske, J. (1992) 'British Cultural Studies and television', in R. C. Allen (ed.), *Channels of Discourse, Reassembled: Television and Contemporary Criticism*, 2nd edition, Chapel Hill, The University of North Carolina Press, pp. 284–326.

Fore, S. (1993) 'America, America this is you! The curious case of *America's Funniest Home Videos*', *Journal of Popular Film & Television*, 21:1, pp. 37–45.

Friedman, J. (ed.) (2002) *Reality Squared: Televisual Discourse on the Real*, New Brunswick, NJ, Rutgers University Press.

Friend, T. (2006) 'The paper chase; on television', *The New Yorker*, 11 December, p. 94.

Fullerton, T. (2008) '"Documentary" games: putting the player in the path of history', in Z. Whalen and L. N. Taylor (eds) *Playing the Past: History and Nostalgia in Video Games*, Nashville, TN, Vanderbilt University Press.

Fürsich, E. (2003) 'Between credibility and commodification: nonfiction entertainment as a global media genre', *International Journal of Cultural Studies*, 6:2, pp. 131–53.

Galloway, A. (2004) 'Social realism in gaming', *Game Studies* 4:1, www.gamestudies.org/0401/galloway/, accessed November 2007.

Gaut, B. (2003) 'Naked film: dogma and its limits', in M. Hjort and S. MacKenzie (eds) *Purity and Provocation*, pp. 89–101.

Geraghty, C. (2003) 'Aesthetics and quality in popular television drama', *International Journal of Cultural Studies*, 6:1, pp. 25–45.

Gettings, M. (2007) 'The fake, the false, and the fictional: *The Daily Show* as news source', in J. Holt (ed.) The Daily Show *and Philosophy*, pp. 16–27.

Gilbert, M. (2003) 'Ignoring sitcom conventions, *Office* supplies biting humor', *Boston Globe*, 9 October, B.10.

Gilbert, M. (2005) 'On many sitcoms, the laugh track's not on us anymore', *Boston Globe*, 6 October, p. E.1.

Gilbert, M. (1997) '*ER* live: a successful operation', *Boston Globe*, 26 September, pp. D1–D2.

Giles, D. (2002) 'Welcome to *Frontline*', *Australian Screen Education*, 30, ATOM Publishing, pp. 120–4.

Gitlin, T. (2000) *Inside Prime Time*, Berkeley, CA, University of California Press.

Gray, J. (2006) *Watching with The Simpsons: Television, Parody and Intertextuality*, New York, Routledge.

Greene, N. (2007) *The French New Wave: A New Look*, London, Wallflower Press.

Hall, J. (2006) *The Rough Guide to British Cult Comedy*, London, Rough Guides Ltd.

Harries, D. (2000) *Film Parody*, London, British Film Institute.

Hay, J. (2001) 'Locating the televisual', *Television New Media*, 2:3, pp. 205–34.

Hight, C. (2001) 'Webcam sites: the documentary genre moves online?', *Media International Australia incorporating Culture and Policy*, 100, pp. 81–93.

Hight, C. (2003) '"It isn't always Shakespeare, but it's genuine": cinema's commentary on documentary hybrids', in S. Holmes and D. Jermyn (eds) *Understanding Reality Television*, pp. 373–405.

Hight, C. (2005) 'Making-of documentaries on DVD: the *Lord of the Rings* trilogy and special editions', *Velvet Light Trap*, 56, pp. 4–17.

Hight, C. (2007) '*American Splendor*: translating comic autobiography into drama-documentary', in I. Gordon, M. Jancovich and M. P. McAllister (eds) *Films and Comic Books*, Jackson, MS, University Press of Mississippi, pp. 180–98.

Hight, C. (2008a) 'Primetime digital documentary animation: the photographic and graphic within play', *Studies in Documentary Film*, 2:1, pp. 9–31.

Hight, C. (2008b) 'Mockumentary: a call to play', in T. Austin and W. de Jong (eds) *Rethinking Documentary*, pp. 203–14.

Hight, C. and J. Roscoe (2006) '*Forgotten Silver*: a New Zealand television hoax and its audience', in A. Juhasz and J. Lerner (eds) *F Is for Phony*, pp. 171–86.

Higley, S. L. (2004) '"People just want to see something": art, death, and document in *Blair Witch*, *The Last Broadcast*, and *Paradise Lost*', in S. L. Higley and J. A. Weinstock (eds) *Nothing That Is*, pp. 87–110.

Higley, S. L. and J. A. Weinstock (2004) 'Introduction: the *Blair Witch* controversies', in S. L. Higley and J. A. Weinstock (eds) *Nothing That Is*, pp. 11–35.

Higley, S. L. and J. A. Weinstock (eds) (2004) *Nothing That Is: Millennial Cinema and the Blair Witch Controversies*, Contemporary Approaches to Film and Television Studies, Detroit, MI, Wayne State University Press.

Hill, A. (2005) *Reality TV: Audiences and Popular Factual Television*, London, New York, Routledge.

Hill, A. (2007) *Restyling Factual TV: Audiences and News, Documentary and Reality Genres*, London, Routledge.

Hill, A. (2008) 'Documentary modes of engagement', in T. Austin and W. de Jong (eds) *Rethinking Documentary*, pp. 216–30.

Hjort, M. (2003) 'Dogma 95: a small nation's response to globalisation', in M. Hjort and S. MacKenzie (eds) *Purity and Provocation*, pp. 31–47.

Hjort, M. and S. MacKenzie (2003) 'Introduction', in M. Hjort and S. MacKenzie (eds) *Purity and Provocation*, pp. 1–28.

Hjort, M. and S. MacKenzie (eds) (2003) *Purity and Provocation: Dogma 95*, London, British Film Institute.

Hogarth, D. (2006) *Realer Than Reel: Global Directions in Documentary*, Austin, TX, University of Texas Press.

Hoijer, B. (1990) 'Studying viewers' reception of television programmes: theoretical and methodological considerations', *European Journal of Communication*, 5:1, pp. 29–56.

Holmes, S. and D. Jermyn (eds) (2004) *Understanding Reality Television*, London, Routledge.

Holt, J. (ed.) (2007) The Daily Show *and Philosophy: Moments of Zen in the Art of Fake News*, Malden, MA, Blackwell Publishing.

Hopgood, F. (2005) 'Before *Big Brother*, there was *Blair Witch*: the selling of "reality"', in G. D. Rhodes and J. P. Springer (eds) *Docufictions*, pp. 237–52.

Humphrys, G. (1999) 'Fooled by the media', *Contemporary Review*, 274, pp. 209–10.

Hurwitz, M. (2004) 'Tanner on Tanner', *Videography*, 29:11, pp. 38–40.

Hutcheon, L. (2000) *A Theory of Parody: The Teachings of Twentieth-Century Art Forms*, Chicago, IL, University of Illinois Press.

Jacobs, D. (2000) *Revisioning Film Traditions: The Pseudo-Documentary and the NeoWestern*, Lewiston, The Edwin Mellen Press.

Jacobs, J. (2001) 'Issues of judgement and value in television studies', *International Journal of Cultural Studies*, 4:4, pp. 427–47.

Jameson, R. T. (1988) '*Tanner '88*: For Real is for now', *Film Comment*, 24:3, pp. 73–5.

Jancovich, M. (1992) 'David Morley, the *Nationwide* studies', in M. Barker and A. Beezer (eds), *Reading into Cultural Studies*, Routledge, London.

Jauregui, C. G. (2004) '"Eat it alive and swallow it whole!" Resavoring *Cannibal Holocaust* as a Mockumentary', *Invisible Culture*, 7, www.rochester.edu/in_visible_culture/Issue_7/Jauregui/jauregui.html, accessed September 2008.

Jenkins, H. (2006) *Convergence Culture: Where Old and New Media Collide*, New York, New York University Press.

Jenkins, H. (2007) 'Narrative spaces', in F. v. Borries, S. P. Walz and M. Böttger (eds) *Space Time Play*, pp. 56–60.

Jensen, K. B., and K. E. Rosengren (1990) 'Five traditions in search of the audience', *European Journal of Communication*, 5:2–3, pp. 207–38.

John, W. S. (2004) 'The Power of Fake News', *New York Times Upfront*, 15 November, pp. 14–15.

Johnson, D. (2005) '*Star Wars* fans, DVD, and cultural ownership: an interview with Will Brooker', *The Velvet Light Trap*, 56, pp. 36–44.

Johnson, S. (2005) *Everything Bad Is Good for You: How Today's Popular Culture Is Actually Making Us Smarter*, New York, Riverhead Books.

Jones, S. (2005) 'MTV: the medium was the message', *Critical Studies in Media Communication*, 22, pp. 83–8.

Juhasz, A. (2008) 'Documentary on YouTube: the failure of the direct cinema of the slogan', in T. Austin and W. de Jong (eds) *Rethinking Documentary*, pp. 299–312.

Juhasz, A. and J. Lerner (2006) 'Introduction', in A. Juhasz and J. Lerner (eds) *F Is for Phony*, pp. 1–35.

Juhasz, A. and J. Lerner (eds) (2006) *F Is for Phony: Fake Documentary and Truth's Undoing*, Visible Evidence Series, Minneapolis, MN, University of Minnesota Press.

Katz, R. (1997) 'Get the gaffer up here, stat!', *Mediaweek*, 8 September, p. 28.

Keller, J. (2004) '"Nothing that is not there and the nothing that is": language and the *Blair Witch* phenomenon', in S. L. Higley and J. A. Weinstock (eds) *Nothing That Is*, pp. 53–63.

Kellner, D. (1999) 'The *X-Files* and the aesthetics and politics of postmodern pop', *Journal of Aesthetics & Art Criticism*, 57:2 pp. 161–75.

Kendzior, S. (1999) 'Fact and Fiction: 1999's horror hit *The Blair Witch Project* isn't all that is seems. Just ask the makers of *The Last Broadcast*', *11th Hour*, www.the11thhour.com/archives/091999/features, accessed October 2004.

Kilborn, R. (1998a) 'Shaping the real: democratization and commodification in UK factual broadcasting', *European Journal of Communication*, 13:2, pp. 201–18.

Kilborn, R. (1998b) 'The price of faking it', *DOX*, 18, pp. 20–1.

Kilborn, R. (2003) *Staging the Real: Factual TV Programming in the Age of* Big Brother, Manchester, Manchester University Press.

Kilborn, R. (2006) 'A walk on the wild side: the changing face of TV wildlife documentary', *Jump Cut: A Review of Contemporary Media*, 48, www.ejumpcut.org/archive/jc48.2006/AnimalTV/index.html, accessed January 2007.

Kleinhans, C. (2008) 'Webisodic mock vlogs: HoShows as commercial entertainment new media', *Jump Cut: A Review of Contemporary Media*, 50, http://216.131.117.136/archive/jc50.2008/WeHoGirls/index.html, accessed November 2007.

Kompare, D. (2004) 'Extraordinary ordinary: *The Osbournes* as *An American Family*', in S. Murray and L. Ouellette (eds) *Reality TV*, pp. 97–116.

Kooistra, P. G., J. S. Mahoney and S. D. Westervelt (1998) 'The world of crime according to *Cops*', in M. Fishman and G. Cavender (eds) *Entertaining Crime: Television Reality Programs*, New York, Aldine de Gruyter, pp. 141–58.

Kraszewski, J. (2004) 'Country hicks and urban cliques: mediating race, reality and liberalism on MTV's *The Real World*', in S. Murray and L. Ouellette (eds) *Reality TV*, pp. 179–96.

Landy, M. (2005) *Monty Python's Flying Circus*, Detroit, MI, Wayne State University Press.

Lane, J. (2002) *The Autobiographical Documentary in America*, Madison, WI, The University of Wisconsin Press.

Lavery, D. and S. L. Dunne (eds) (2006) *Seinfeld, Master of Its Domain: Revisiting Television's Greatest Sitcom*, New York, Continuum.

Lay, S. (2002) *British Social Realism: From Documentary to Brit Grit*, London, Wallflower Press.

Lebow, A. (2006) 'Faking what? making a mockery of documentary', in A. Juhasz and J. Lerner (eds) *F Is For Phony*, pp. 223–37.

Lee, J. (2003) 'Good morning, Senator! You rocked on *K Street*', *New York Times*, 5 October, p. 9.1.

Lewisohn, M. (2003) *Radio Times Guide to TV Comedy*, London, BBC Worldwide Ltd.

Lilley, C. (2006) *We Can Be Heroes: Finding the Australian of the Year: The Journey*, Sydney, ABC Books.

Lipkin, S. N. (2002) *Real Emotional Logic: Film and Television Docudrama as Persuasive Practice*, Carbondale, IL, Southern Illinois University Press.

Lipkin, S. N., D. Paget, and J. Roscoe (2005) 'Docudrama and mock-documentary: defining terms, proposing canons', in G. D. Rhodes and J. P. Springer (eds) *Docufictions*, pp. 11–26.

McAleer, S. (2008) 'The virtues of humor: what *The Office* can teach us about Aristotle's ethics', in J. J. Wisnewski (ed.) The Office *and Philosophy*, pp. 49–64.

McCarthy, A. (2001) *Ambient Television: Visual Culture and Public Space*, Durham, NC, Duke University Press.

McClure, K. R. and L. L. McClure (2001) 'Postmodern parody: *Zelig* and the rhetorical subversion of documentary form', *Communication Quarterly*, 49:2, pp. 81–8.

McDowell, S. D. (2001) 'Method filmmaking: an interview with Daniel Myrick, co-director of *The Blair Witch Project*', *Journal of Film and Video*, 53:2–3, pp. 140–7.

McGonigal, J. (2003) 'A real little game: the performance of belief in pervasive play', in Level Up, Proceedings of DiGRA Conference, Utrecht, Netherlands, Digital Games Research Association (DiGRA), November, available at www.digra.org/dl/db/05097.11067.

McGonigal, J. (2007) 'Ubiquitous gaming: a vision for the future of enchanted spaces', in F. v. Borries, S. P. Walz and M. Böttger (eds) *Space Time Play*, pp. 233–7.

McKain, A. (2005) 'Not necessarily not the news: gatekeeping, remediation, and *The Daily Show*', *The Journal of American Culture*, 28:4, pp. 415–30.

MacKenzie, S. (2003) 'Manifest destinies: Dogma 95 and the future of the film manifesto', in M. Hjort and S. MacKenzie (2003) *Purity and Provocation*, pp. 48–57.

Manovich, L. (2006) 'After effects or the velvet revolution', *Millennium Film Journal*, 45–46, pp. 5–19.

Mapplebeck, V. (1997) 'The tabloid formula', *DOX*, 13, pp. 10–12.

Marin, R. (2000) 'The great and wonderful wizard of odds' *New York Times*, 16 July, p. 9.1.

Mathijs, E. and J. Jones (eds) (2004) *Big Brother International: Formats, Critics and Publics*, London, Wallflower Press.

Meyer, M. P. and G. J. Schneider (2008) 'Being-in-*The Office*: Sartre, the look, and the viewer', in J. J. Wisnewski (ed.) The Office *and Philosophy*, pp. 130–40.

Middleton, J. (2002) 'Documentary comedy', *Media International Australia incorporating Culture and Policy*, 104, pp. 55–66.

Mills, B. (2004) 'Comedy verité: contemporary sitcom form', *Screen*, 45:1, pp. 63–78.

Mills, B. (2005) *Television Sitcom*, London, British Film Institute.

Morley, D. (1992) *Television, Audiences, and Cultural Studies*, London, Routledge.

Morreale, J. (2003) 'Revisiting *The Osbournes*: the hybrid reality-sitcom', *Journal of Film and Video*, 55:1, pp. 3–15.

Motavalli, J. (2003) '*K Street* reaches a dead end', *TelevisionWeek*, 17 November, p. 0.1.

Muir, J. K. (2004) *Best in Show: The Films of Christopher Guest and Company*, New York, Applause Theatre & Cinema Books.

Murray, J. (2000) *Hamlet on the Holodeck: The Future of Narrative in Cyberspace*, Cambridge, MA, MIT Press.

Murray, S. and L. Ouellette (eds) (2004) *Reality TV: Remaking Television Culture*, New York, New York University Press.

Neale, S. and F. Krutnik (1990) *Popular Film and Television Comedy*, London, Routledge.

Newman, M. Z. (2006) 'lonelygirl15: the Pleasures and Perils of Participation', *Flow*, 4:12, http://jot.communcaition.utexas.edu/flow/?jot=view&id=1967, accessed August 2006.

Nichols, B. (1991) *Representing Reality: Issues and Concepts in Documentary*, Bloomington, IN, Indiana University Press.

Nichols, B. (1994) *Blurred Boundaries: Questions of Meaning in Contemporary Culture*, Bloomington, IN, Indiana University Press.

Ostrow, J. (2003) 'Inept cops aim for laughs in improvisational *Reno*', *Denver Post*, 14 July, p. F.01.

Ostrow, J. (2004a) 'The evolution of the sitcom', *Denver Post*, 2 May, p. F.01.

Ostrow, J. (2004b) '*Arrested Development* has its own pace', *Denver Post*, 7 November, p. F.15.

Ouellette, L. (1995) 'Camcorder dos and don'ts: popular discourses on amateur video and participatory television, *The Velvet Light Trap*, 36, pp. 33–44.

Paget, D. (1998) *No Other Way To Tell It: Dramadoc/Docudrama on Television*, Manchester, Manchester University Press.

Paget, D. and J. Roscoe (2006) 'Giving voice: performance and authenticity in the documentary musical', *Jump Cut: A Review of Contemporary Media*, 48, www.ejumpcut.org/archive/jc48.2006/MusicalDocy/index. html, accessed January 2007.

Palmer, G. (2002) '*Big Brother*: an experiment in governance', *Television New Media*, 3:3, pp. 295–310.

Palmer, G. (2003) *Discipline and Liberty: Television and Governance*, Manchester, Manchester University Press.

Peters, J. D. (2001) 'Witnessing', *Media Culture Society*, 23:6, pp. 707–23.

Philo, G. (1990) *Seeing and Believing: The Influence of Television*, London, Routledge.

Plantinga, C. (1998) 'Gender, power and a cucumber: satirizing masculinity in *This is Spinal Tap*', in B. K. Grant and J. Sloniowski (eds) *Documenting the Documentary: Close Readings of Documentary Film and Video*, Detroit, MI, Wayne State University Press, pp. 318–32.

Poole, S. (2000) *Trigger Happy: The Inner Life of Videogames*, London, Fourth Estate Limited.

Posner, A. (2004) 'Can this man save the sitcom?' *New York Times*, 1 August, p. 2.1.

Postman, N. (1985) *Amusing Ourselves to Death: Public Discourse in the Age of Show Business*, New York, Penguin.

Press, J. (2003) 'The comedy of cringe', *The Village Voice*, 48:4, p. 50.

Raessens, J. (2006) 'Reality play: documentary computer games beyond fact and fiction', *Popular Communication*, 4:3, pp. 213–24.

Raphael, C. (1997) 'Political economy of reali-TV', *Jump Cut: A Review of Contemporary Media*, 41, pp. 102–9.

Rapping, E. (2004) 'Aliens, nomads, mad dogs, and road warriors: the changing face of criminal violence on TV', in S. Murray and L. Ouellette (eds) *Reality TV*, pp. 214–30.

Reed, K. (2004) 'Televised dogfight: Jetblue and song launch ads to lure air travellers', *Boston Globe*, 28 April, p. C.1.

Reincheld, A. (2006) '"Saturday Night Live" and Weekend Update: the formative years of comedy news dissemination', *Journalism History*, 31:4, pp. 190–7.

Renov, M. (2004) *The Subject of Documentary*, Minneapolis, MN, University of Minnesota Press.

Rhodes, G. D. and J. P. Springer (eds) (2005) *Docufictions: Essays On the Intersection of Documentary and Fictional Filmmaking*, Jefferson, NC, McFarland & Company, Inc.

Rice, L. (1997) 'Live "ER" powers Peacock', *Broadcasting & Cable*, 127:40, pp. 6–8.

Rickard, B. (1999) 'Season of the witch', *Fortean Times: The Journal of Strange Phenomena*, 128, pp. 34–40.

Rochlin, M. (2003) 'Finding humor in the everyday horror of the office', *New York Times*, 20 January, p. 234.

Rochlin, M. (2004) 'In British TV shorts, the science sounds almost familiar enough to be real', *New York Times*, 2 December, E9.

Rocknak, S. (2008) 'Pam and Jim on the make: the epistemology of self-deception', in J. J. Wisnewski (ed.) The Office *and Philosophy*, pp. 67–77.

Roscoe, J. (1997) '*Man Bites Dog*: deconstructing the documentary look', *Metro Education*, 13, pp. 7–12.

Roscoe, J. (2000) '*The Blair Witch Project*: mock-documentary goes mainstream', *Jump Cut: A Review of Contemporary Media*, 43, pp. 3–8.

Roscoe, J. (2001a) '*Big Brother* Australia: performing the "real" twenty-four-seven', *International Journal of Cultural Studies*, 4:4, pp. 473–88.

Roscoe, J. (2001b) 'Real entertainment: new factual hybrid television', *Media International Australia incorporating Culture and Policy*, 100, pp. 9–20.

Roscoe, J. and C. Hight (2001) *Faking It: Mock-documentary and the Subversion of Factuality*, Manchester, Manchester University Press.

Roscoe, J., H. Marshall and K. Gleeson (1995) 'The television audience: a reconsideration of the "taken-for-granted" terms "active", "social" and "critical"', *European Journal of Communication*, 10:1, pp. 87–108.

Rose, B. (2003) 'TV genres re-viewed', *Journal of Popular Film & Television*, 31:1, pp. 2–4.

Rosenthal, A. (ed.) (1999) *Why Docudrama? Fact-Fiction on Film and TV*, Carbondale, IL, Southern Illinois University Press.

Ruby, J. (1977) 'The image mirrored: reflexivity and the documentary film', in A. Rosenthal and J. Corner (eds) (2005) *New Challenges for Documentary* Manchester, Manchester University Press, pp. 34–47.

Ruoff, J. (2002) *An American Family: A Televised Life*, Minneapolis, MN, University of Minnesota Press.

Russell, C. (2006) 'Surrealist ethnography: *Las Hurdes* and the documentary unconscious', in A. Juhasz and J. Lerner (eds) *F Is For Phony*, pp. 99–115.

Russo, J. L. (2005) 'Inside out: television on television', www.j-l-r.org/docs/jlr_tvontv.pdf, accessed March 2006.

Saunders, D. (2007) *Direct Cinema: Observational Documentary and the Politics of the Sixties*, London, Wallflower Press.

Scannell, P. (2002) 'Big Brother as a television event', *Television New Media*, 3:3, pp. 271–82.

Schreier, M. (2004) '"Please help me; all I want to know is: is it real or not?" How recipients view the reality status of *The Blair Witch Project*', *Poetics Today*, 25:2, pp. 305–34.

Scott, K. D. and A. M. White (2003) 'Unnatural history? deconstructing the *Walking with Dinosaurs* phenomenon', *Media Culture Society*, 25:3, pp. 315–32.

Sexton, J. (2003) '"Televerite" hits Britain: documentary, drama and the growth of 16mm filmmaking in British television', *Screen*, 44:4, pp. 429–44.

Shiel, M. (2006) *Italian Neorealism: Rebuilding the Cinematic City*, London, Wallflower Press.

Siegel, L. (2003) 'What was *K Street*?', *New Republic*, 15 December, pp. 38–43.

Smith, M. J. and A. F. Wood (eds) (2003) *Survivor Lessons: Essays on Communication and Reality Television*, Jefferson, NC, McFarland & Company, Inc.

Smithies, G. (2008) 'Past master', *Sunday Star Times Magazine*, 19 October, pp. 14–19.

Sobchack, V. (2004) *Carnal Thoughts: Embodiment and Moving Image Culture*, Berkeley, CA, University of California Press.

Stahl, R. (2000) 'Blair Witchery: simulacra, propaganda, and documentary', *Mythosphere*, 2, pp. 307–19.

Stern, D. A. (ed.) (1999) *The Blair Witch Project: A Dossier*, New York, Onyx.

Stern, D. A. (2000) *Blair Witch: The Secret Confession of Justin Parr*, New York, Pocket Books.

Sterritt, D. and L. Rhodes (2001) '*Monty Python*: lust for glory', *Cineaste*, 26:4, pp. 18–23.

Stratton, J. and I. Ang (1994) '*Sylvania Waters* and the spectacular exploding family', *Screen*, 35:1, pp. 1–21.

Szulborski, D. (2007) '*The Beast*: an alternative reality game defines the future', in F. v. Borries, S. P. Walz and M. Böttger (eds) *Space Time Play*, pp. 228–9.

Telotte, J. P. (2004) 'The *Blair Witch Project* project: film and the internet', in S. L. Higley and J. A. Weinstock (eds) *Nothing That Is*, pp. 37–51.

Terjesen, A. (2008) '*Can* Michael ever learn? Empathy and the self-other', in J. J. Wisnewski (ed.) The Office *and Philosophy*, pp. 26–37.

Thompson, R. J. (1997) *Television's Second Golden Age: From Hill Street Blues to ER*, New York, Syracuse University Press.

Torchin, L. (2008) 'Cultural learnings of *Borat* make for benefit of glorious study of documentary', *Film & History*, 38:1, pp. 53–63.

Trudeau, G. (2002) 'Now what?', *Electronic Media*, 28 October, pp. 23–5.

Tufte, E. R. (1990) *Envisioning Information*, Graphics Press, Cheshire.

Tufte, E. R. (1997) *Visual Explanations: Images and Quantities, Evidence and Narrative*, Graphics Press, Cheshire.

Tufte, E. R. (2001) *The Visual Display of Quantitative Information*, 2nd edition, Graphics Press, Cheshire.

Tufte, E. R. (2006) *Beautiful Evidence*, Graphics Press, Cheshire.

Turnbull, S. (2004) '"Look at Moiye, Kimmie, Look at Moiye!" *Kath and Kim* and the Australian comedy of taste', *Media International Australia incorporating Culture and Policy*, 113, pp. 98–109.

Turner, C. (2004) *Planet Simpson: How a Cartoon Masterpiece Documented an Era and Defined a Generation*, London, Ebury Press.

Waisbord, S. (2004) 'McTV: understanding the global popularity of television formats', *Television New Media*, 5:4, pp. 359–83.

Walker, J. S. (2004) 'Mom and the Blair Witch: narrative, form, and the feminine', in S. L. Higley and J. A. Weinstock (eds) *Nothing That Is*, pp. 163–80.

Walters, B. (2005) *The Office*, London, British Film Institute.

Walters, B. (2007) 'A guaranteed premonition', *Film Quarterly* 61:2, pp. 66–8.

Ward, P. (2005a) *Documentary: The Margins of Reality*, London, Wallflower Press.

Ward, P. (2005b) 'The future of documentary? "Conditional tense" documentary and the historical record', in G. D. Rhodes and J. P. Springer (eds) *Docufictions*, pp. 270–83.

Warner, J. (2007) 'Political culture jamming: the dissident humor of *The Daily Show with Jon Stewart*', *Popular Communication*, 5:1, pp. 17–36.

Winston, B. (1999). 'Documentary: how the myth was deconstructed', *Wide Angle*, 21:2, pp. 70–86.

Winston, B. (2000) *Lies, Damn Lies and Documentaries*, London, British Film Institute.

Wisnewski, J. J. (ed.) (2008) The Office *and Philosophy: Scenes from the Unexamined Life*, Malden, MA, Blackwell Publishing Ltd.

Witchell, D. (2008) 'Do ya think I'm sexy', *Listener*, 15 November, pp. 34–5

Zimmermann, P. R. (1995) *Reel Families: A Social History of Amateur Film*, Bloomington, IN, Indiana University Press.

Zoonen, L. v. (2001) 'Desire and resistance: *Big Brother* and the recognition of everyday life', *Media, Culture & Society*, 23:5, pp. 669–77.

Index